POWER NOTES

COST ACCOUNTING
NINTH EDITION
A MANAGERIAL EMPHASIS

POWER NOTES

William O. Stratton
University of Southern Colorado

COST ACCOUNTING
A MANAGERIAL EMPHASIS

NINTH EDITION

HORNGREN • FOSTER • DATAR
Stanford University   *Stanford University*   *Stanford University*

PRENTICE HALL, Upper Saddle River, NJ 07458

Project editor: Richard Bretan
Acquisitions editor: P.J. Boardman
Associate editor: Diane deCastro
Manufacturing buyer: Paul Smolenski

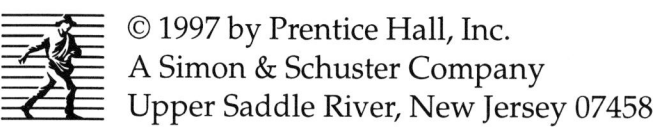 © 1997 by Prentice Hall, Inc.
A Simon & Schuster Company
Upper Saddle River, New Jersey 07458

All rights reserved. No part of this book may be
reproduced, in any form or by any means,
without permission in writing from the publisher.

Printed in the United States of America

10 9 8 7 6 5 4 3 2 1

ISBN 0-13-567322-4

Prentice-Hall International (UK) Limited, *London*
Prentice-Hall of Australia Pty. Limited, *Sydney*
Prentice-Hall Canada Inc., *Toronto*
Prentice-Hall Hispanoamericana, S.A., *Mexico*
Prentice-Hall of India Private Limited, *New Delhi*
Prentice-Hall of Japan, Inc., *Tokyo*
Simon & Schuster Asia Pte. Ltd., *Singapore*
Editora Prentice-Hall do Brasil, Ltda., *Rio de Janeiro*

Contents

Chapter 1		The Accountant's Role in the Organization	1-1
Chapter 2		An Introduction to Cost Terms and Purposes	2-1
Chapter 3		Cost-Volume-Profit Relationships	3-1
Chapter 4		Costing Systems and Activity-Based Costing I: Service and Merchandising Applications	4-1
Chapter 5		Costing Systems and Activity-Based Costing II: Manufacturing Applications	5-1
Chapter 6		Master Budget and Responsibility Accounting	6-1
Chapter 7		Flexible Budgets, Variances, and Management Control: I	7-1
Chapter 8		Flexible Budgets, Variances, and Management Control: II	8-1
Chapter 9		Income Effects of Alternative Inventory-Costing Methods	9-1
Chapter 10		Determining How Costs Behave	10-1
Chapter 11		Relevant Revenues, Relevant Costs, and the Decision Process	11-1
Chapter 12		Pricing Decisions, Product Profitability Decisions, and Cost Management	12-1
Chapter 13		Cost Allocation I	13-1
Chapter 14		Cost Allocation II	14-1
Chapter 15		Cost Allocation: Joint Products and Byproducts	15-1
Chapter 16		Revenues, Revenue Variances, and Customer-Profitability Analysis	16-1

Contents (cont.)

Chapter 17	Process Costing Systems	17-1
Chapter 18	Spoilage, Reworked Units, and Scrap	18-1
Chapter 19	Cost Management: Quality, Time, and the Theory of Constraints	19-1
Chapter 20	Operation Costing, Backflush Costing, and Project Control	20-1
Chapter 21	Inventory Management and Just-in-Time	21-1
Chapter 22	Capital Budgeting and Cost Analysis	22-1
Chapter 23	Capital Budgeting: A Closer Look	23-1
Chapter 24	Measuring Mix, Yield, and Productivity	24-1
Chapter 25	Control Systems, Transfer Pricing and Multi-national Considerations	25-1
Chapter 26	Systems Choice: Performance Measurement, Compensation and Multinational Considerations	26-1

PowerNotes for Cost Accounting: A Managerial Emphasis, Ninth Edition

The Accountant's Role in the Organization

NOTES

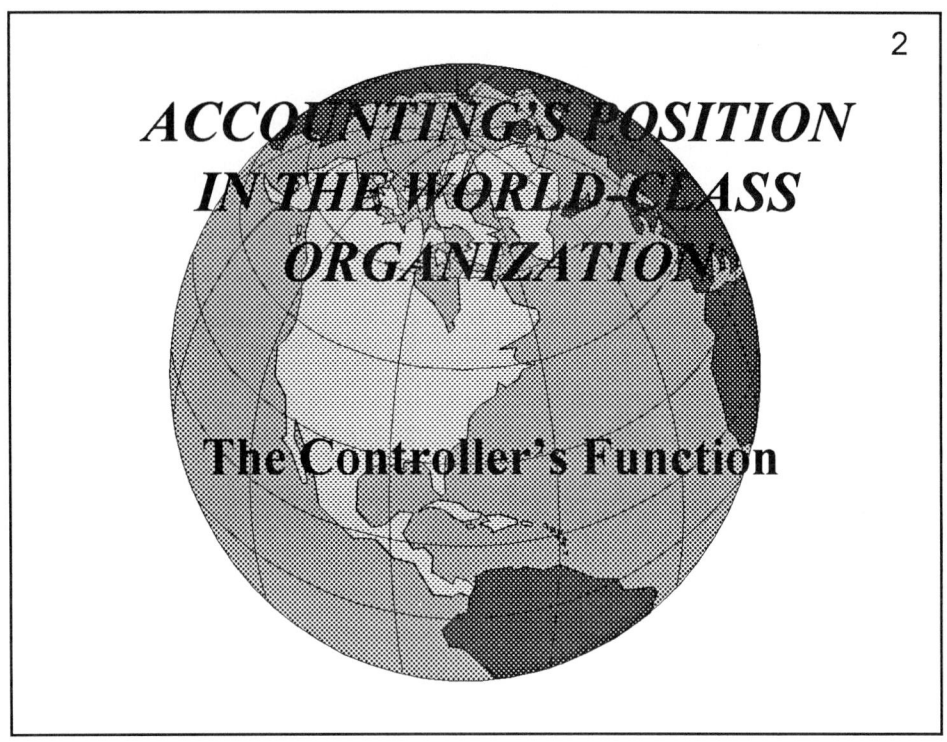

ACCOUNTING'S POSITION IN THE WORLD-CLASS ORGANIZATION

The Controller's Function

NOTES

The role of accountants in today's highly competitive, global market is quite different than in the past. The following series of job descriptions, survey results, and experiences demonstrate the importance of the accounting function and its nature and scope.

It is also important to note that "non-accountants" must develop a solid understanding of basic management accounting principles.

This course expands upon the basic management accounting concepts that are used on a daily basis by accountants and other managers.

NOTES

PowerNotes for Cost Accounting: A Managerial Emphasis, Ninth Edition

SAMPLES OF JOB DESCRIPTIONS TAKEN FROM CURRENT ADVERTISED POSITION ANNOUNCEMENTS

NOTES

TITLE	DUTIES	QUALIFICATIONS
COST MANAGER Suburban Machine Manufacturer	Selecting and implementing new cost system. Manage department, financial statement preparation, budget planning.	Strong communication skills; works with minimum direction. Salary to $70,000.
COST ACCOUNTANT Multi-Media Software Company	Inventory tracking and costing; variance analysis; design, develop, and implement costing system; establish costs for new products.	Technical expertise; big picture mentality; communication skills; software experience; degree in accounting or finance. Salary to $45,000.
DIVISION CONTROLLER Consumer and Industrial Products Manufacturer	Cost accounting, budgeting/forecasting, financial reporting to headquarters, computer system enhancements, analysis of results, process improvement.	Process and standard costing, budgeting experience including variable and overhead budgeting; strong systems experience; BS in Accountng. Salary to $60,000 + profit sharing.

NOTES

TITLE	DUTIES	QUALIFICATIONS
CONTROLLER Major Trade Association	Oversee three companies, monitor general ledger activity, financial statement preparation and analysis, budgeting and forecasting.	Ability to interact with others at various levels, communication skills, big picture perspective, B.S. in Accounting, computer literacy in Windows, knowledge of spreadsheets. Salary to $65,000.
VP FINANCE Financial Services Holding Company	Manage multiple departments with staff of 30+; corporate accounting, information systems, tax, treasury, risk management.	Analytical, problem-solving and team-building skills, ability to interface with Senior Operating Management and external regulatory bodies. CPA/CMA with 10+ years experience.

NOTES

SAMPLES OF JOB DESCRIPTIONS AND ROLES TAKEN FROM CURRENT SURVEYS AND ACTUAL EXPERIENCES

MOST IMPORTANT KNOWLEDGE, SKILLS, AND ABILITIES FOR WORK

- **WORK ETHIC**
- **ANALYTICAL AND PROBLEM SOLVING SKILLS**
- **INTERPERSONAL SKILLS**
- **LISTENING SKILLS**
- **USE OF COMPUTERIZED SPREADSHEETS**
- **UNDERSTANDING THE BUSINESS**
- **UNDERSTANDING THE BOTTOM-LINE IMPLICATIONS OF DAY-TO-DAY BUSINESS AND ACCOUNTING DECISIONS**
- **WRITING SKILLS**

SOURCE: "The Practice Analysis of Management Accounting," G. Siegel and C. Kulesza, Management Accounting *(April 1996), pp. 20-28. Four thousand corporate accountants from membership rosters of IMA, Financial Executives Institute, AICPA, and the Institute of Internal Auditors were survied.*

NOTES

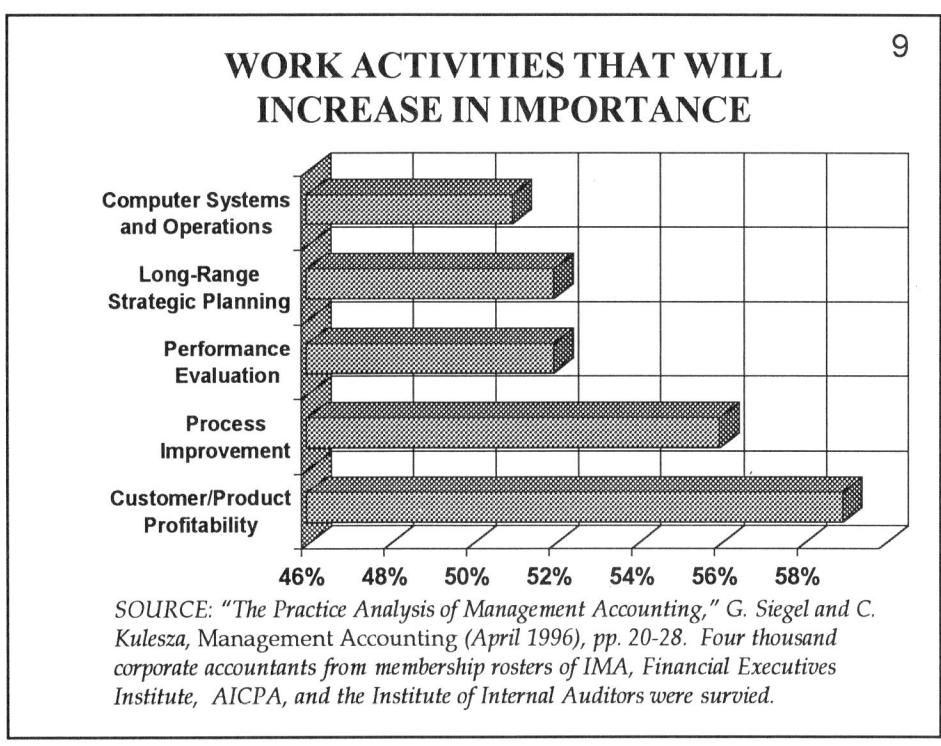

SOURCE: "The Practice Analysis of Management Accounting," G. Siegel and C. Kulesza, Management Accounting *(April 1996), pp. 20-28. Four thousand corporate accountants from membership rosters of IMA, Financial Executives Institute, AICPA, and the Institute of Internal Auditors were survied.*

NOTES

PowerNotes for Cost Accounting: A Managerial Emphasis, Ninth Edition

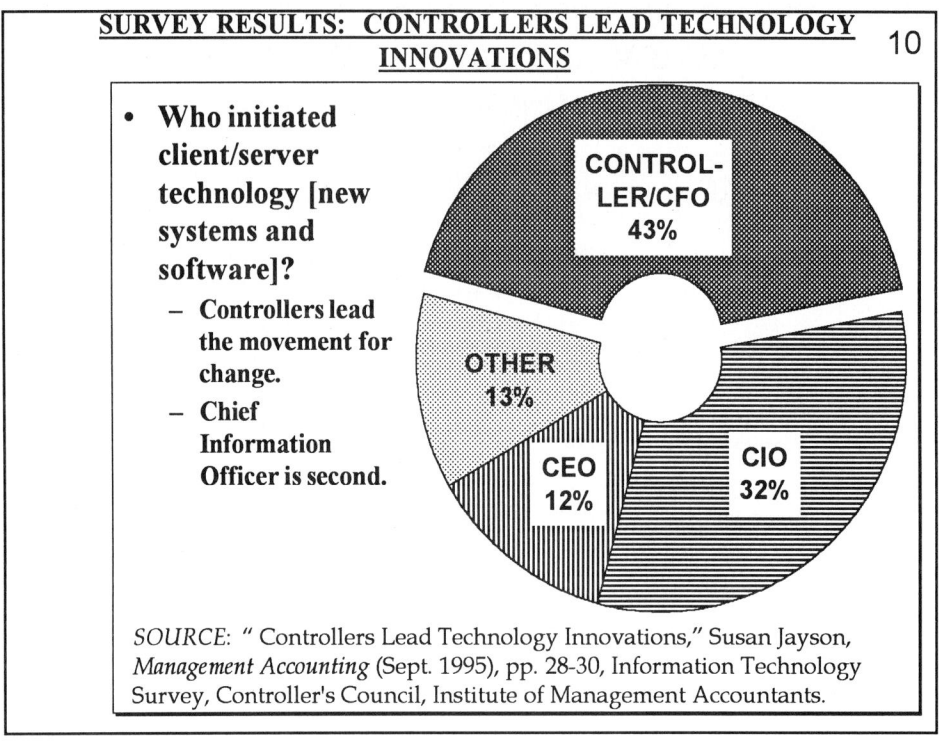

NOTES

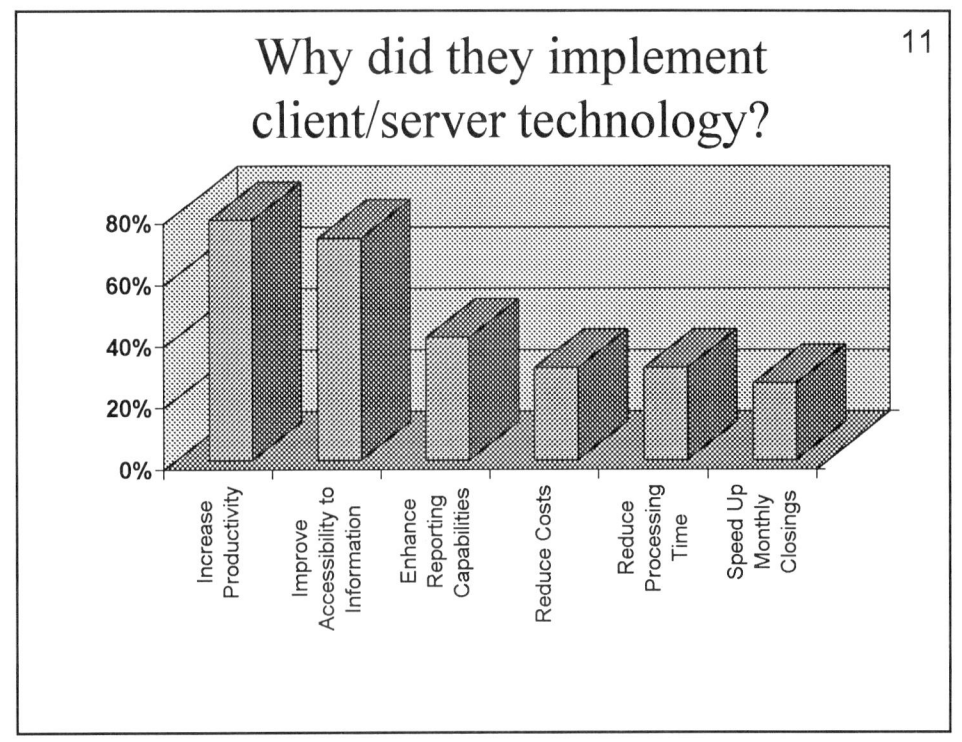

NOTES

12

"Accountants who have shed the bean counter image to play on the management team have done so by becoming active members of information system development projects. We are the obvious choice for leadership in the design of new cost accounting systems. Management accounting is more alive than ever! Some of us have become analytical team players, but we have only scratched the surface." -- "Shedding the Bean Counter Image," William Baker, Management Accounting (Oct. 1994), pp. 29-31.

Southwire Company is America's largest wire maker, with annual revenue of $1.3 billion. Like many large companies, Southwire has a quality process. Management accountants at Southwire play a big role in the drive towards business excellence. They are called on to assume leadership in the areas of personal application [customer visits, training, benchmarking], communication [developing vision and mission statement, defining customer/product and service relationships], and public promotion [attending quality conferences]. -- "Implementing the Quality Process at Southwire Company," G. Agacer, D. Baker, and L. Miles, Management Accounting (Nov. 1994), pp. 59-62.

NOTES

WHAT ARE CURRENT TRENDS IN THE MANAGEMENT ACCOUNTING FIELD?

NOTES

CURRENT TRENDS

14

- **INCREASED OUTSOURCING OF FINANCE FUNCTIONS [Pension Management, Taxes, Payroll]**
  - **Impact on the controller's role -- "It lets him or her partner with management and be a powerful part of the business process and strategy." Michael Brown, CFO, Microsoft**
  - **"It also lets the controller spend less time on day-to-day routine tasks and play a key role in running the company." Dennis Torkko, Managing Partner, Arthur Andersen's Consulting Services Practice**

  SOURCE: "Will Your Finance Function Be Outsourced?", K. Williams, Editor, *Management Accounting* (Dec. 1995), pp. 20-21.

NOTES

CURRENT TRENDS 15

- **IN 7 YEARS [2003], WHAT WILL THE WORKPLACE BE LIKE?**
  - "More people will choose to work on a temporary basis as opportunities in this sector grow. ... Accountants will place their job security on the fact that they're good cost accountants and not on their longevity with an employer." Max Messmer, President, Robert Half International
  - "American business will have fewer layers of management. The typical organization will consist of a core group of permanent employees, a tested cadre of outsourced staff, and temporary workers to handle the peak loads. ... For the individual, the major change will be the switch from reliance upon the employers to concentration on developing skills that will provide a true value-added service." Donald DeCamp, Vice President of Operations, Romac Associates

NOTES

CURRENT TRENDS

- **WHAT ARE SOME JOB-RICH AREAS FOR MANAGEMENT ACCOUNTANTS?**
    - "Cost accounting, businesses must understand internal cost structures in order to control them; credit and collections, many firms will attack the opposite side of the ledger as aggressively as the cost side; SEC and financial reporting, more stock offerings and an increased desire for accurate, usable, and timely reports will create more jobs; forensic accounting, skilled investigative accountants and auditors; international tax and accounting, knowledge of foreign taxation and accounting are in demand as firms expand globally." Max Messmer

    SOURCE: "Career Forecast for the '90s," Susan Jayson, *Management Accounting* (June 1993), pp. 38-40.

NOTES

An Introduction to Cost Terms and Purposes

NOTES

MANAGEMENT INFLUENCE ON COST BEHAVIOR

CAPACITY DECISIONS AT GENERAL MOTORS CORPORATION AND FORD MOTOR COMPANY

NOTES

How Management Influences Costs

- Management influences cost behavior through decisions on product or service attributes, policies that create incentives to control costs, capacity, and technology choice.
- Capacity decisions relate to strategic decisions about the scale and scope of an organization's activities.
- These decisions generally result in fixed levels of capacity costs.
- In industries with long-term variations in demand, caution should be exercised when making capacity decisions.

NOTES

For example, during the economic recession in the early 1990s, General Motors had much more difficulty in controlling its production costs. From an article appearing in U.S. News & World Report:

"GM's losses stem from a decline in volume and stepped up labor and marketing incentive costs, say analysts. According to Wertheim's Casesa, the auto maker also has four to five too many plants in North America, adding up to excess capacity of about a million vehicles. Auto analyst Maryann Keller of Furman Selz points out that with its broad array of products, GM is faced with the prospect of having to eliminate whole car lines in order to pare capacity, since some products are made in only one underutilized factory. "

SOURCE: *U.S. News & World Report*, April 15, 1991, v110 n14 p51(3)

NOTES

Another illustration of the risk associated with capacity and technology investments:

"THE LAUNCH OF THE 1995 Chevrolet Cavalier and sister Pontiac Sunfire at the Lordstown, Ohio plant has been a disaster, probably the worst car launch in modern history, yet one more sign that GM's big problems are not yet behind it.

"Job 1, the first car off the line, rolled last August. Fast startups roll without a lost day. Six to 12 weeks is a generous ramp-up time from Job 1 to full production. By mid-February, six months after Job 1, the Cavalier and Pontiac Sunfire hadn't reached full production; they were running around 60% of capacity, an average 50 cars an hour against a target of 80. By late March the rate was only 70%.

NOTES

The inescapable fact is that GM has blown the '95 model year for its newest car. Maybe the damage isn't permanent, and all the momentum of a new model launch will be recovered next year. Maybe, but you never recover the tens of millions of dollars in slow time (idle capacity) at the factory..."

SOURCE: *Forbes,* April 24, 1995, v155 n9 p116(1)

Ford was faced with a similar capacity dilemma in the mid-1980s. But the option of building new and expensive plants and assembly lines was rejected by Ford:

"We know in 1986 and 1987 we lost some sales. We could have probably had a higher market share. But we felt it was worth it to keep our costs under control."

Source: Text, page 84.

NOTES

Controlling Risk, Capacity Decisions, Technology Decisions

- Consider one of Ford's automotive production plants. Assume the plant is currently running at full capacity and that Ford is considering building a new, fully-automated plant that will increase its capacity. The cost of the new plant is $20 million.

- The cost of labor in the new plant would be significantly reduced but capacity costs would be much greater due to the cost of the high-technology equipment.
- Currently, Ford is using overtime and outsourcing production in order to meet demand. This is a costly practice which is why Ford is considering building a new plant facility.
- Cost data for the two options described above are given in the following table (millions of dollars).
- **Would you recommend committing Ford to building automated facilities? Give your reasoning**.

NOTES

Build & Outsource/Overtime Options Expected Costs (Millions)

	Build Option			Outsource/Overtime Option		
Percent of Current Capacity	60	100	120	60	100	120
Material Costs	$18	$30	$36	$18	$30	$36
Labor Costs	6	10	12	18	30	44
Other Costs	40	40	40	20	20	20
Total Costs	$64	$80	$88	$56	$80	$100

NOTES

ANALYSIS OF COST BEHAVIOR

- In order to gain a better understanding of the cost behavior associated with the capacity and technology choice decision facing Ford, we will prepare line and pie charts using the data provided.

NOTES

TOTAL COSTS (MILLIONS)
BUILD VERSUS OUTSOURCE/OVERTIME OPTIONS

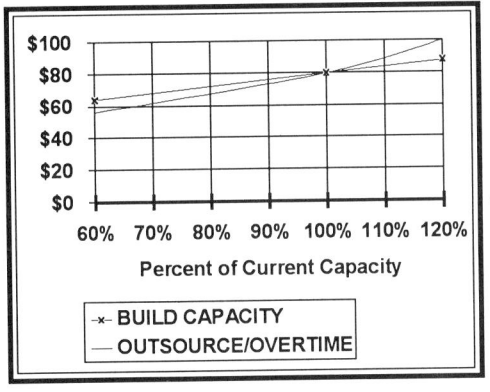

- At operating levels below 100% of (current) capacity, outsourcing with overtime yields the lower total cost. Above 100%, building capacity yields the lower total cost.
- Building new capacity will expose Ford to added risk due to the increased fixed costs associated with the high technology. During business downturns, Ford will not be able to cover these costs with decreased revenues.

UNDERSTANDING COSTS

- A better understanding of cost behavior can be gained by considering the cost structure under each option more carefully.
- To do this we construct pie charts for each option and economic scenario.

NOTES

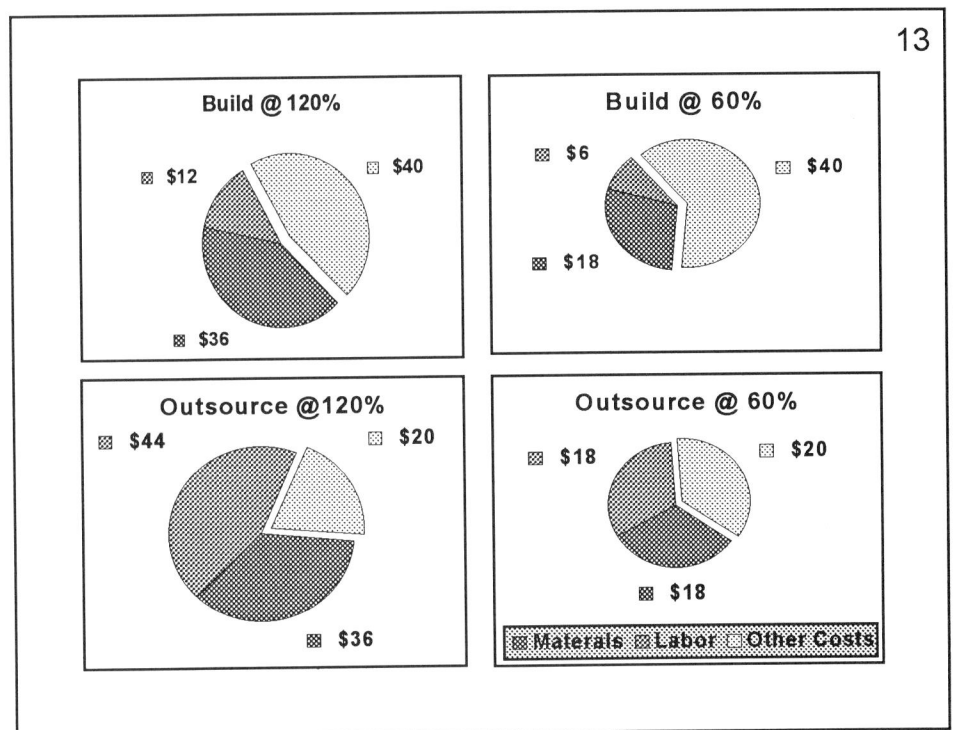

NOTES

PowerNotes for Cost Accounting: A Managerial Emphasis, Ninth Edition

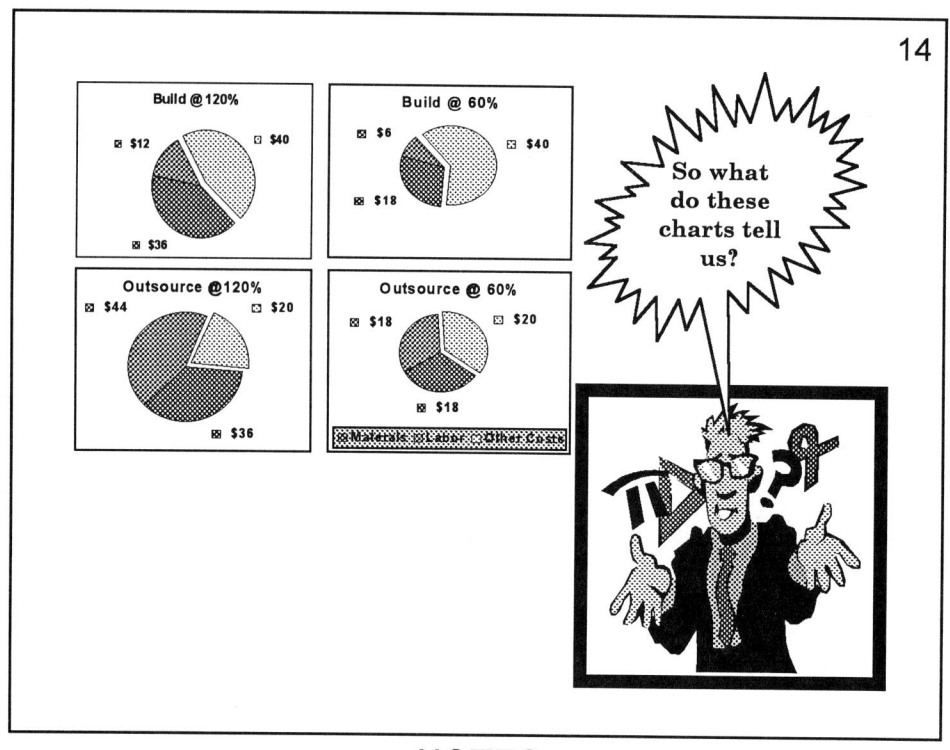

NOTES

2-14

Cost Behavior of Capacity Costs [Millions]
Build Option @ 120% of Capacity

- What is the cost behavior of each cost component?
- What happens to costs if demand drops to 60% of capacity?

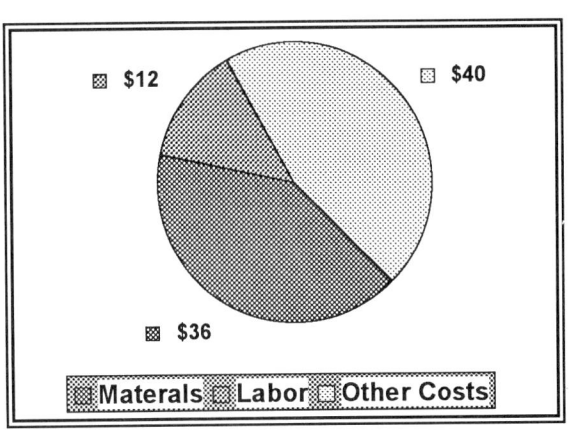

$12, $40, $36 — Materals, Labor, Other Costs

NOTES

Cost Behavior of Capacity Costs [Millions]
Build Option @ 120% & 60% of Capacity

- At 120% of capacity, fixed costs are 45% of total costs.
- When demand declines, fixed costs remain at $40 but variable costs decline in proportion. So...
- At 60% of capacity, fixed costs increase to 63% of total costs.

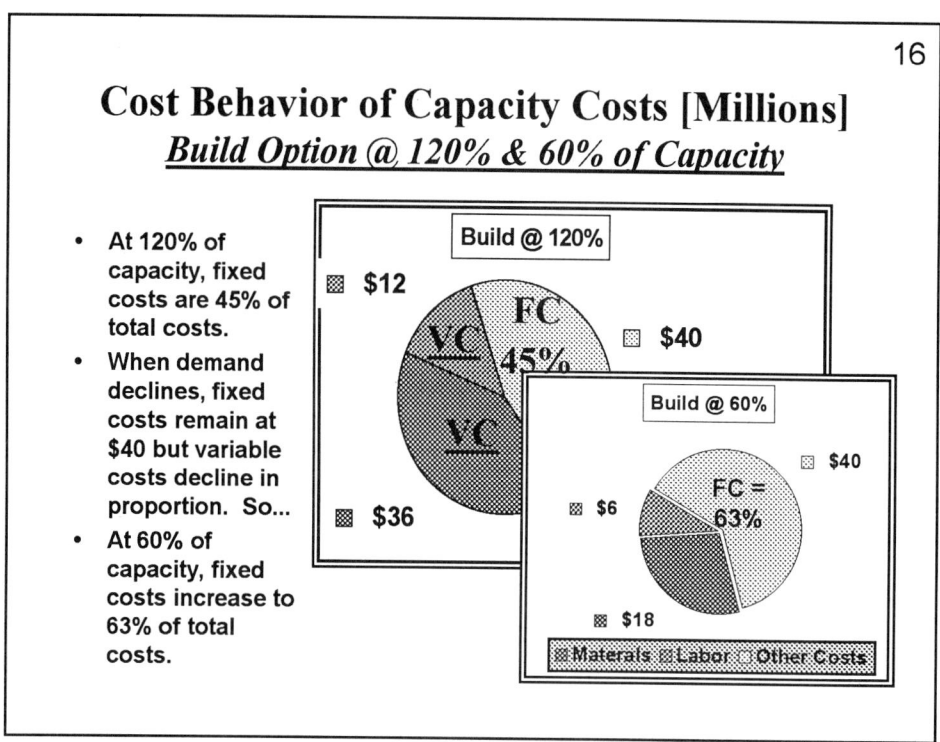

NOTES

PowerNotes for Cost Accounting: A Managerial Emphasis, Ninth Edition

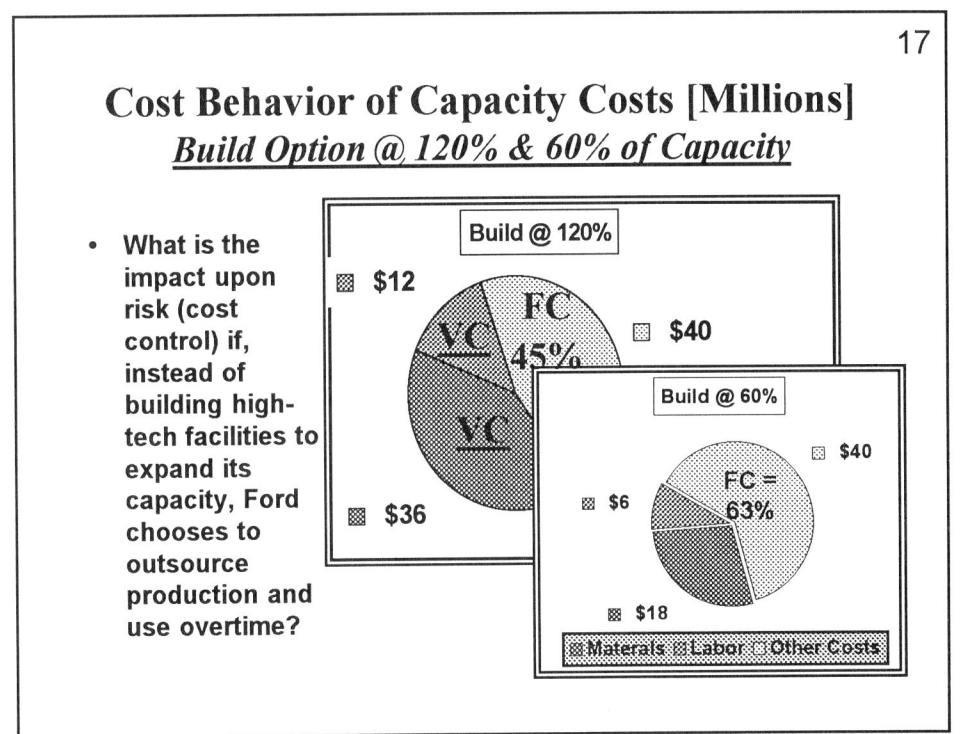

Cost Behavior of Capacity Costs [Millions]
Build Option @ 120% & 60% of Capacity

- What is the impact upon risk (cost control) if, instead of building high-tech facilities to expand its capacity, Ford chooses to outsource production and use overtime?

NOTES

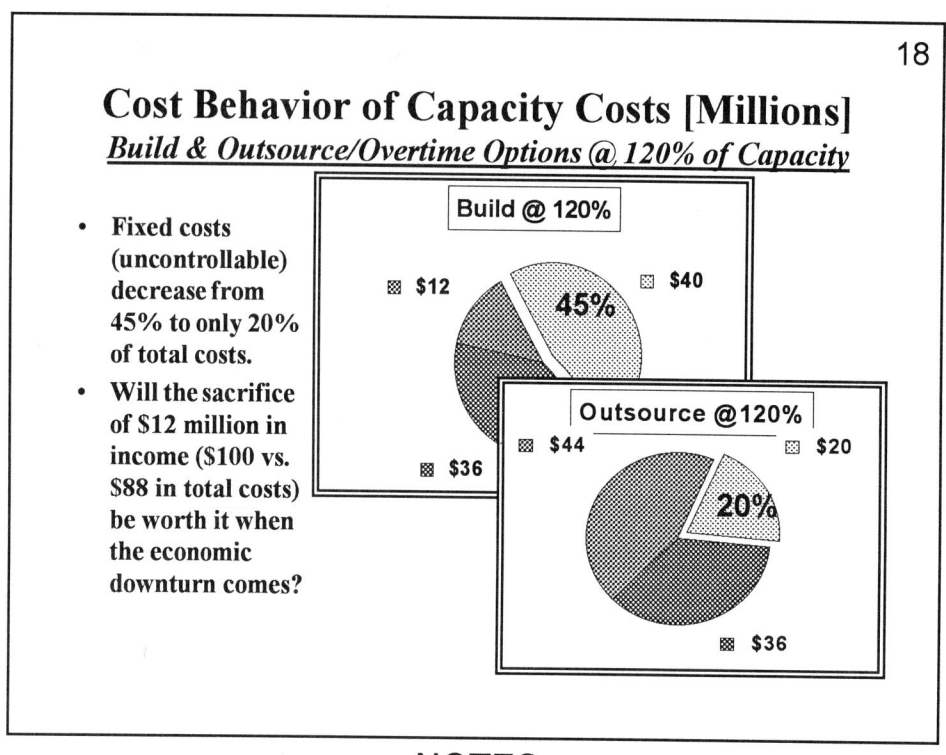

Cost Behavior of Capacity Costs [Millions]
Build & Outsource/Overtime Option @ 60% of Capacity

- During the downturn (60% of capacity), total costs under the outsource/overtime option are $56 million or $8 less than under the build option.
- Ford is willing to sacrifice short-term profit ($12 million) for cost (risk) control. Ford is also considering the long-term average utilization level - normally less than 100%.

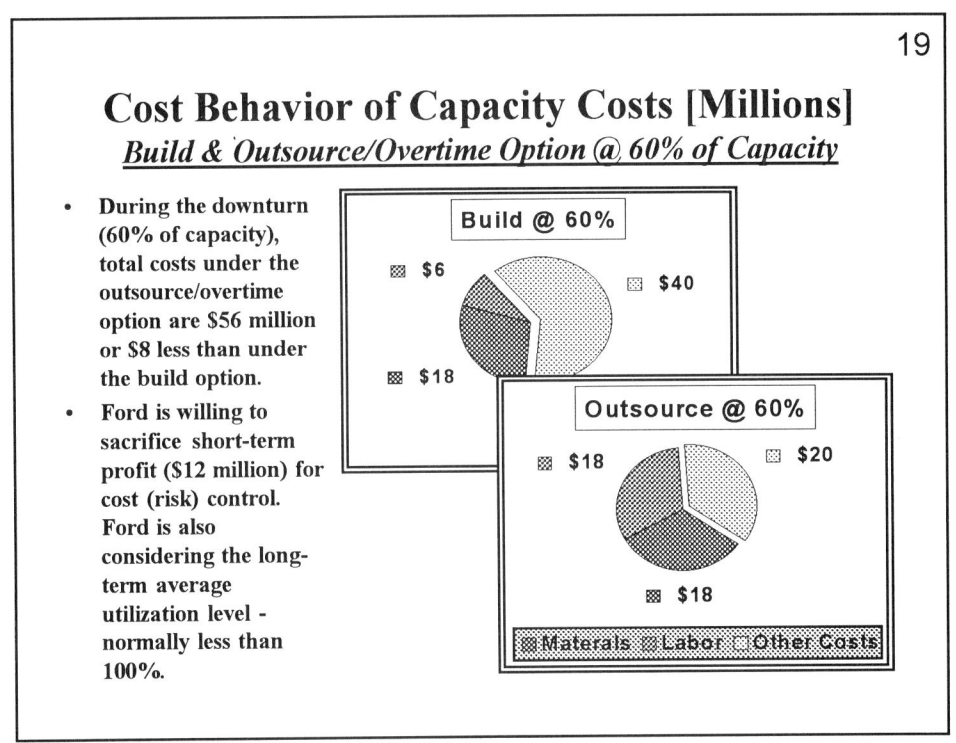

PowerNotes for Cost Accounting: A Managerial Emphasis, Ninth Edition

3

Cost-Volume-Profit Relationships

NOTES

UNDERSTANDING COST BEHAVIOR

COST-VOLUME-PROFIT AND SENSITIVITY ANALYSIS

NOTES

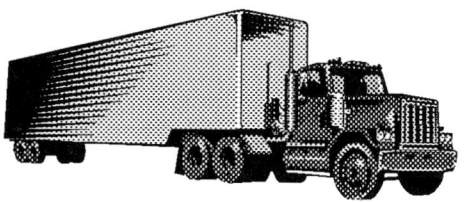

- **Cost-volume-profit (CVP) analysis** examines the behavior of total revenues, total costs, and operating income as changes occur in the output level, selling price, variable costs, or fixed costs.
- **Sensitivity analysis** is a what-if technique that examines how a result will change if the original predicted data are not achieved or if an underlying assumption changes.

NOTES

COST-VOLUME-PROFIT SCENARIO

Union Moving Company hauls household goods. The company uses revenue miles as the cost driver for all its operating costs. The following data are budgeted for the next year and are based on expected revenue miles of 700,000. The relevant range of demand is from 300,000 to 1,000,000 revenue miles.

	Per Revenue Mile
Average Selling Price	$1.90
Average Variable Costs	$1.60

Fixed Costs, $150,000

Prepare a bar graph that shows the budgeted profit for revenue miles from 300,000 to 1,000,000. Evaluate the impact of a 10% increase in promotion costs (fixed) that will enable a 5% increase in sales price with no change in revenue miles.

NOTES

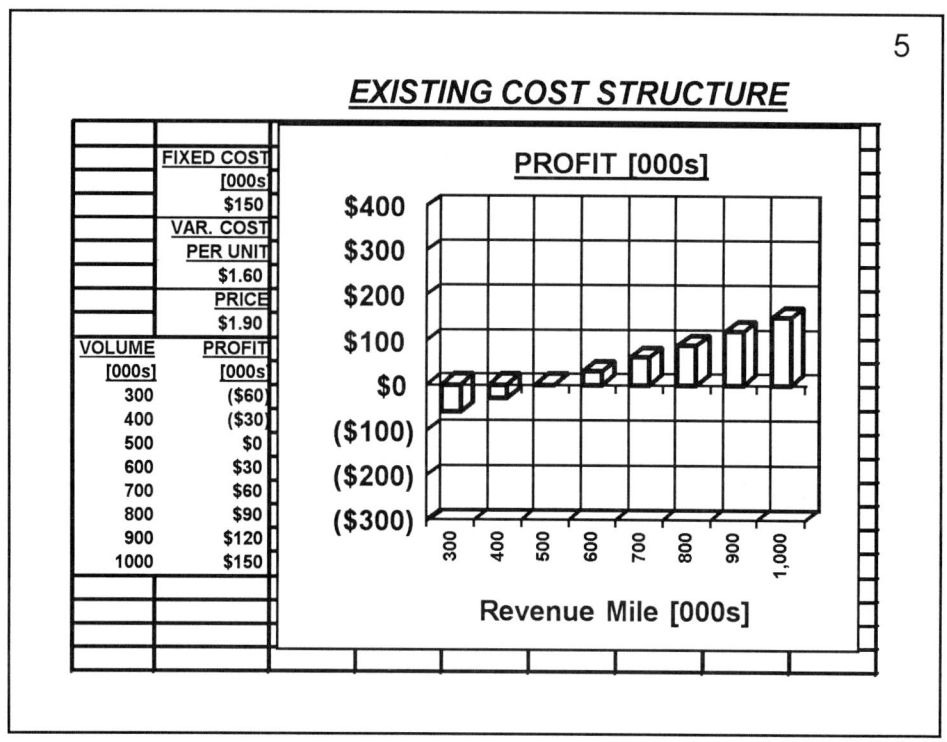

NOTES

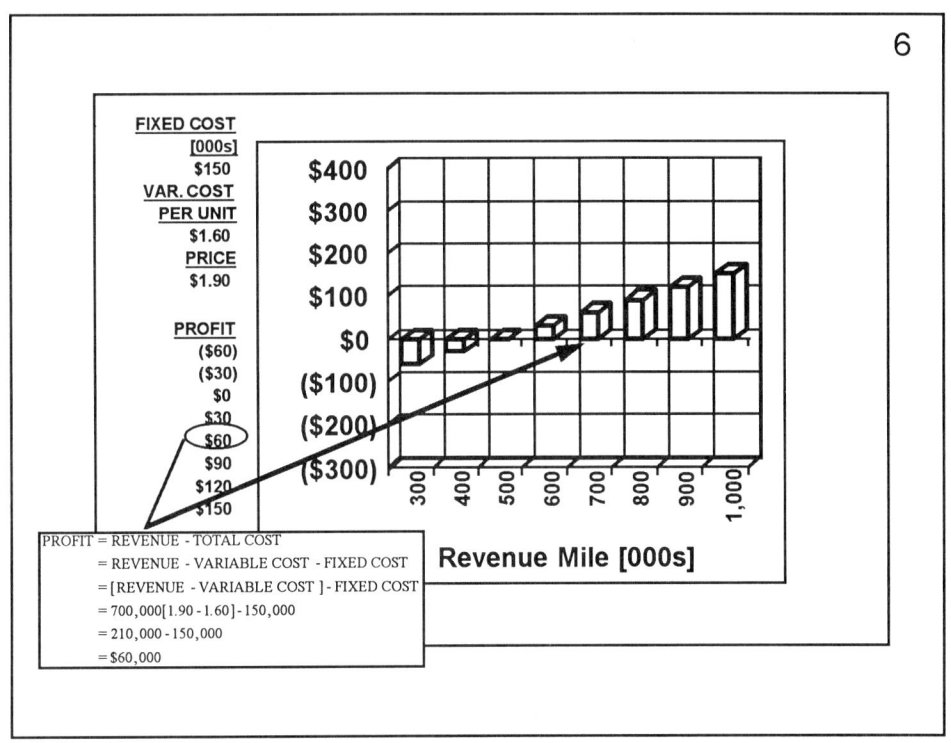

NOTES

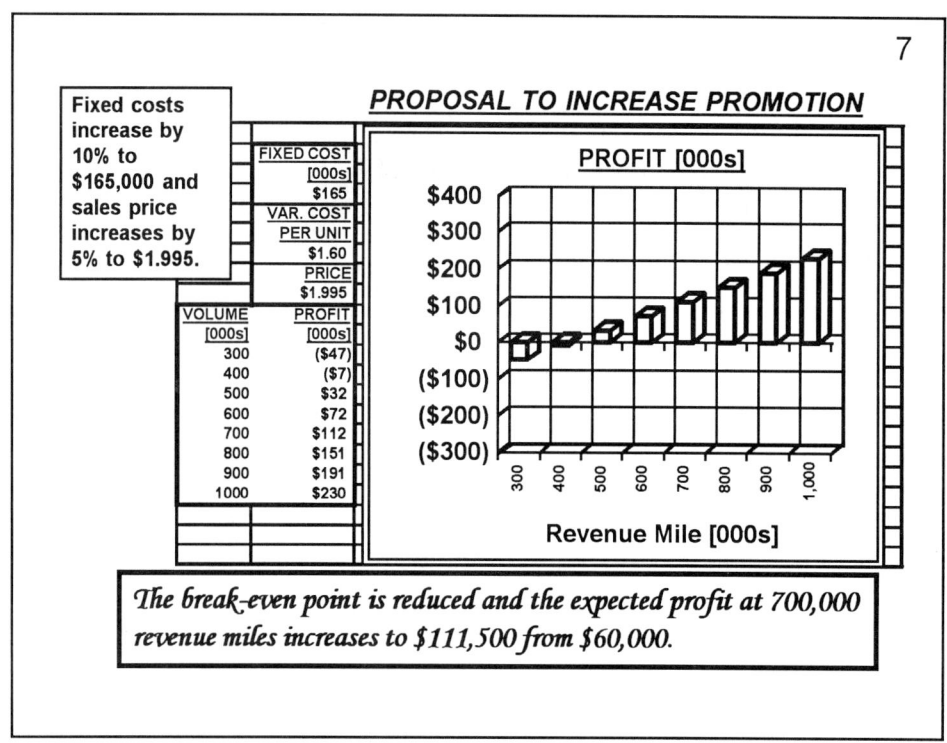

NOTES

> Union is considering the purchase of equipment that will improve its operations. This will enable a significant reduction in the labor force. The result on their cost structure is an increase in fixed costs (equipment depreciation) from $150,000 to $430,000 and a decrease in the variable cost of labor from $1.60 to $1.20 per revenue mile.
>
> Construct a bar graph that shows this new cost-volume-profit structure over the same relevant range. Compare the relative risks to the company of this option to the existing operating system if expected demand varies from 300,000 to 1,000,000 revenue miles.

NOTES

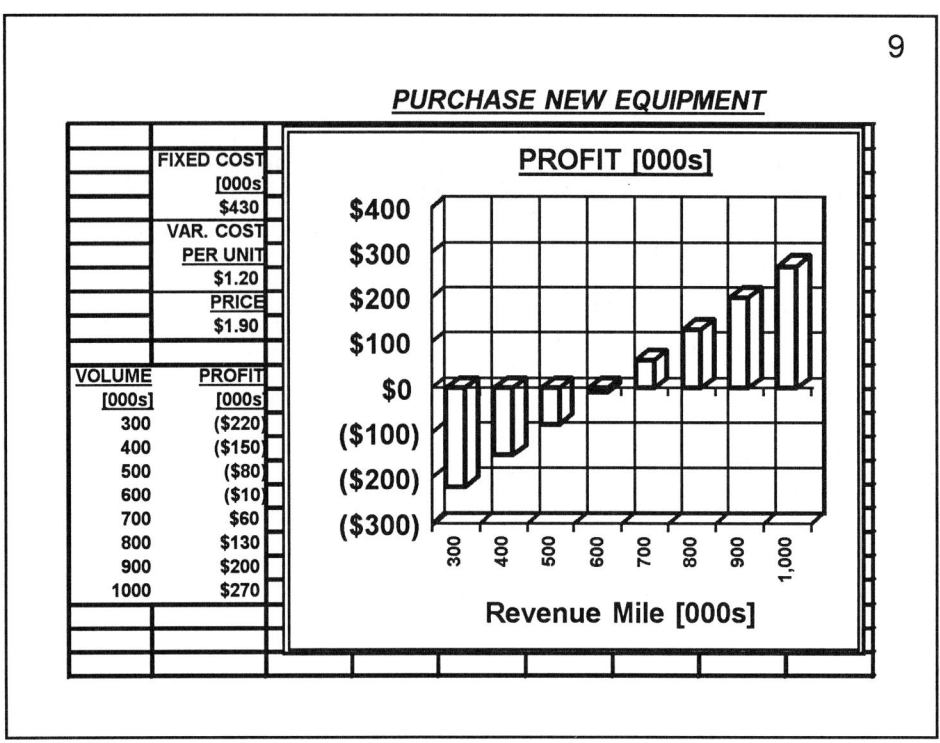

NOTES

PowerNotes for Cost Accounting: A Managerial Emphasis, Ninth Edition

NOTES

Costing Systems and Activity-Based Costing (I): Service and Merchandising Applications

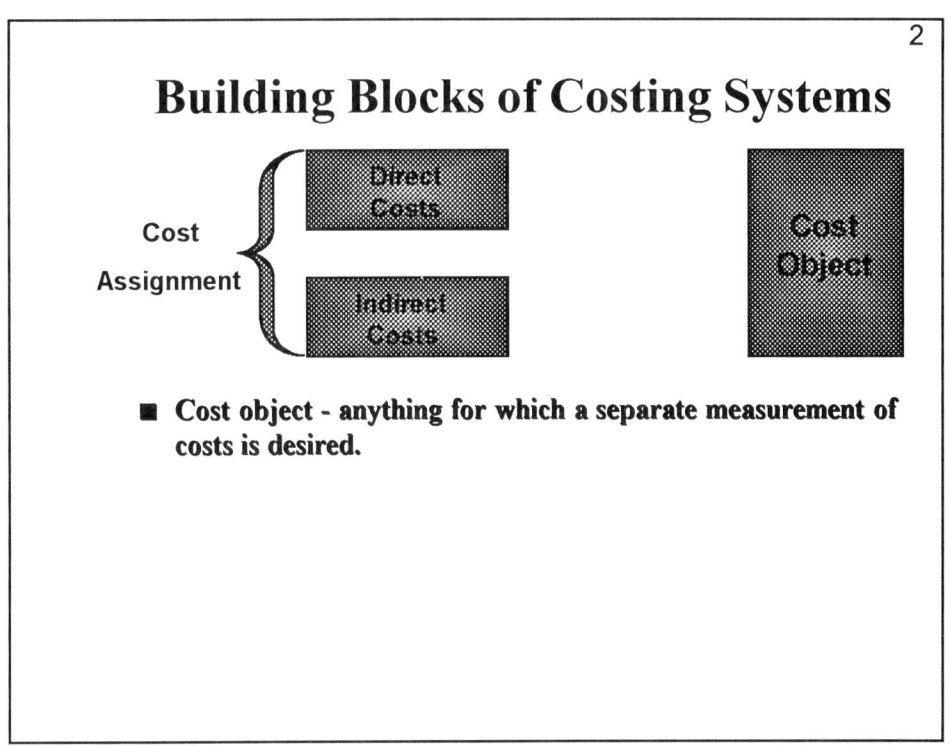

Building Blocks of Costing Systems

Cost Assignment { Direct Costs / Indirect Costs }   Cost Object

- Cost object - anything for which a separate measurement of costs is desired.

Building Blocks of Costing Systems

- Cost object - anything for which a separate measurement of costs is desired.
- Direct costs of a cost object - costs that are related to the particular cost object and can be traced to it in an economically feasible (cost-effective) way.

NOTES

Building Blocks of Costing Systems

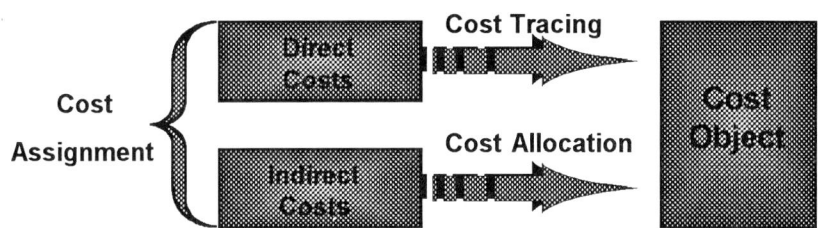

- Cost object - anything for which a separate measurement of costs is desired.
- Direct costs of a cost object - costs that are related to the particular cost object and can be traced to it in an economically feasible (cost-effective) way.
- Indirect costs of a cost object - costs that are related to the particular cost object but cannot be traced to it in an economically feasible way. Indirect costs are allocated to the cost object.

NOTES

Six-Step Approach to Costing

- Identify Cost Objects
- Identify Direct Costs
- Identify Indirect-Cost Pools [Activity Centers in the ABC Approach]
- Select Cost-Allocation Base for Each Indirect Cost Pool [Activity Center]
- Develop the Rate Per Unit of the Cost-Allocation Base Used to Allocate Indirect Costs
- Assign Costs to the Cost Ojbects

NOTES

NOTES

Company Background and Key Business Issue

The billing department (BD) of Portland Power Company (PPC) provides account inquiry and billing services to residential and commercial customers. The BD will experience significant increases in demand over the next year.

Since current capacity will not be sufficient to service the expected demand increases, PPC is considering a proposal by a local service bureau to provide all functions of the BD at a cost of $3.50 per customer. The BD's cost per customer for residential and commercial accounts is $3.69 and $6.15, respectively, based on the existing traditional costing system that allocates all BD costs based on the *number of inquiries* received by each customer class [see Exhibit 1].

Management was uncomfortable with the cost data currently provided and decided to refine the costing system by using an activity-based [ABC] approach. ABC focuses on activities as the fundamental cost objects [see page 107].

NOTES

PowerNotes for Cost Accounting: A Managerial Emphasis, Ninth Edition

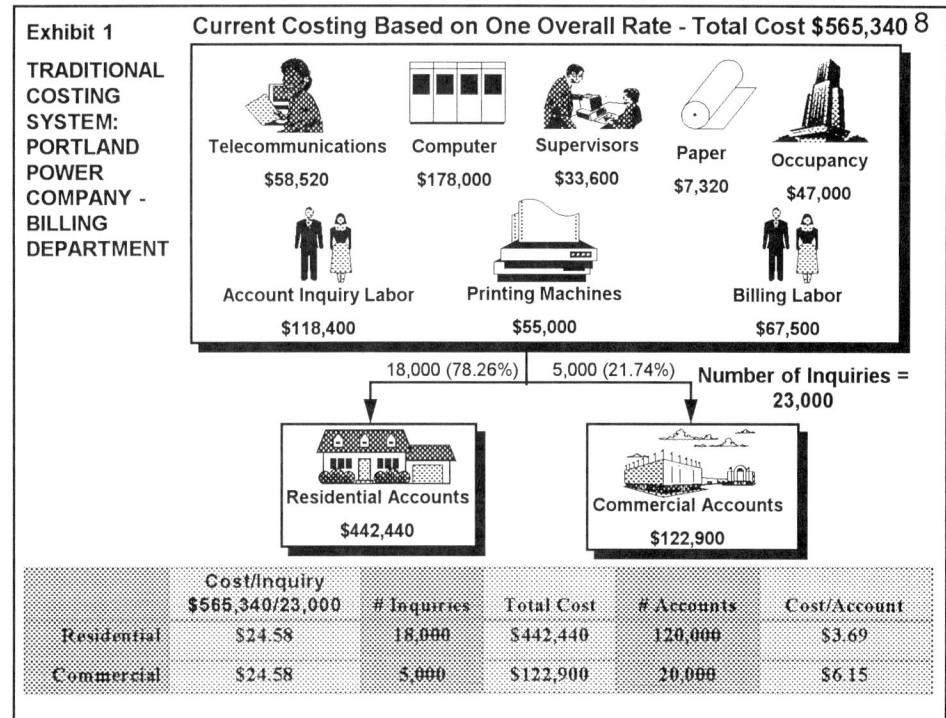

NOTES

Steps 1-4: Determine Cost Objectives, Activity Centers, Resources, and Cost Drivers

- Cost objects are the two customer classes - Residential and Commercial
- Based on interviews of key operating personnel, four key activity centers and associated cost drivers were determined to be:
  - Correspondence — *Letters*
  - Account billing — *Lines*
  - Bill verification — *Accounts*
  - Account inquiry — *Labor-Hours*
- Resources used to support the above activities were shown in Exhibit 1

NOTES

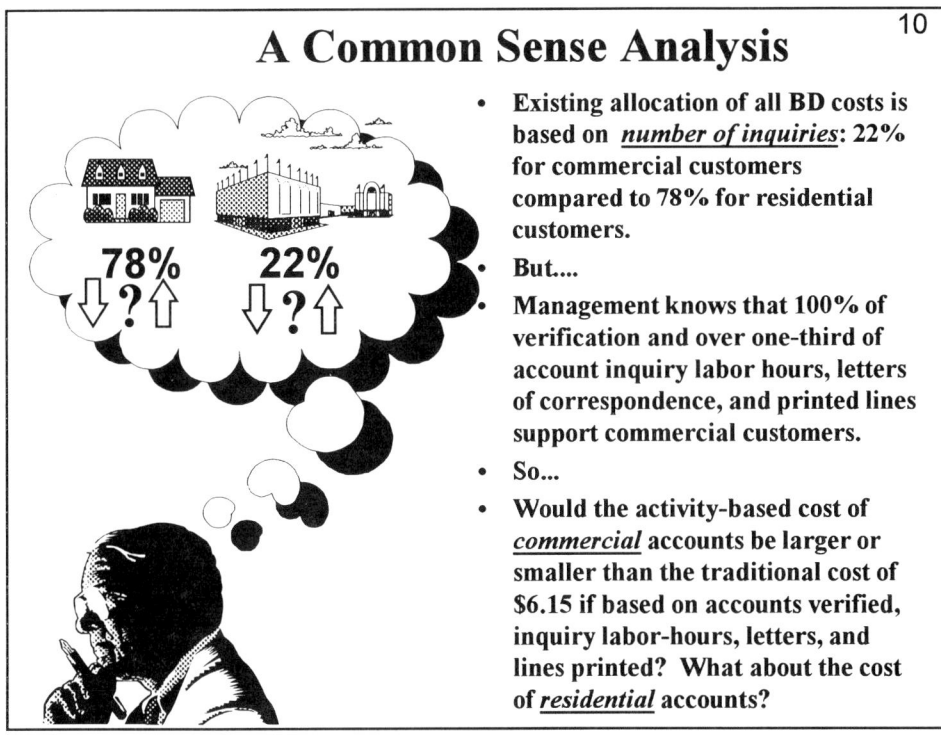

A Common Sense Analysis

- Existing allocation of all **BD** costs is based on *number of inquiries*: 22% for commercial customers compared to 78% for residential customers.
- But....
- Management knows that 100% of verification and over one-third of account inquiry labor hours, letters of correspondence, and printed lines support commercial customers.
- So...
- Would the activity-based cost of *commercial* accounts be larger or smaller than the traditional cost of $6.15 if based on accounts verified, inquiry labor-hours, letters, and lines printed? What about the cost of *residential* accounts?

Building the Process Map

- In complex systems, it is often useful to develop a process-based map of operations to gain an understanding of how costs flow through activity centers.
- Determine the cost objects - the products or services that generate the demand for activities.
- For PPC, the cost objects are the two customer classes - residential and commercial.
- Cost objects can also be product lines, departments, distribution channels, etc.

RESIDENTIAL ACCOUNT SUMMARY

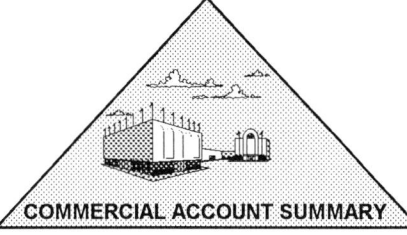
COMMERCIAL ACCOUNT SUMMARY

NOTES

PowerNotes for Cost Accounting: A Managerial Emphasis, Ninth Edition

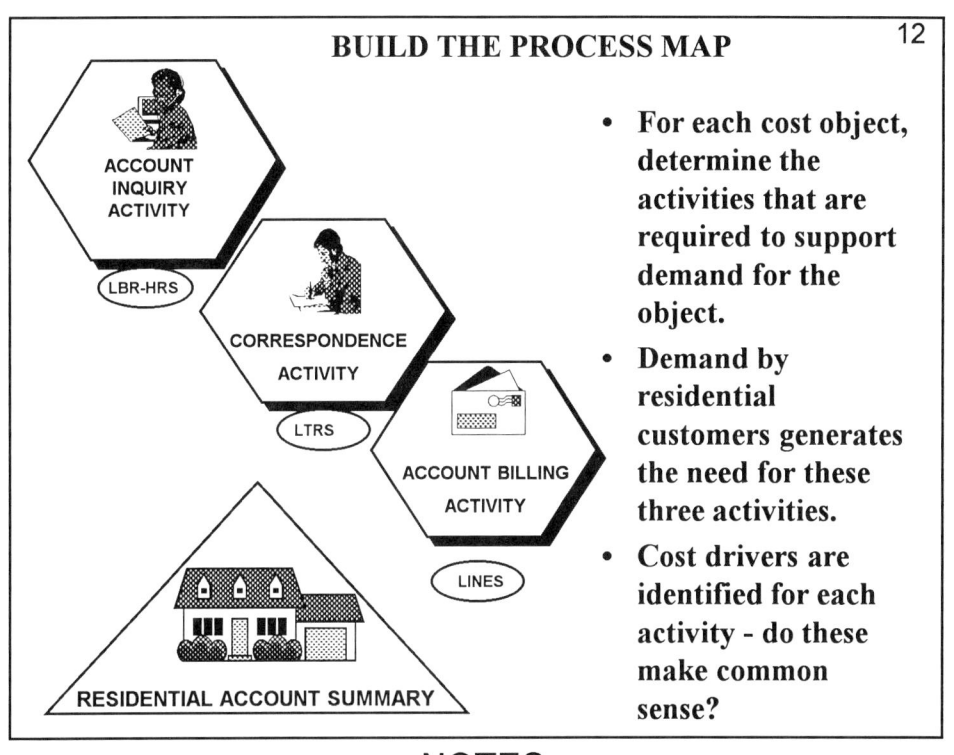

BUILD THE PROCESS MAP

- For each cost object, determine the activities that are required to support demand for the object.
- Demand by residential customers generates the need for these three activities.
- Cost drivers are identified for each activity - do these make common sense?

NOTES

PowerNotes for Cost Accounting: A Managerial Emphasis, Ninth Edition

BUILD THE PROCESS MAP

- **For each activity, determine the resources (or other activities) required to support the activity. Identify cost drivers.**
- **Account billing activity requires printing machines and billing labor.**
- **Note that costs are associated with resources that are consumed by activities.**

PRINTING MACHINES — LINES

BILLING LABOR — LBR-HRS

ACCOUNT BILLING ACTIVITY — LINES

NOTES

BUILD THE PROCESS MAP

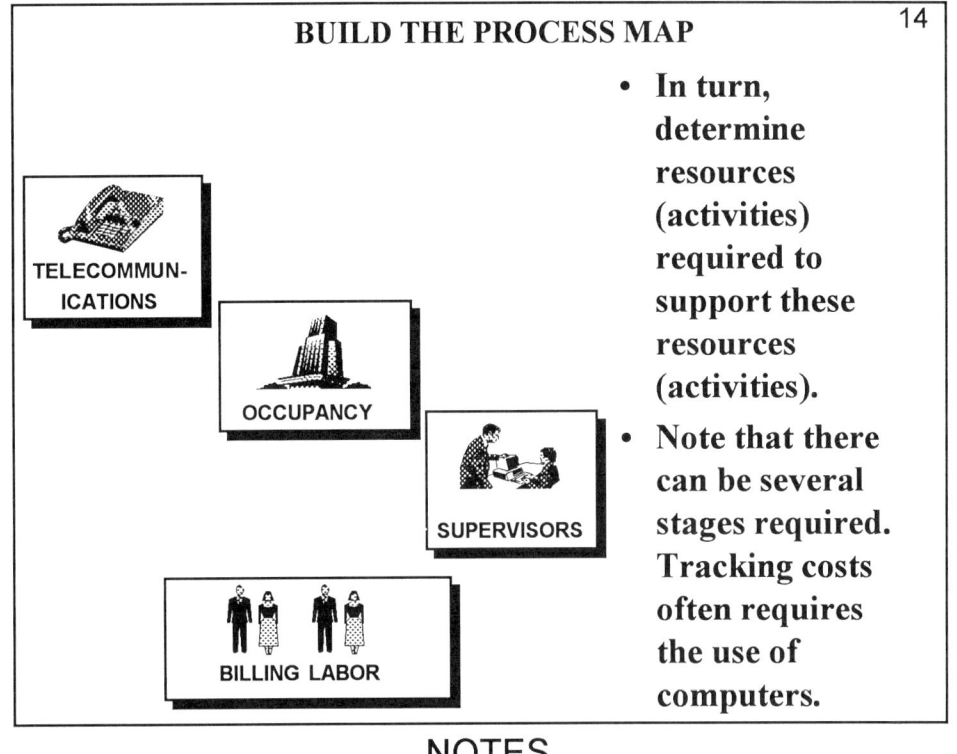

- **In turn, determine resources (activities) required to support these resources (activities).**
- **Note that there can be several stages required. Tracking costs often requires the use of computers.**

NOTES

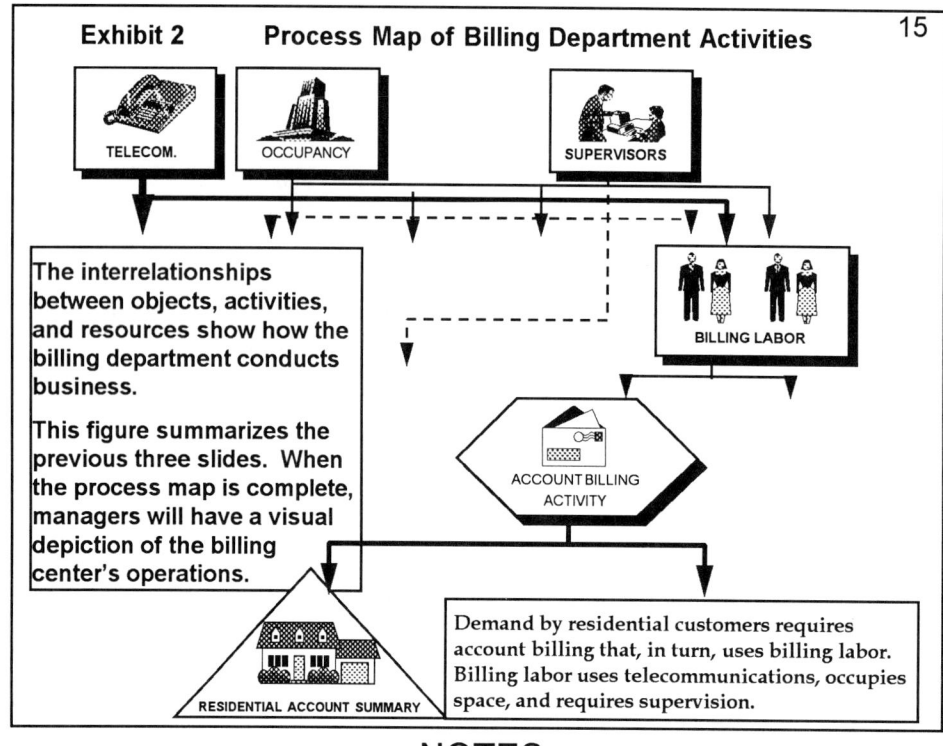

NOTES

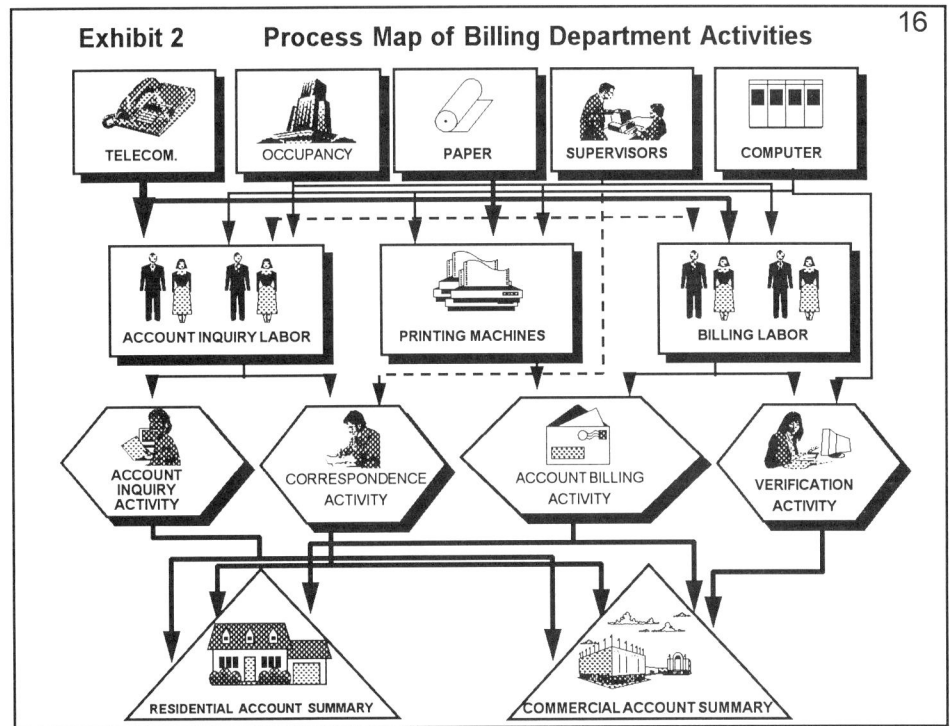

Exhibit 2 — Process Map of Billing Department Activities

NOTES

Collect Relevant Data

- Further interviews were conducted to collect data to be input into a computer program [NetProphet II ™] that automatically computes ABC results.
- A computer model was used to track the costs from resources to the final activity centers.
- The next two slides are sample outputs of NetProphet II. Compare the computer-generated results to Exhibits 3 and 4. Note that the "Traceable Costs" used in Exhibit 3 was taken from the NetProphet II results since their derivation by hand would be too complex.

NOTES

PowerNotes for Cost Accounting: A Managerial Emphasis, Ninth Edition

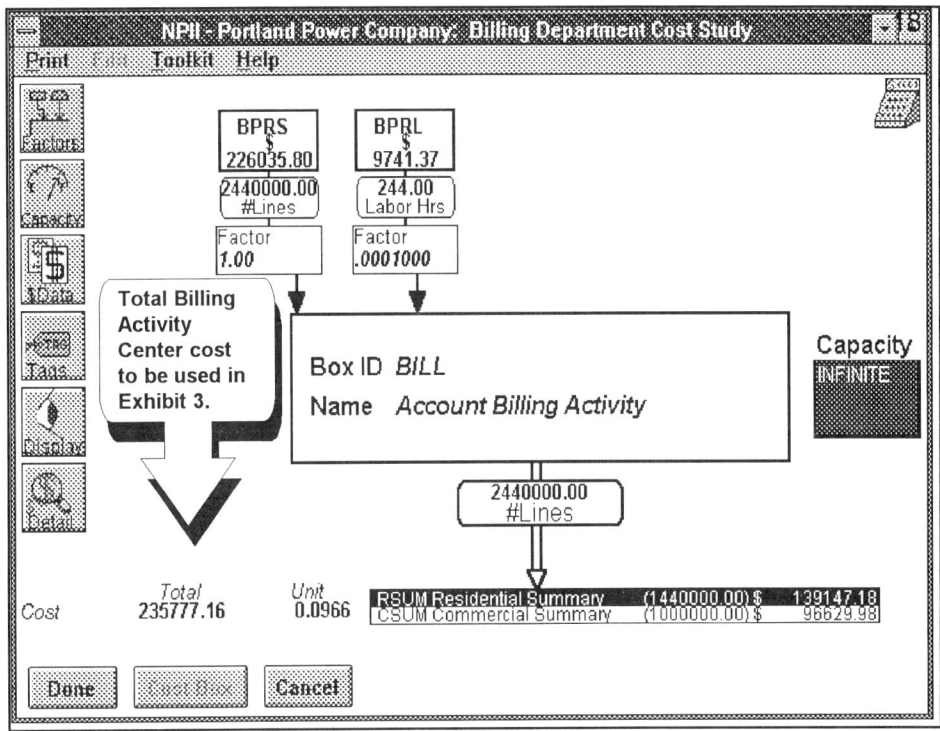

NOTES

PowerNotes for Cost Accounting: A Managerial Emphasis, Ninth Edition

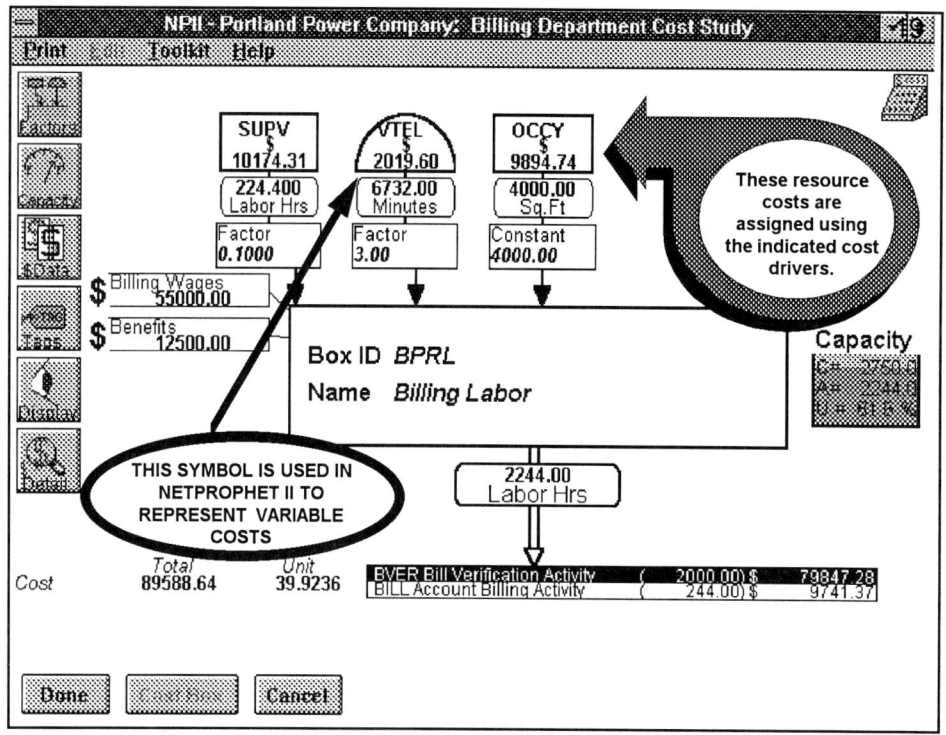

NOTES

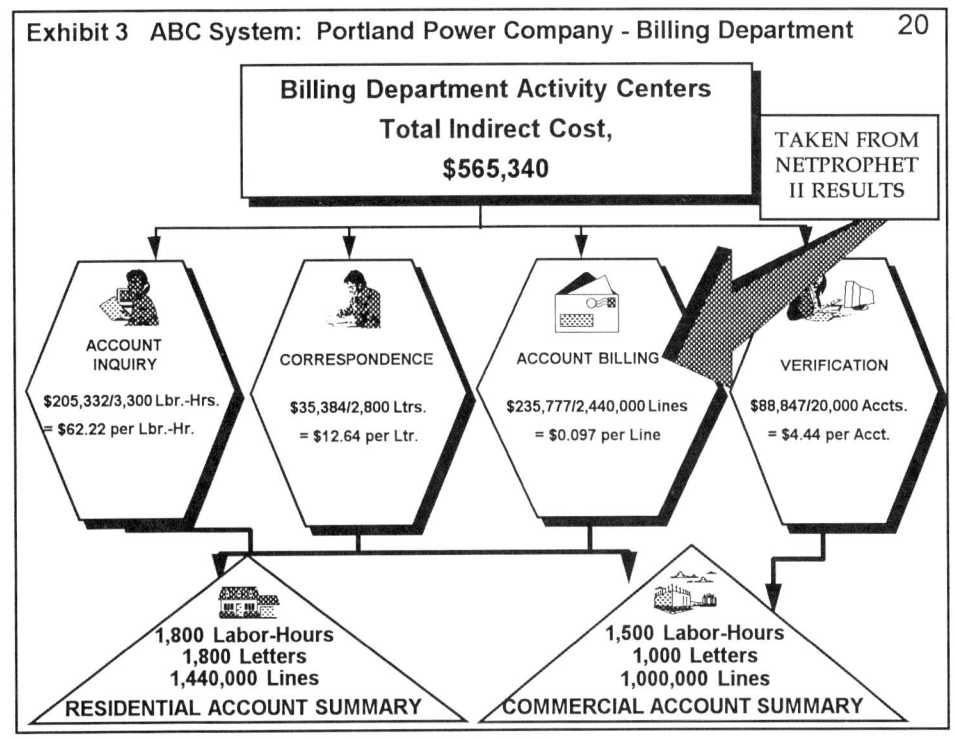

NOTES

Steps 5-6: Calculate and Interpret New Activity-Based Information

- The calculation of activity-based costs is shown in Exhibit 4. For most real-world applications, a computer program such as NetProphet II is used.

NOTES

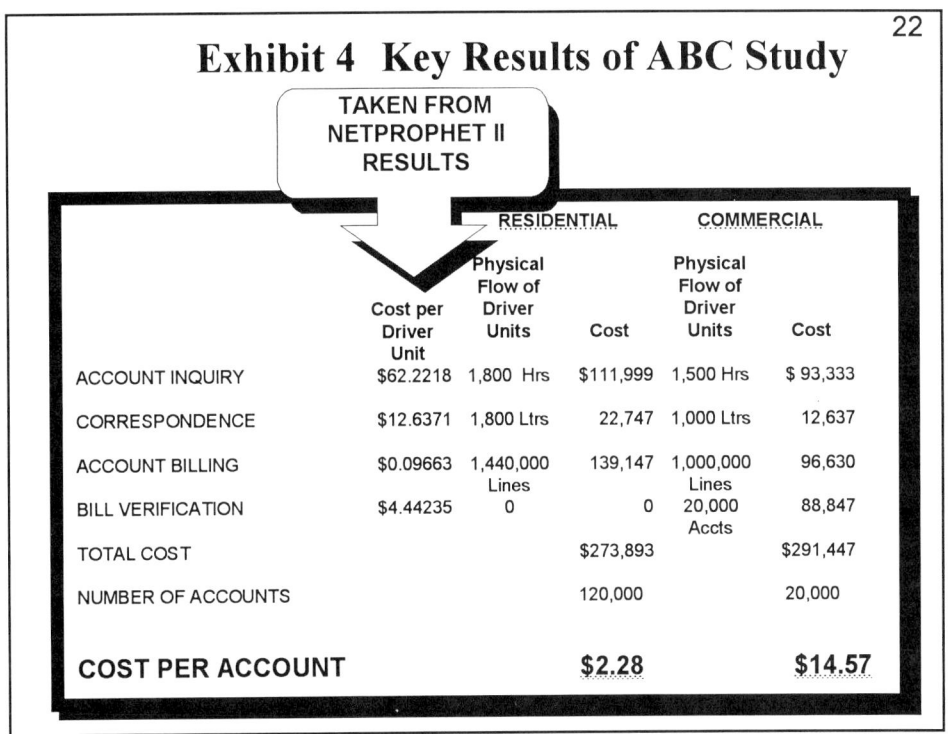

NOTES

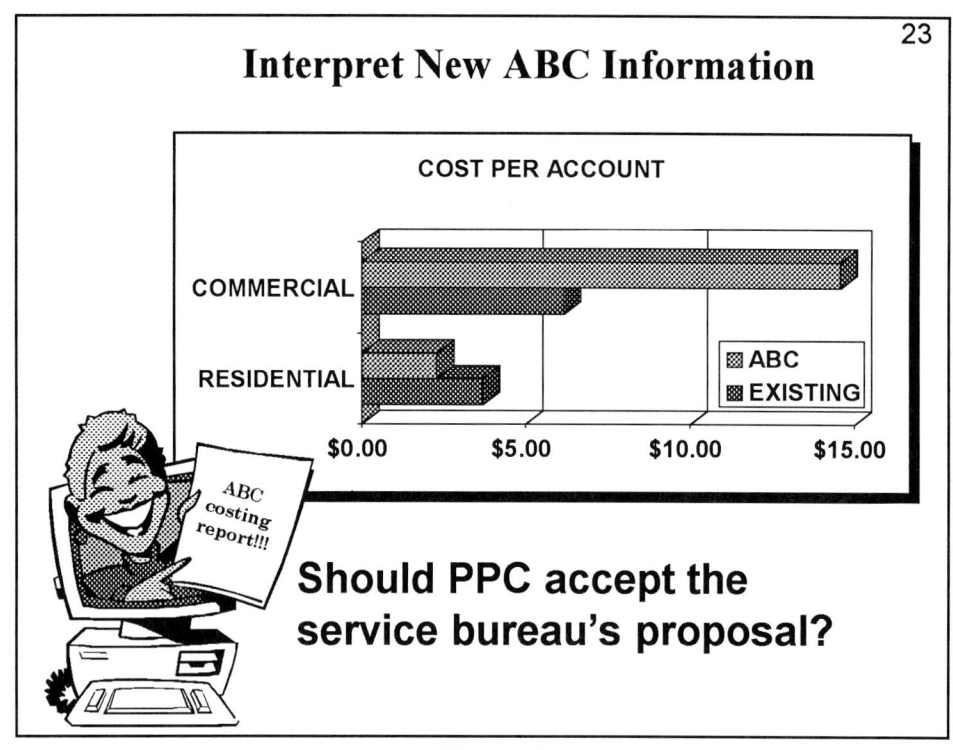

NOTES

NOTES

PowerNotes for Cost Accounting: A Managerial Emphasis, Ninth Edition

Costing Systems and Activity-Based Costing (II): Manufacturing Applications

NOTES

Basic Journal Entries and General Ledger Postings

Consider the following data for Buckinghamshire Printing Company - a British-based firm (in thousands of pounds):

Inventories, December 31, 19X6

Direct Materials	£ 16
Work-in-Process	31
Finished Goods	90

NOTES

Buckinghamshire uses a normal costing method - that is, actual costs for direct-cost items and budgeted costs for indirect-cost items. Exhibit 1 is an overivew of the job-costing system at London.

NOTES

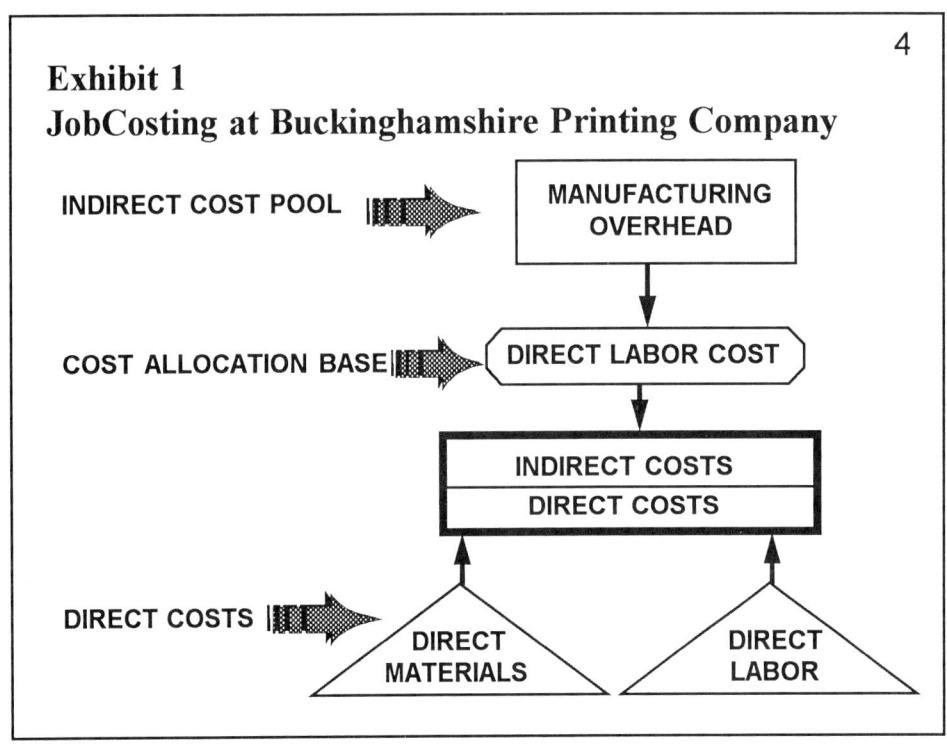

Exhibit 1
JobCosting at Buckinghamshire Printing Company

NOTES

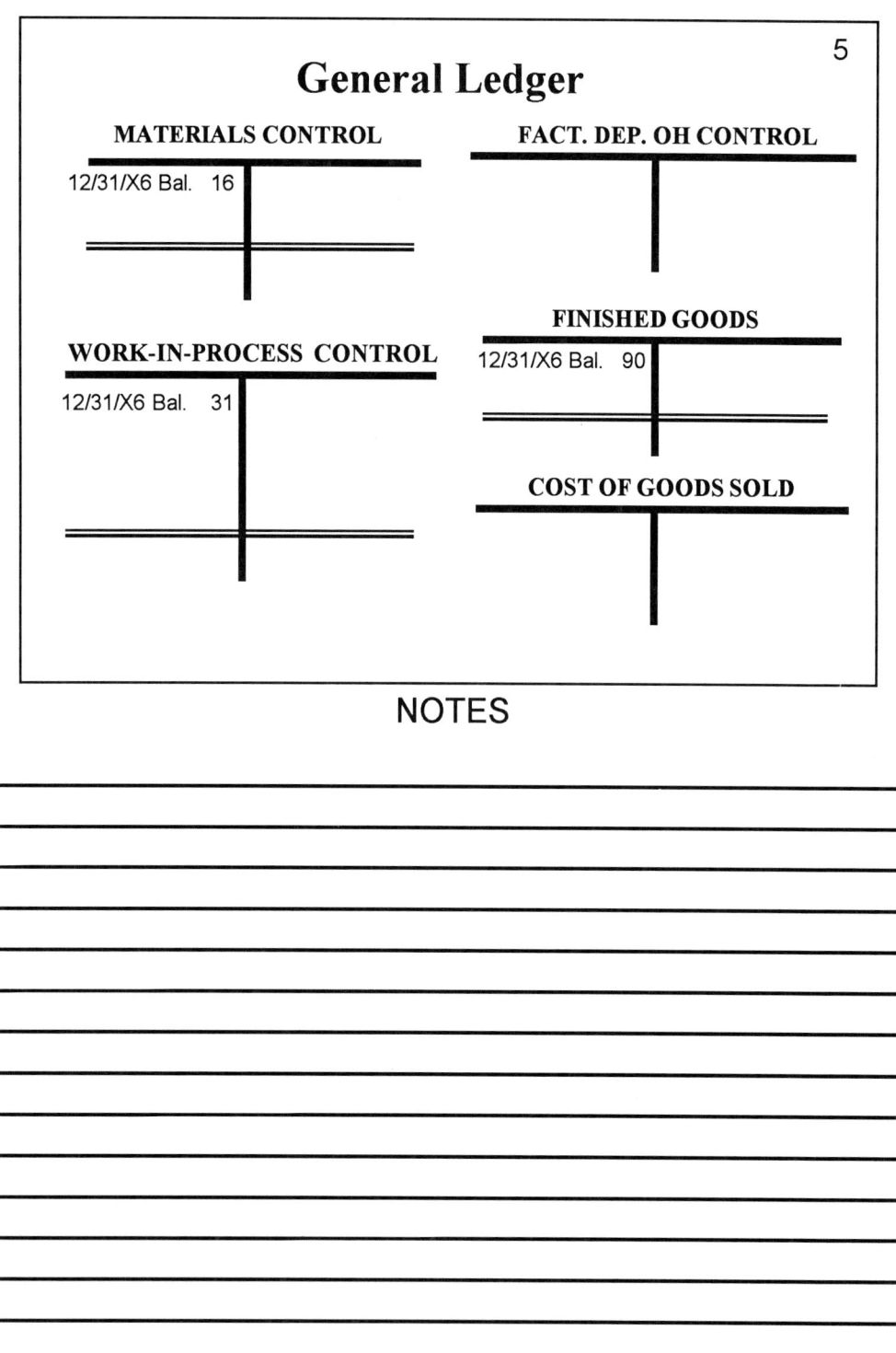

NOTES

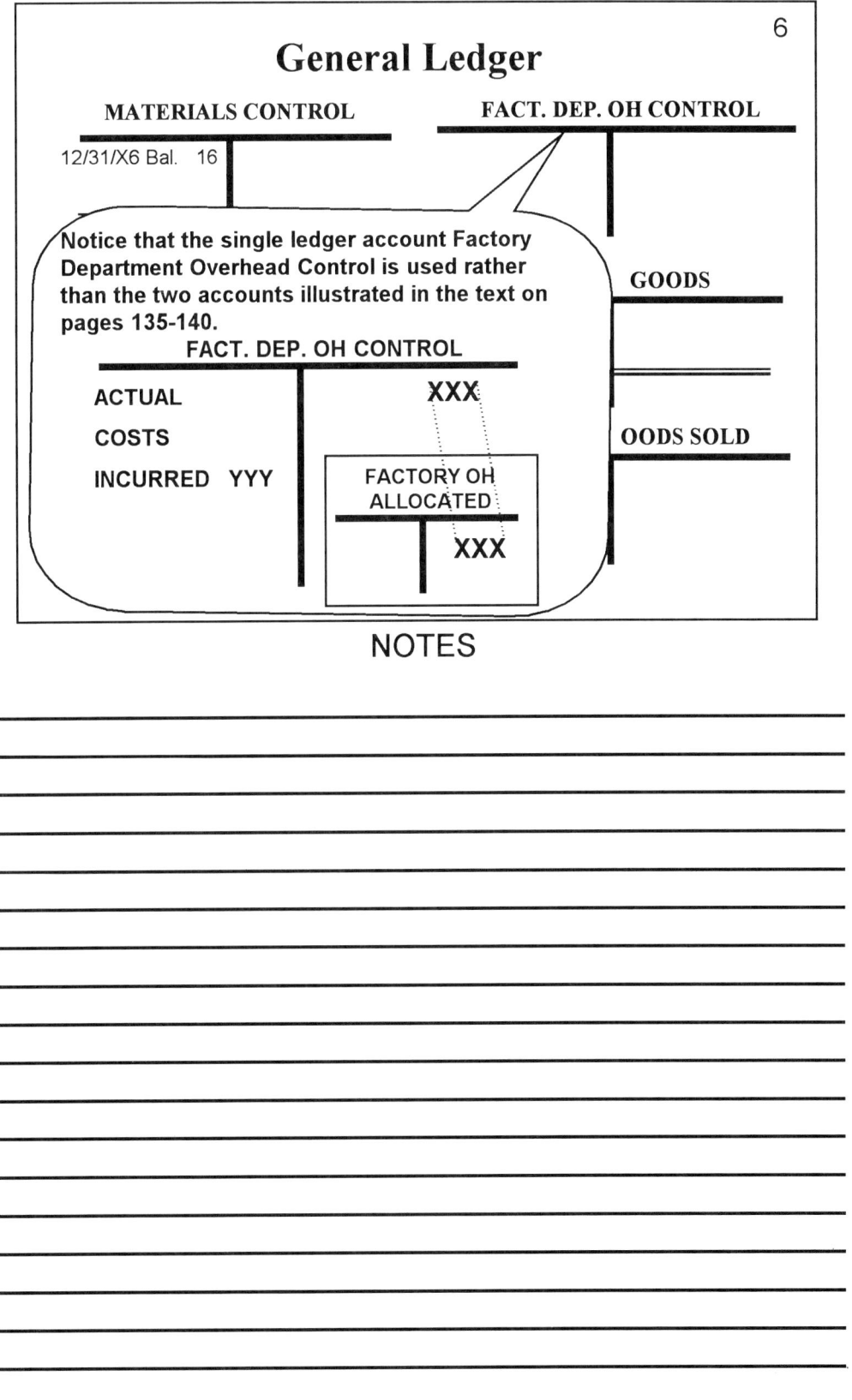

Summarized transactions for 19X7:

a.	Purchases of direct materials	£ 91
b.	Direct materials used	77
c.	Direct labor	90
d.	Factory overhead incurred	80
e.	Factory overhead allocated, 80% of direct labor	?
f.	Cost of goods completed and transferred to finished goods	220
g.	Cost of goods sold	210
h.	Sales on account	400

NOTES

Summary Journal Entries

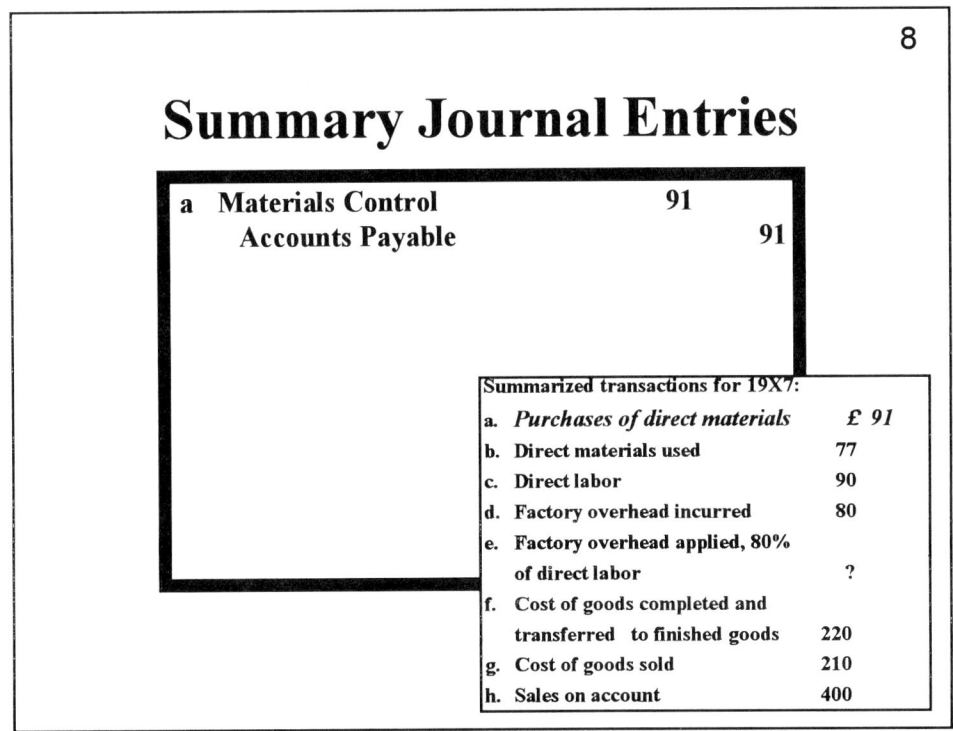

a	Materials Control	91	
	Accounts Payable		91

Summarized transactions for 19X7:
a. *Purchases of direct materials* — £ 91
b. Direct materials used — 77
c. Direct labor — 90
d. Factory overhead incurred — 80
e. Factory overhead applied, 80% of direct labor — ?
f. Cost of goods completed and transferred to finished goods — 220
g. Cost of goods sold — 210
h. Sales on account — 400

NOTES

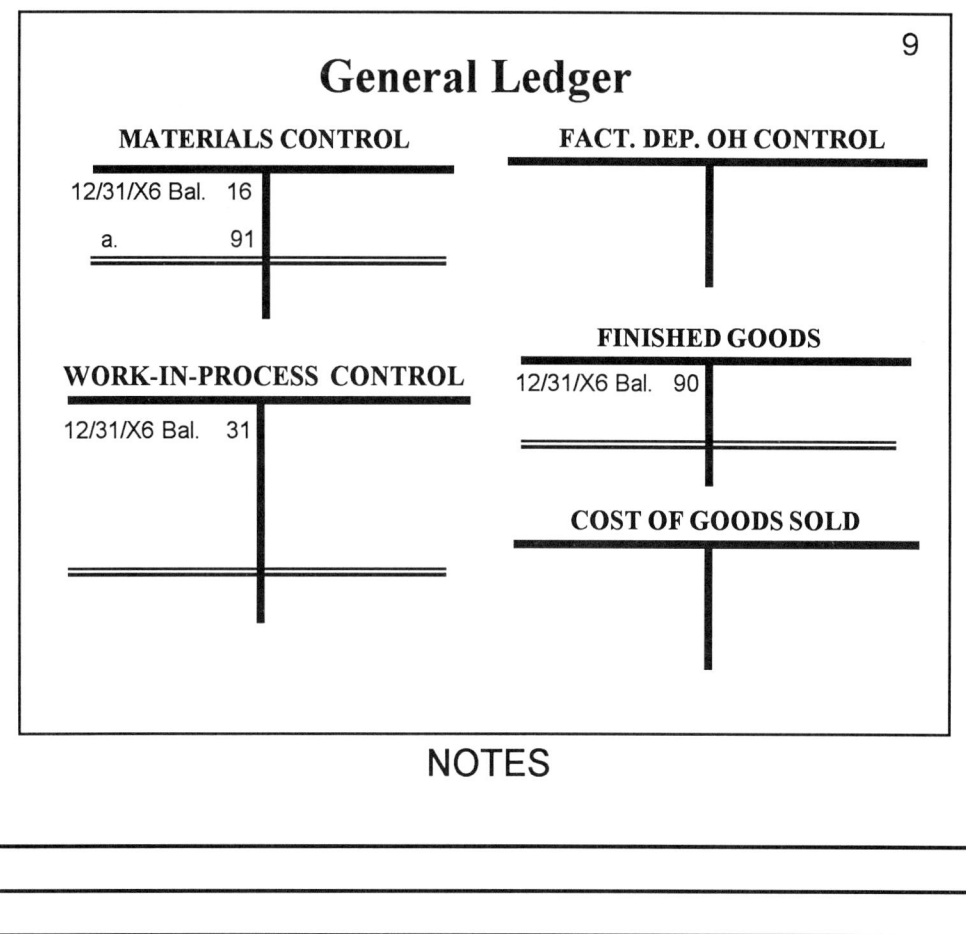

NOTES

Summary Journal Entries

a	Materials Control	91	
	Accounts Payable		91
b	Work-in-Process Control	77	
	Materials Control		77

Summarized transactions for 19X7:
a. Purchases of direct materials £ 91
b. Direct materials used 77
c. Direct labor 90
d. Factory overhead incurred 80
e. Factory overhead applied, 80% of direct labor ?
f. Cost of goods completed and transferred to finished goods 220
g. Cost of goods sold 210
h. Sales on account 400

General Ledger

MATERIALS CONTROL

12/31/X6 Bal. 16	b. 77
a. 91	
12/31/X7 Bal. 30	

WORK-IN-PROCESS CONTROL

12/31/X6 Bal. 31	
b. 77	

FACT. DEP. OH CONTROL

FINISHED GOODS

12/31/X6 Bal. 90	

COST OF GOODS SOLD

NOTES

Journal Entries

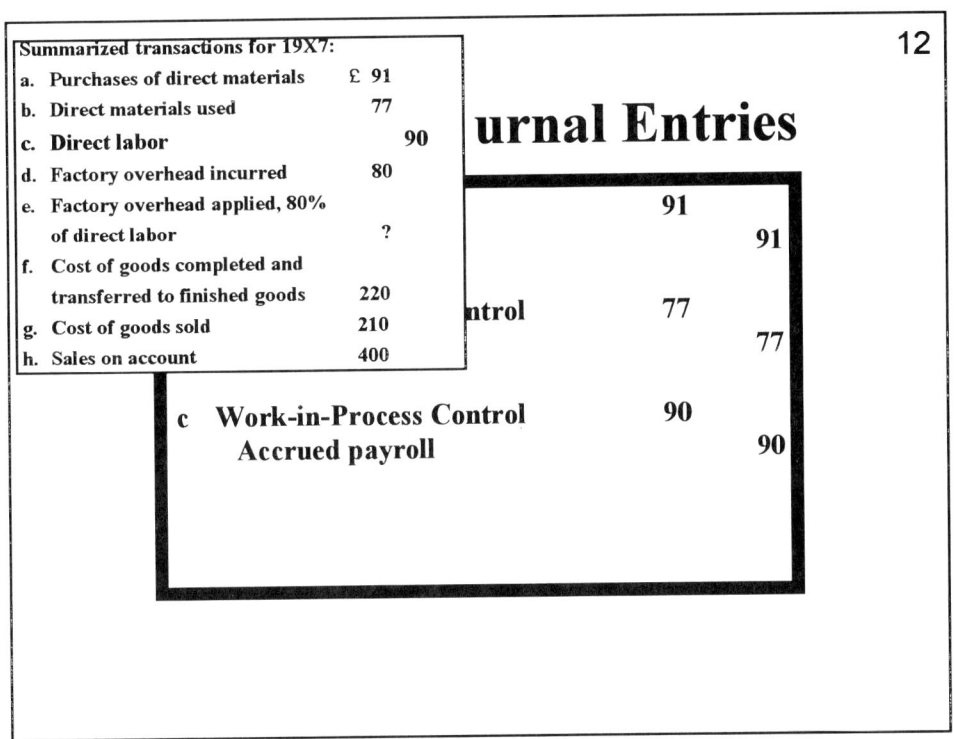

Summarized transactions for 19X7:
a. Purchases of direct materials £ 91
b. Direct materials used 77
c. Direct labor 90
d. Factory overhead incurred 80
e. Factory overhead applied, 80% of direct labor ?
f. Cost of goods completed and transferred to finished goods 220
g. Cost of goods sold 210
h. Sales on account 400

	91	
		91
ntrol	77	
		77
c Work-in-Process Control	90	
Accrued payroll		90

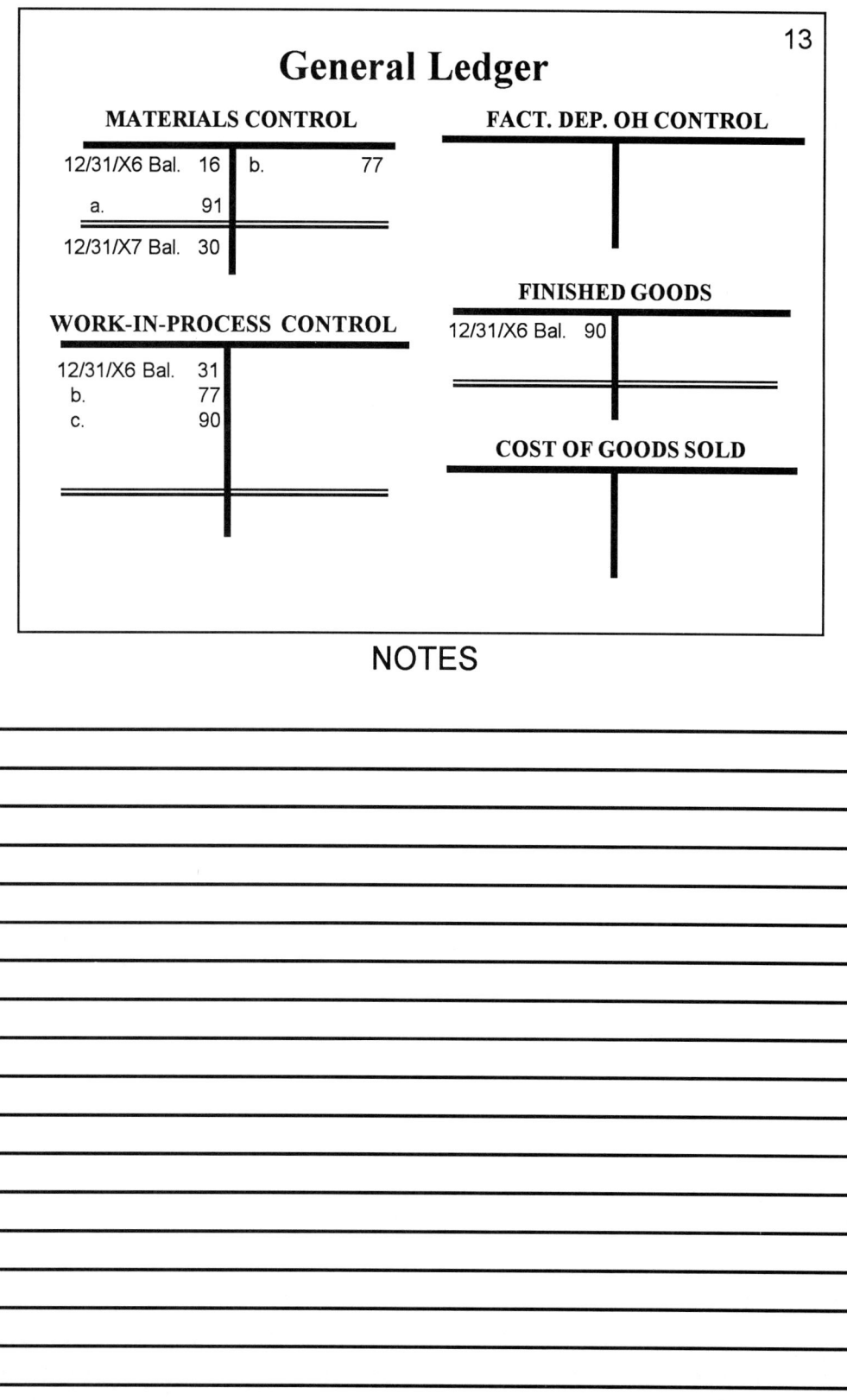

PowerNotes for Cost Accounting: A Managerial Emphasis, Ninth Edition

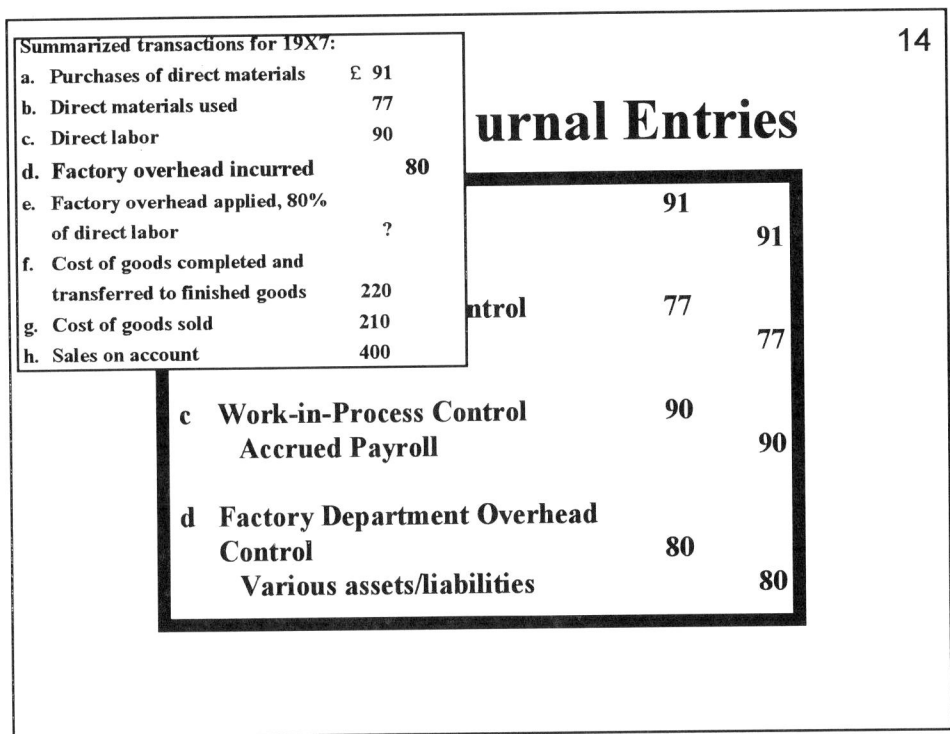

Journal Entries

Summarized transactions for 19X7:	
a. Purchases of direct materials	£ 91
b. Direct materials used	77
c. Direct labor	90
d. Factory overhead incurred	80
e. Factory overhead applied, 80% of direct labor	?
f. Cost of goods completed and transferred to finished goods	220
g. Cost of goods sold	210
h. Sales on account	400

```
a   Materials Control                           91
        Accounts Payable                            91

b   Work-in-Process Control                     77
        Materials Control                           77

c   Work-in-Process Control                     90
        Accrued Payroll                             90

d   Factory Department Overhead
    Control                                     80
        Various assets/liabilities                  80
```

NOTES

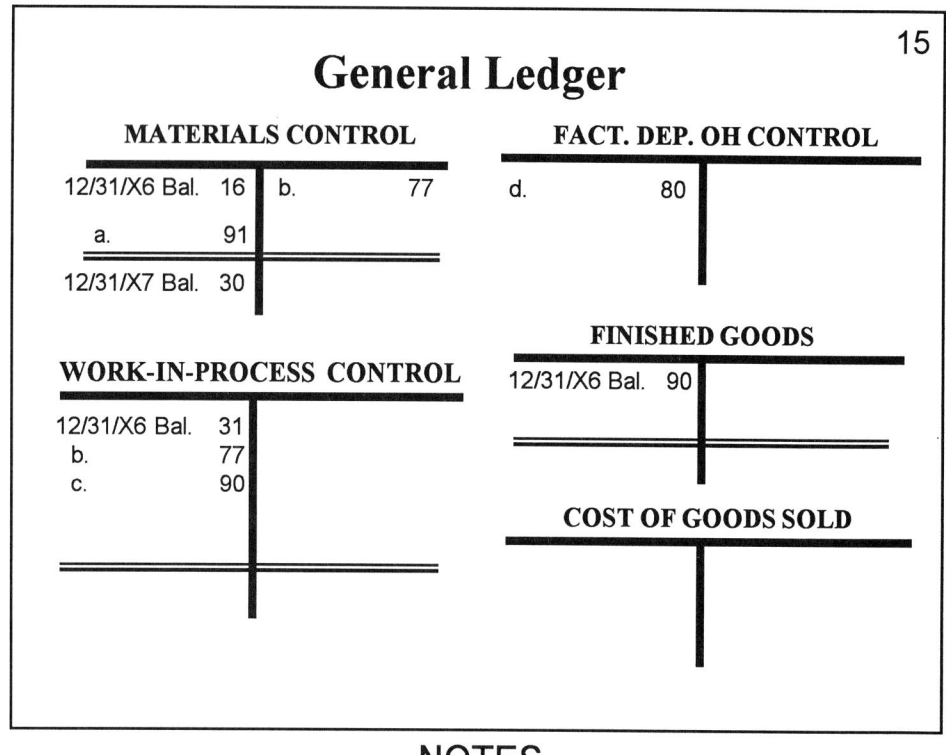

NOTES

Summary Journal Entries

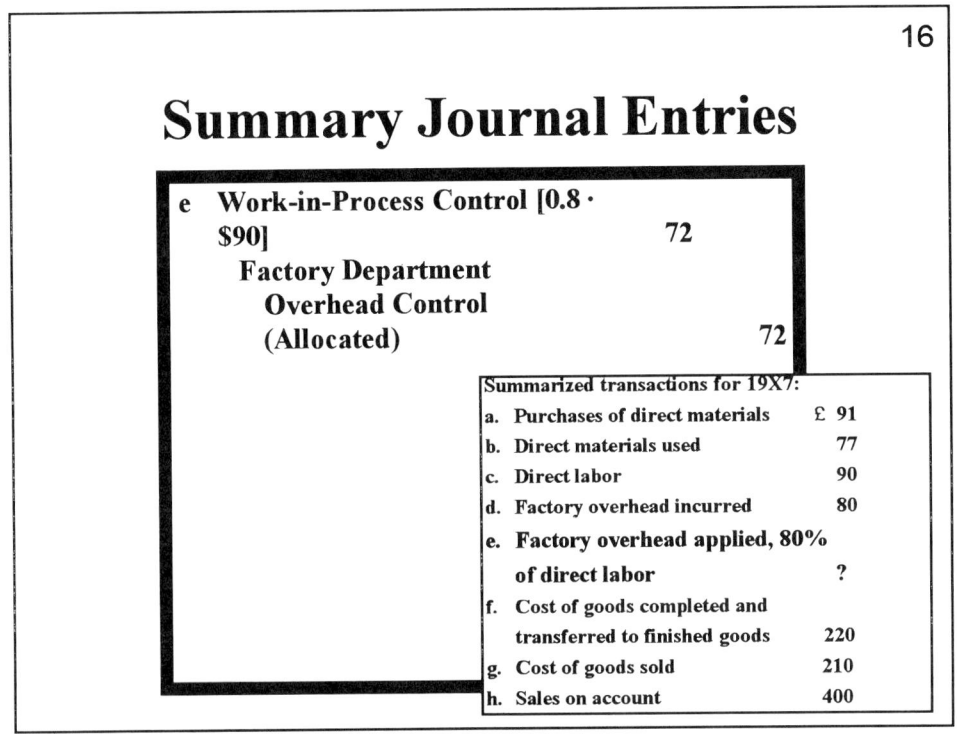

e	Work-in-Process Control [0.8 · $90]	72	
	Factory Department Overhead Control (Allocated)		72

Summarized transactions for 19X7:
a.	Purchases of direct materials	£ 91
b.	Direct materials used	77
c.	Direct labor	90
d.	Factory overhead incurred	80
e.	Factory overhead applied, 80% of direct labor	?
f.	Cost of goods completed and transferred to finished goods	220
g.	Cost of goods sold	210
h.	Sales on account	400

General Ledger

MATERIALS CONTROL

12/31/X6 Bal.	16	b.	77
a.	91		
12/31/X7 Bal.	30		

WORK-IN-PROCESS CONTROL

12/31/X6 Bal.	31		
b.	77		
c.	90		
e.	72		
	270		

FACT. DEP. OH CONTROL

d.	80	e.	72

FINISHED GOODS

12/31/X6 Bal.	90		

COST OF GOODS SOLD

NOTES

Summary Journal Entries

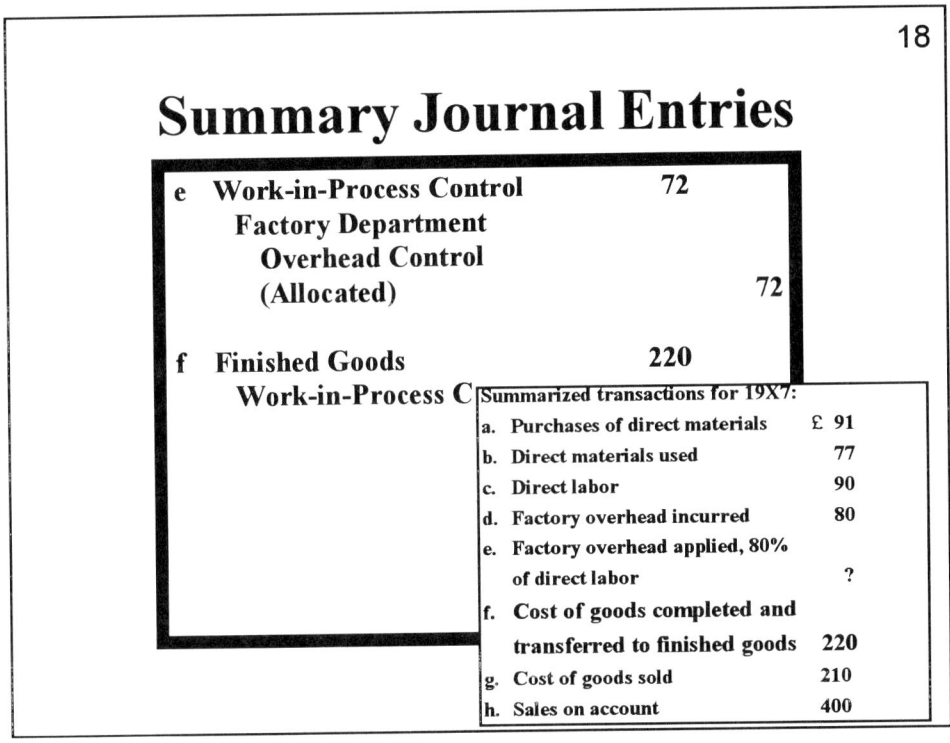

PowerNotes for Cost Accounting: A Managerial Emphasis, Ninth Edition

General Ledger

MATERIALS CONTROL

12/31/X6 Bal.	16	b.	77
a.	91		
12/31/X7 Bal.	30		

WORK-IN-PROCESS CONTROL

12/31/X6 Bal.	31	f.	220
b.	77		
c.	90		
e.	72		
	270		
12/31/X7 Bal.	50		

FACT. DEP. OH CONTROL

d.	80	e.	72

FINISHED GOODS

12/31/X6 Bal.	90	f.	220

COST OF GOODS SOLD

NOTES

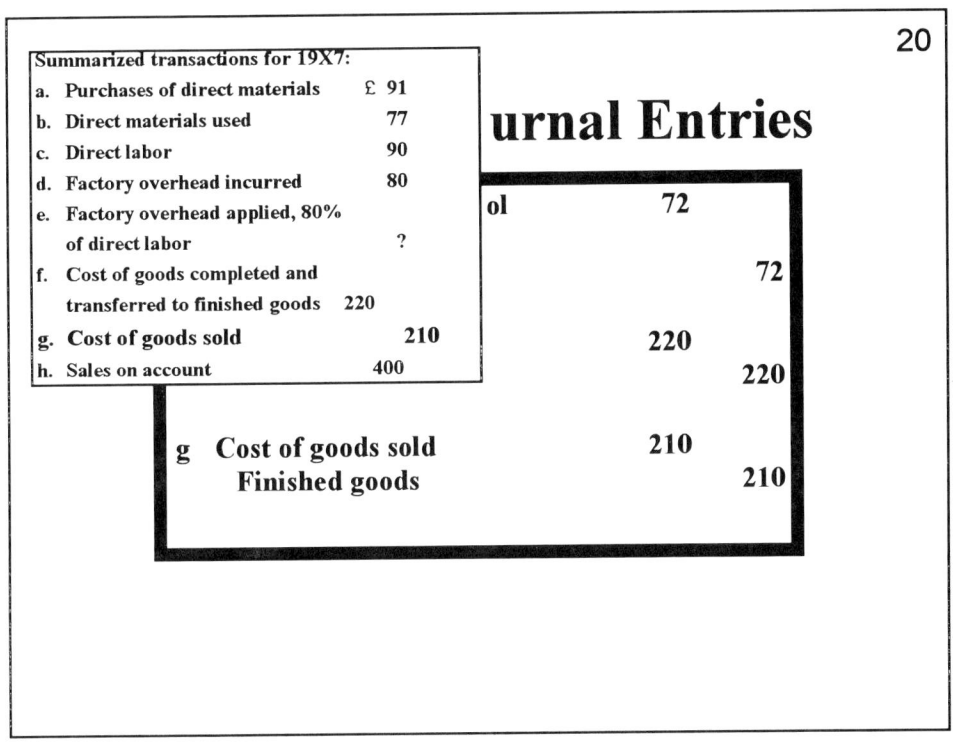

Journal Entries

Summarized transactions for 19X7:	
a. Purchases of direct materials	£ 91
b. Direct materials used	77
c. Direct labor	90
d. Factory overhead incurred	80
e. Factory overhead applied, 80% of direct labor	?
f. Cost of goods completed and transferred to finished goods	220
g. Cost of goods sold	210
h. Sales on account	400

	ol	72	
			72
		220	
			220
g	Cost of goods sold	210	
	Finished goods		210

NOTES

General Ledger

MATERIALS CONTROL

12/31/X6 Bal.	16	b.	77
a.	91		
12/31/X7 Bal.	30		

WORK-IN-PROCESS CONTROL

12/31/X6 Bal.	31	f.	220
b.	77		
c.	90		
e.	72		
	270		
12/31/X7 Bal.	50		

FACT. DEP. OH CONTROL

d.	80	e.	72

FINISHED GOODS

12/31/X6 Bal.	90		
f.	220	g.	210
12/31/X7 Bal.	80		

COST OF GOODS SOLD

g.	210	

NOTES

PowerNotes for Cost Accounting: A Managerial Emphasis, Ninth Edition

Master Budget and Responsibility Accounting

NOTES

PowerNotes for Cost Accounting: A Managerial Emphasis, Ninth Edition

PROFIT PLANNING AND COST REDUCTION

The Budgeting Process at Daihatsu

NOTES

COST REDUCTION

- Companies employ many methods to control (reduce) costs.
- When revenues are set by market conditions, gaining and maintaining a competitive edge is accomplished, in large part, by cost reduction.
- What are the most important *cost estimation tools* and *cost reduction techniques* and how can the annual profit plan (master budget) aid in cost reduction?

NOTES

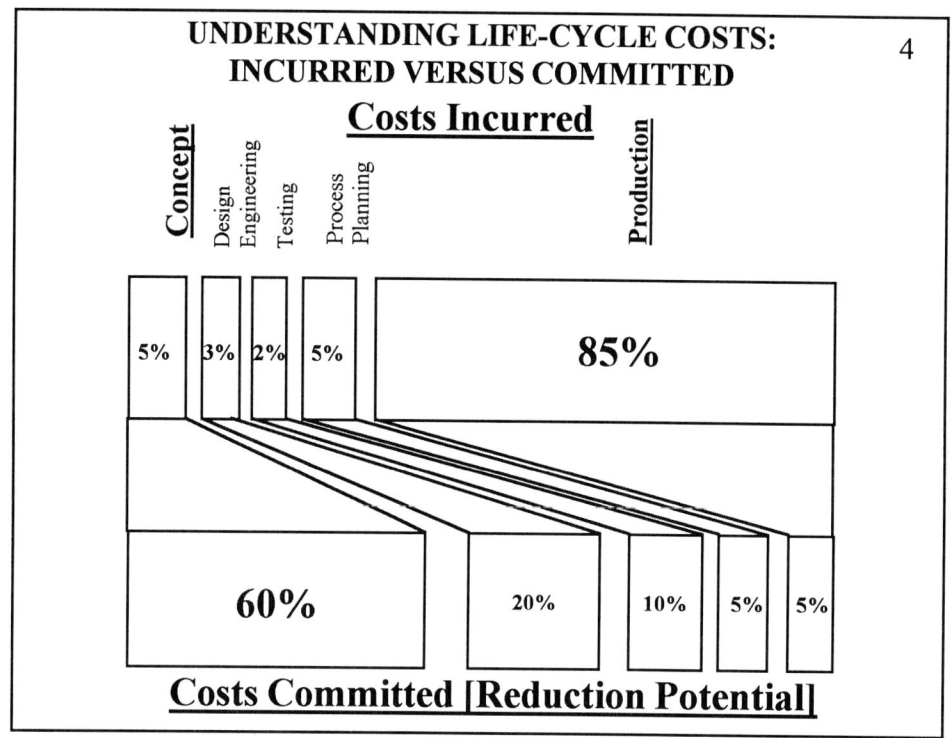

NOTES

PowerNotes for Cost Accounting: A Managerial Emphasis, Ninth Edition

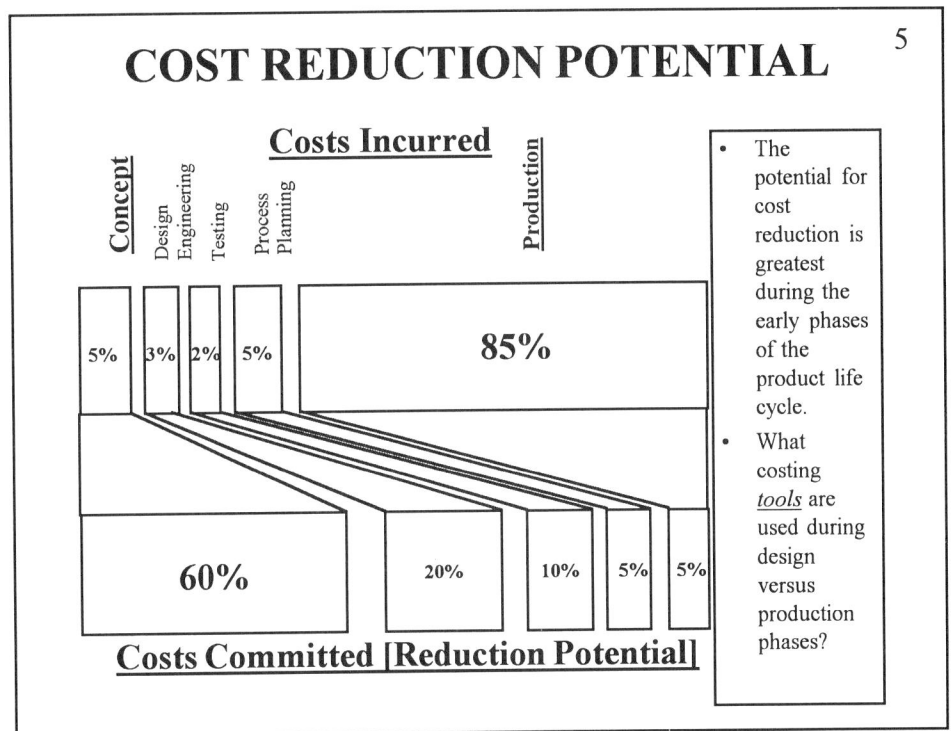

NOTES

TOOLS: TARGET AND KAIZEN COSTING

Concept | Design Engineering | Testing | Process Planning | Production

TARGET COSTING

A tool used to set cost reduction "targets" to be achieved over the product life cycle. Target costing is used primarily during the concept - process planning stages.

KAIZEN COSTING

NOTES

WHEN TARGET AND KAIZEN COSTING IS USED

Concept | Design Engineering | Testing | Process Planning | Production

After the concept - process planning stages of the life cycle, there usually remains a gap between the target life-cycle cost and the estimated cost. The process of continuous improvement during the production stage is kaizen - reaching cost reduction targets set for each department as part of the annual profit plan. *Kaizen costing is the cost tool used to establish short-term reduction targets.* Figure 1 gives <u>techniques</u> used to reduce costs during the product life cycle.

KAIZEN COSTING

NOTES

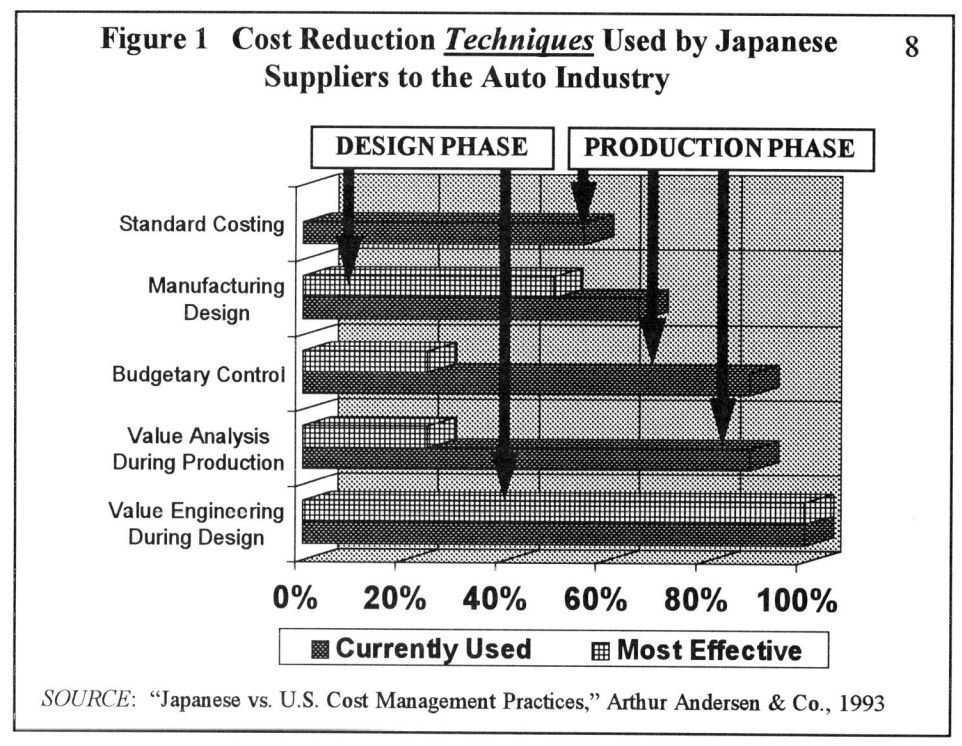

NOTES

DAIHATSU: COMPANY BACKGROUND

- Daihatsu, based in Osaka, Japan, is partly owned by Toyota
- Manufactures minivehicles and compact cars
- 1995 sales of 420,000 units in Japan and 83,000 exported.
- 1995 revenue of over ¥ 700 billion

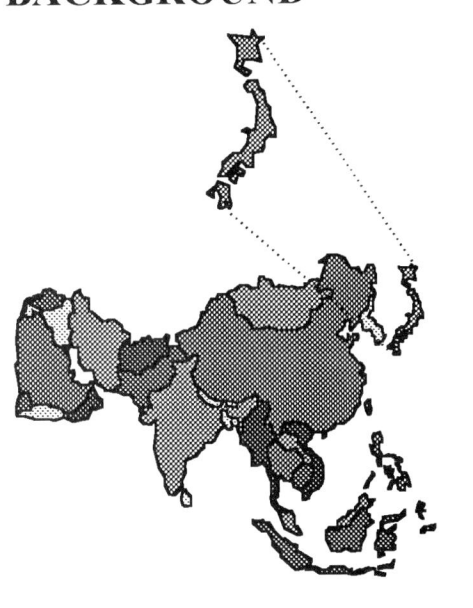

NOTES

COST REDUCTION AT DAIHATSU

- **TARGET COSTING**
  - Used during new product design & development
- **KAIZEN COSTING**
  - Supports continuous improvement and cost reduction during manufacturing phase
  - Is a budgetary control system
  - Daihatsu defines kaizen costing as those activities that *"sustain the current level of the existing car production costs, and further reduce it to the expected level based on the company (profit) plan."*

NOTES

DAIHATSU'S ANNUAL BUDGET

- Daihatsu's annual budget is the first year of the five-year long-range plan
- Each department develops 6 plans as part of the annual budget [see Figure 2]
  - **Plan 1:** the *production, distribution, and sales plan* is the heart of the annual budget
    - The contribution approach is used
    - Costs are *actual **variable** costs* from the previous year-end
    - Forecast *sales less actual variable costs gives contribution margin* before Kaizen improvements

NOTES

Figure 2
Operating Profit Budget

From Plan 1	Sales Forecast
	− Actual Variable Costs
	Contribution Margin
From Plans 2 & 3	− Changes in Variable Costs
	Adjusted Contribution Margin
From Plans 4 - 6	− Expected Fixed Costs
	Budgeted Operating Profit

NOTES

Daihatsu's Annual Budget

- **Plan 2**: *Parts and Materials Plan*
  - Sets targets for the purchasing department
- **Plan 3**: *Plant Rationalization Plan*
  - **Central component of Kaizen costing**
  - Reductions in manufacturing variable costs [See Figure 3]
- Plan 1 less Plans 2 and 3 yields *adjusted contribution margin*

NOTES

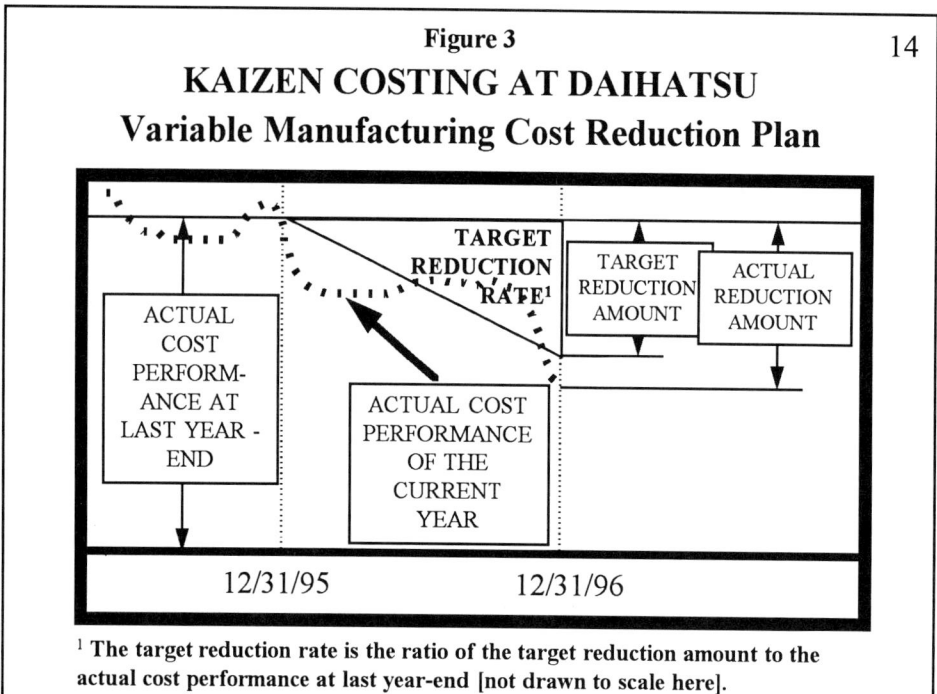

Figure 3

KAIZEN COSTING AT DAIHATSU
Variable Manufacturing Cost Reduction Plan

[1] The target reduction rate is the ratio of the target reduction amount to the actual cost performance at last year-end [not drawn to scale here].

NOTES

Daihatsu's Annual Budget

- **Plan 4**: *Personal Plan*
  - Sets targets for direct labor and service department personnel [fixed costs]
- **Plan 5**: *Facility Investment Plan [Capital Budget]*
  - Depreciation taken from the capital budget - fixed cost - is part of the *operating budget*
  - The capital budget is an example of a *financial budget*
- **Plan 6**: *Fixed Expense Plan*
  - Design, maintenance, advertising, general and administrative costs [fixed costs]

NOTES

PowerNotes for Cost Accounting: A Managerial Emphasis, Ninth Edition

Flexible Budgets, Variances, and Management Control: I

NOTES

FLEXIBLE BUDGETING

Illustration of the General Model

Static and Flexible Budgets Compared

Static Budget
- One level of output
- *Not* adjusted to reflect changes in revenue or cost driver levels

Flexible Budget
- Numerous levels of output
- Adjusted to reflect changes in revenue or cost driver levels

NOTES

Steps in Developing a Flexible Budget

- Determine budgeted selling price per unit, budgeted variable cost per unit, and budgeted fixed costs
- Determine actual quantity of revenue driver
- Determine flexible budget for revenue
- Determine actual quantity of cost driver(s)
- Determine flexible budget for costs

NOTES

Relationships Between Variances

Relationships Between Variances

Level 1 | Static-budget variance |

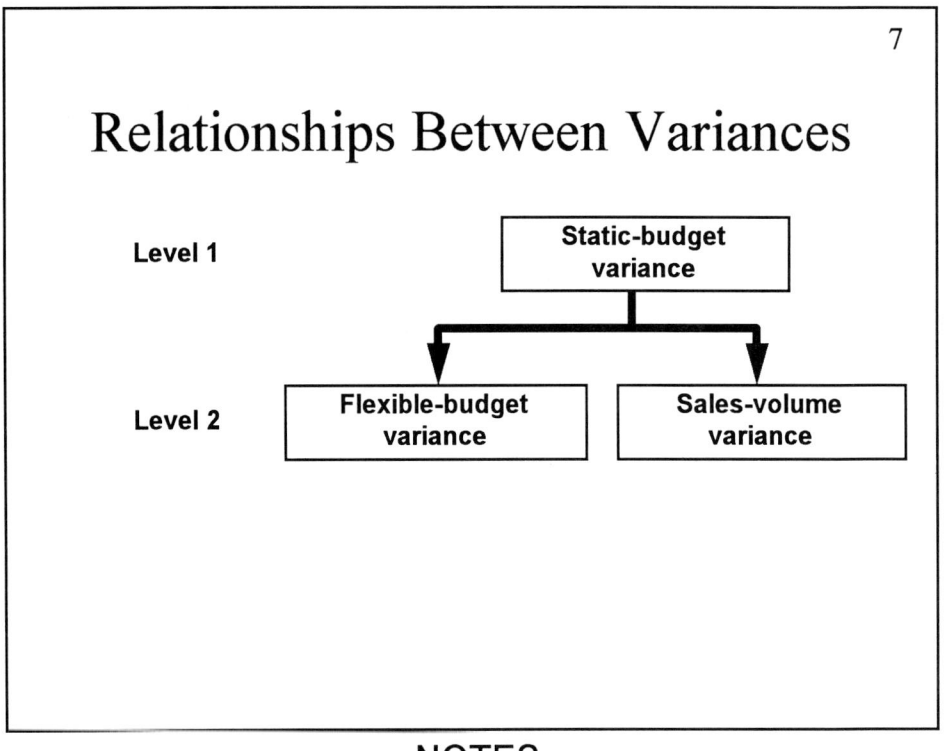

NOTES

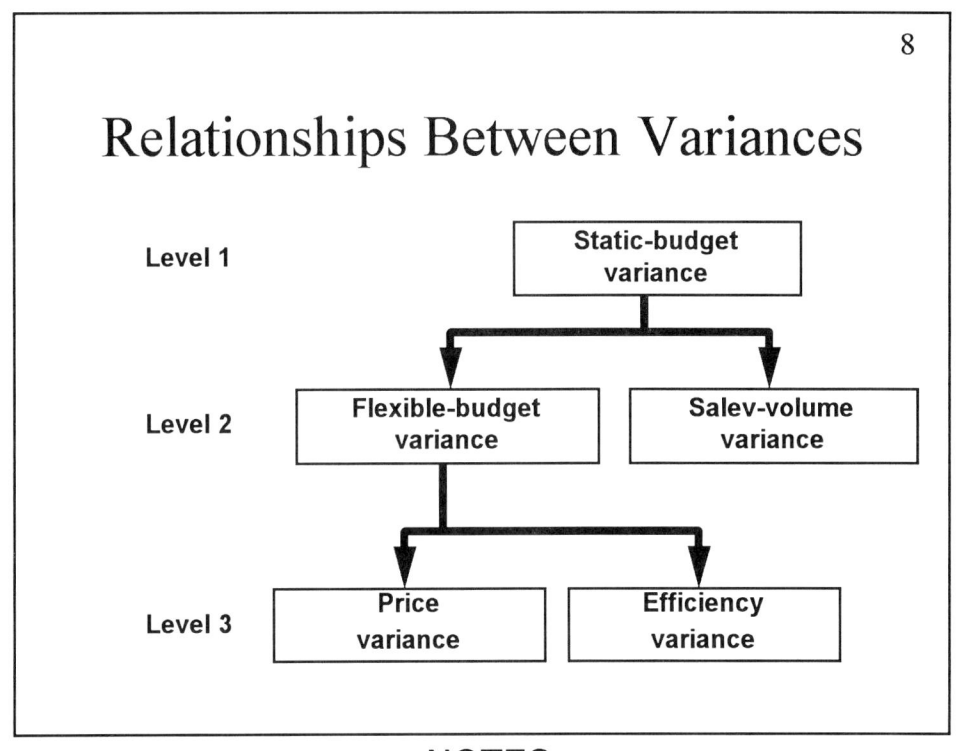

NOTES

General Model for the Evaluation of Financial Performance

	ACTUAL RESULTS AT ACTUAL ACTIVITY LEVEL (1)	FLEXIBLE-BUDGET VARIANCES (2) = (1) - (3)	FLEXIBLE-BUDGET FOR ACTUAL SALES VOLUME (3)	SALES-VOLUME VARIANCES (4) = (3) - (5)	STATIC BUDGET (5)
Units					
Sales					
VC					
CM					
FC					
OI					

NOTES

Illustration of Flexible Budget

	BUDGET	ACTUAL	VARIANCE
Net Revenue	$10,000	$9,500	-$500
Variable Costs	8,000	7,779	221
Contribution Margin	2,000	1,721	-279
Fixed Costs	1,200	1,200	0
Operating Income	800	521	-279

- *The condensed performance report for a recent quarter is given above ($000). Using the format of Exhibit 7-5 on page 229, prepare a table showing the static budget variance, the sales volume variances, and the flexible-budget variances.*

NOTES

PowerNotes for Cost Accounting: A Managerial Emphasis, Ninth Edition

NOTES

	ACTUAL RESULTS AT ACTUAL ACTIVITY LEVEL (1)	FLEXIBLE-BUDGET VARIANCES (2) = (1) - (3)	FLEXIBLE-BUDGET FOR ACTUAL SALES VOLUME (3)	SALES-VOLUME VARIANCES (4) = (3) - (5)	STATIC BUDGET (5)
Sales	$9,500		$9,500	$500	$10,000
VC	$7,779	$179	$7,600	$400	$8,000
CM	$1,721	$179	$1,900	$100	$2,000
FC	$1,200		$1,200		$1,200
OI	$521	$179	$700	$100	$800

NOTES

Understanding the Performance Evaluation Relationship between Static and Flexible Budget

	ACTUAL RESULTS AT ACTUAL ACTIVITY LEVEL (1)	FLEXIBLE-BUDGET VARIANCES (2) = (1) - (3)	FLEXIBLE-BUDGET FOR ACTUAL SALES VOLUME (3)	SALES-VOLUME VARIANCES (4) = (3) - (5)	STATIC BUDGET (5)
Sales	$9,500		$9,500	$500	$10,000
VC	$7,779	$179	$7,600	$400	$8,000
CM	$1,721	$179	$1,900	$100	$2,000
FC	$1,200		$1,200		$1,200
OI	$521	$179	$700	$100	$800

- *Why did actual results differ from the static budget?*
- *Sales volume was lower than expected, resulting in a $100 lower contribution margin.*
- *Variable costs per unit of activity were higher than budgeted, resulting in a $179 lower contribution margin.*

NOTES

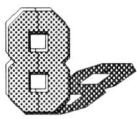

Flexible Budgets, Variances, and Management Control: II

Case 8-1
Fixed Overhead Variances

The Rocky Company is installing an absorption standard-cost system and a flexible-overhead budget. Standard costs have recently been developed for its only product and are as follows:

Direct material, 2 pounds @ $15	$30
Direct labor, 3 hours @ $12	36
Variable overhead, 3 hours @ $4	12
Fixed overhead	-?-
Standard cost per unit of finished product	$?

NOTES

Expected production activity is expressed as 6,000 standard direct-labor-hours per month. Fixed overhead is expected to be $36,000 per month. The predetermined fixed-overhead rate for product costing is not changed from month to month.

NOTES

Fixed Overhead Rate

- Calculate the proper fixed-overhead rate per standard direct-labor-hour and per unit.

Fixed Overhead Rate

- **Calculate the proper fixed-overhead rate per standard direct-labor-hour and per unit.**

$36,000 ÷ 6,000 hrs. = $6.00 per hour or $18.00 per unit ($6.00 • 3 hours)

NOTES

Graph budgeted and allocated *variable* overhead from zero to 7,500 hours.

NOTES

Graph budgeted and allocated *variable* overhead from zero to 7,500 hours.

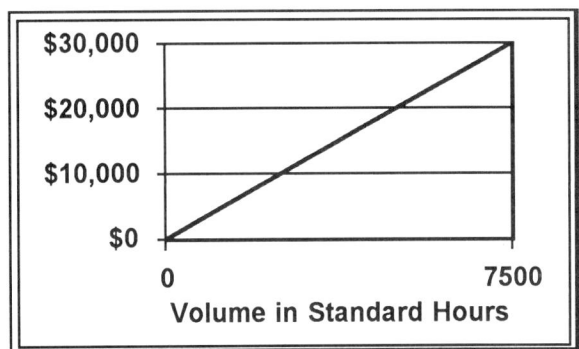

Budgeted and allocated lines are superimposed @ $4.00 per standard direct-labor-hour.

NOTES

Graph budgeted and allocated *fixed* overhead from zero to 7,500 hours.

NOTES

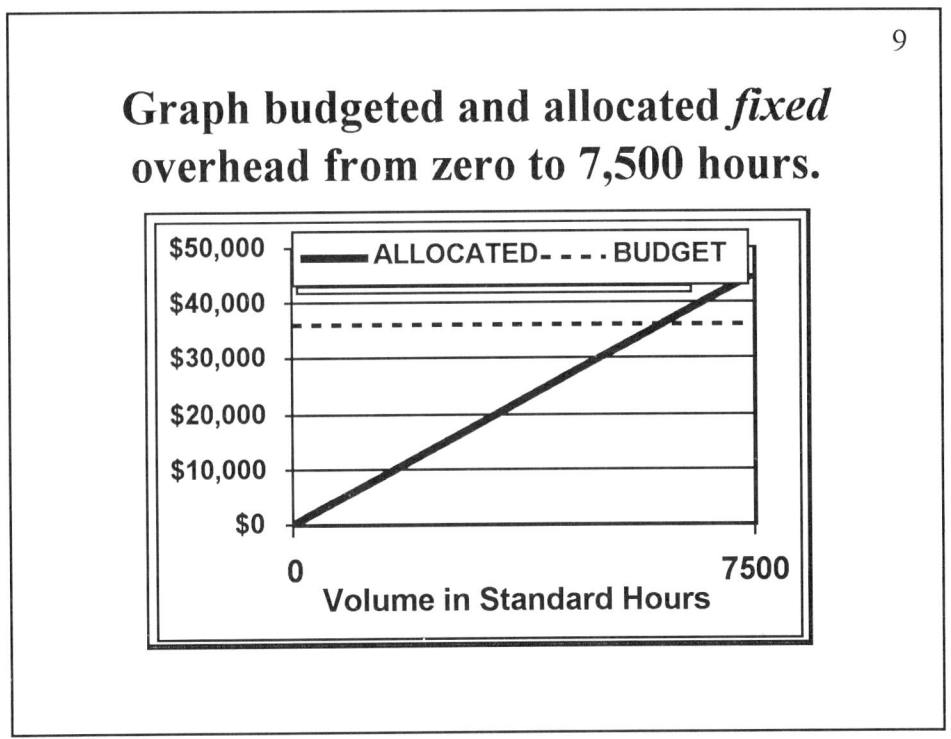

NOTES

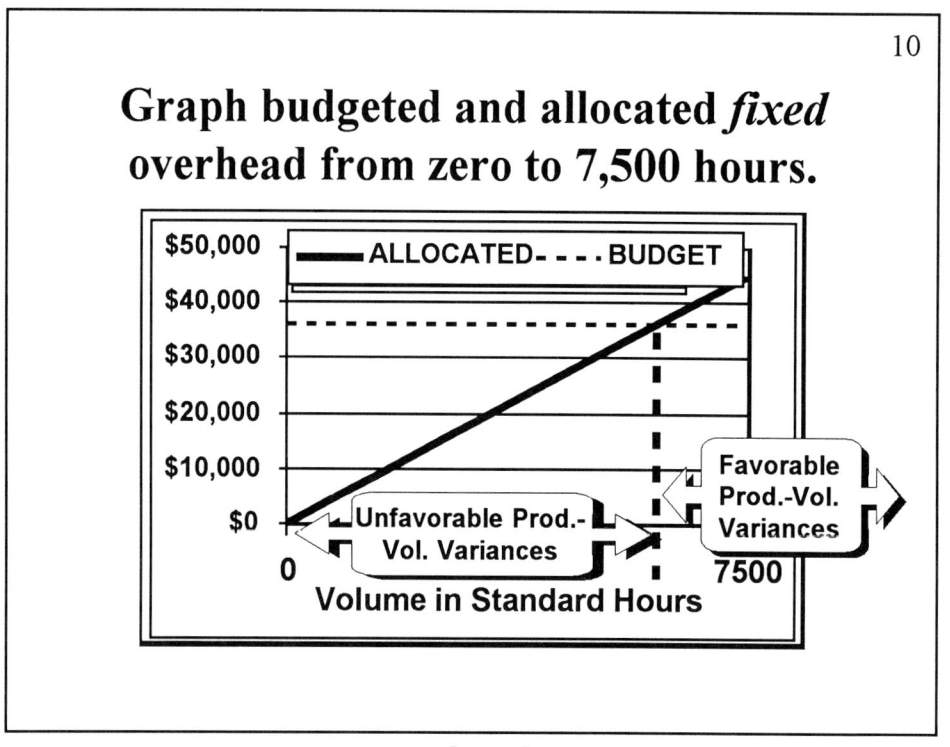

NOTES

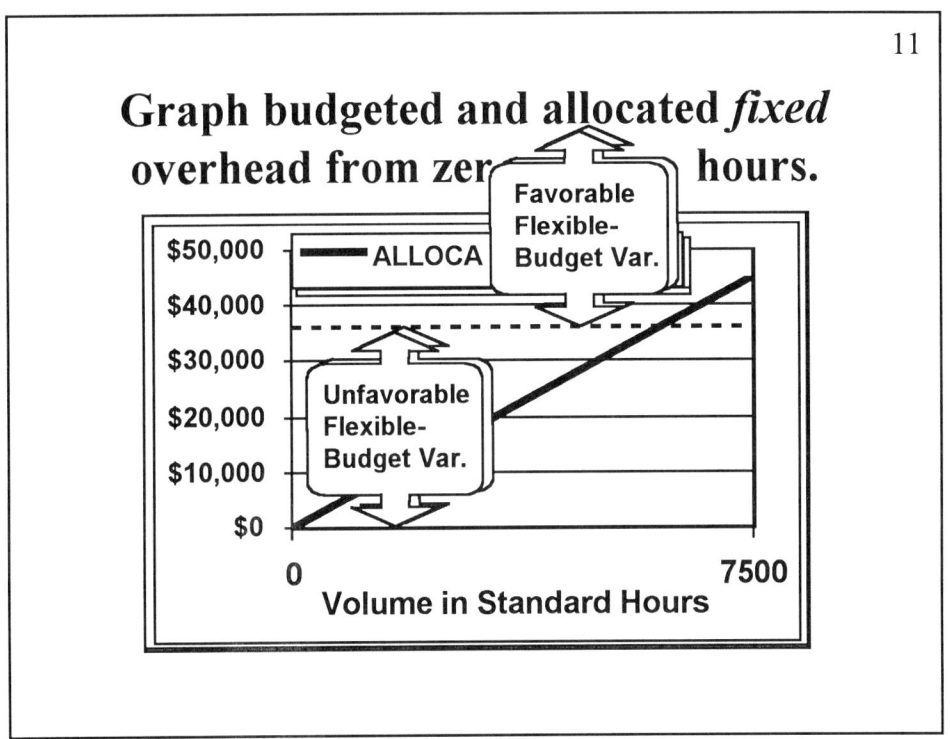

NOTES

8-11

Computing Overhead Variances

Assume that 5,000 standard direct-labor-hours are allowed for the output achieved during a given month. Actual fixed overhead amounted to $43,000.

Calculate the fixed-overhead flexible-budget variance and the production-volume variance.

NOTES

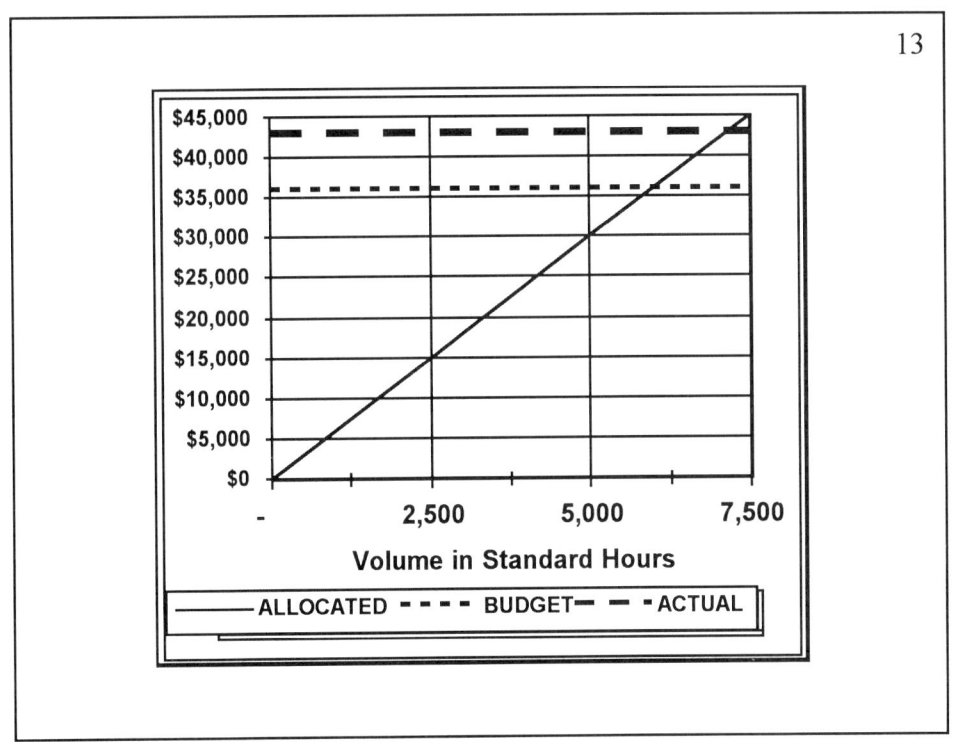

NOTES

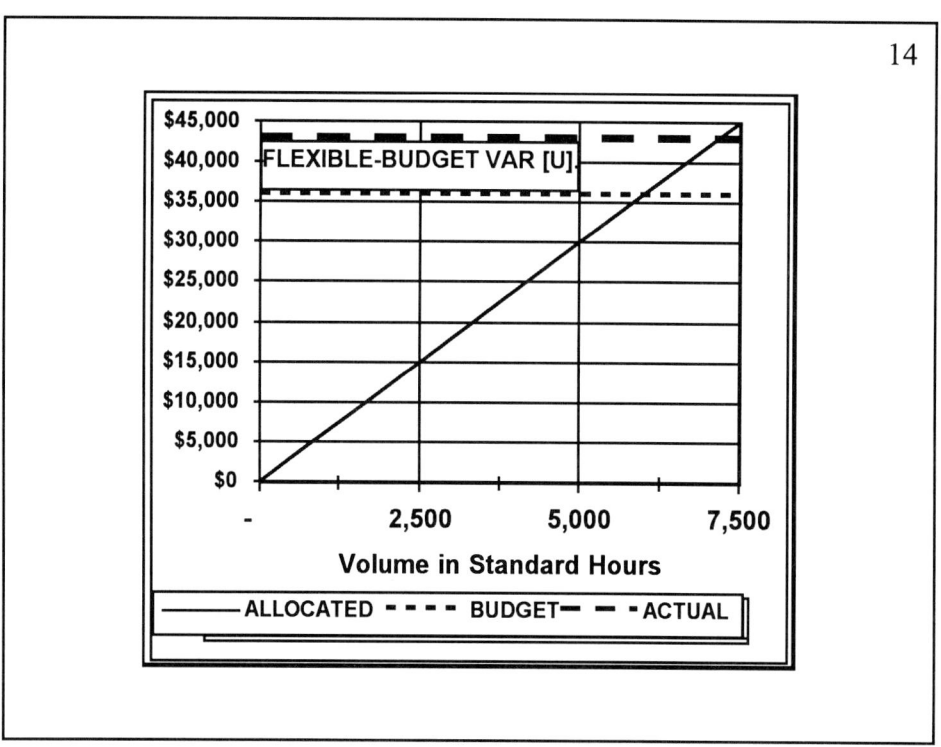

NOTES

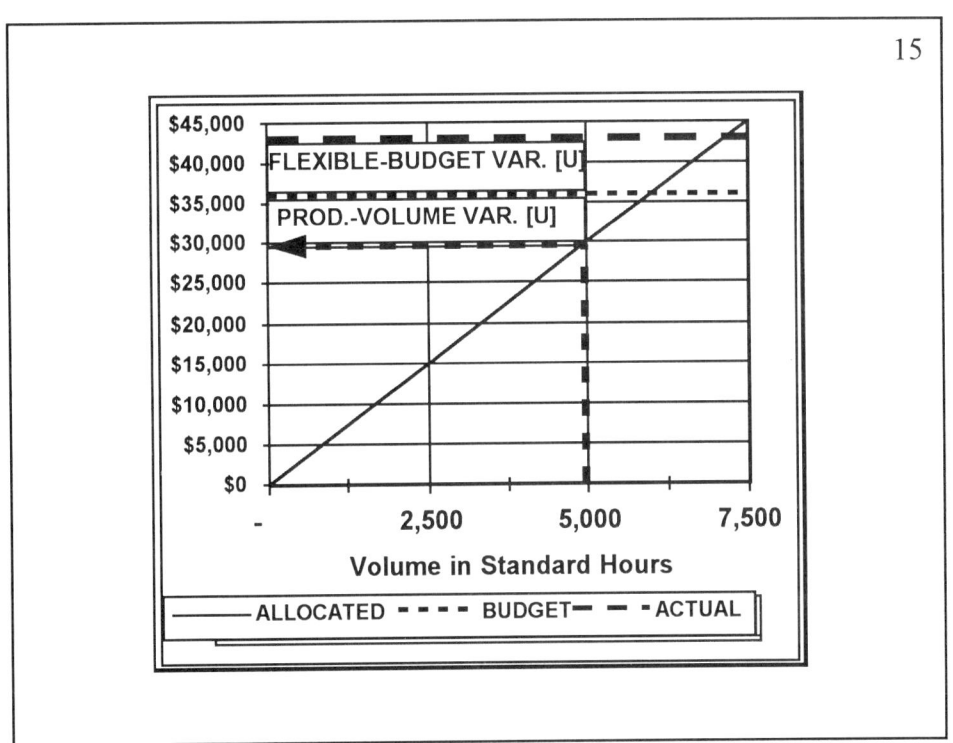

NOTES

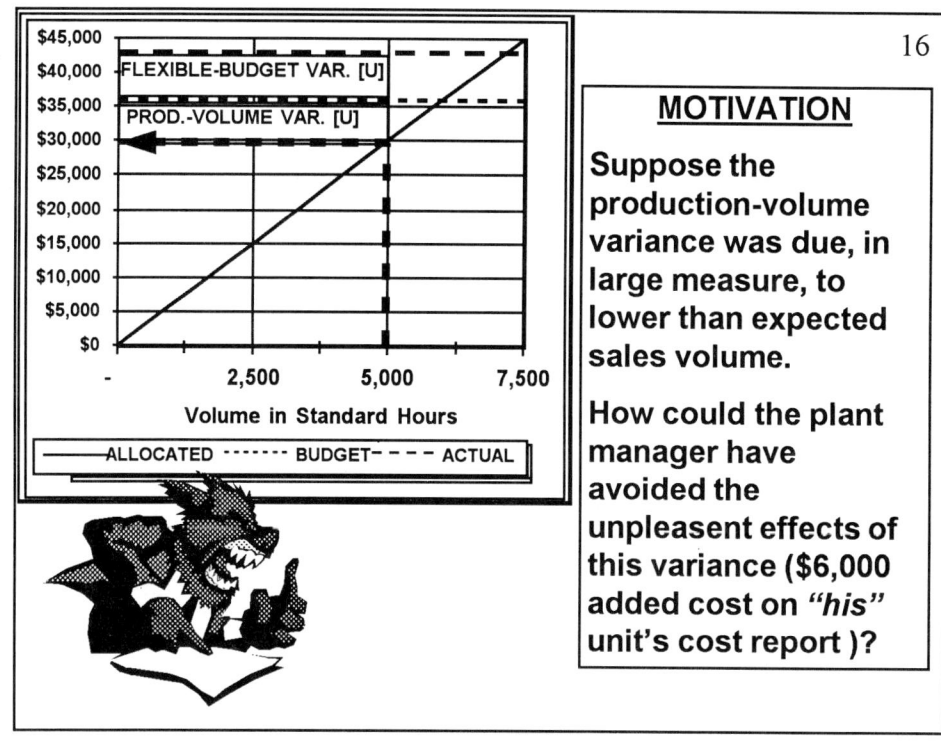

MOTIVATION

Suppose the production-volume variance was due, in large measure, to lower than expected sales volume.

How could the plant manager have avoided the unpleasent effects of this variance ($6,000 added cost on *"his"* unit's cost report)?

NOTES

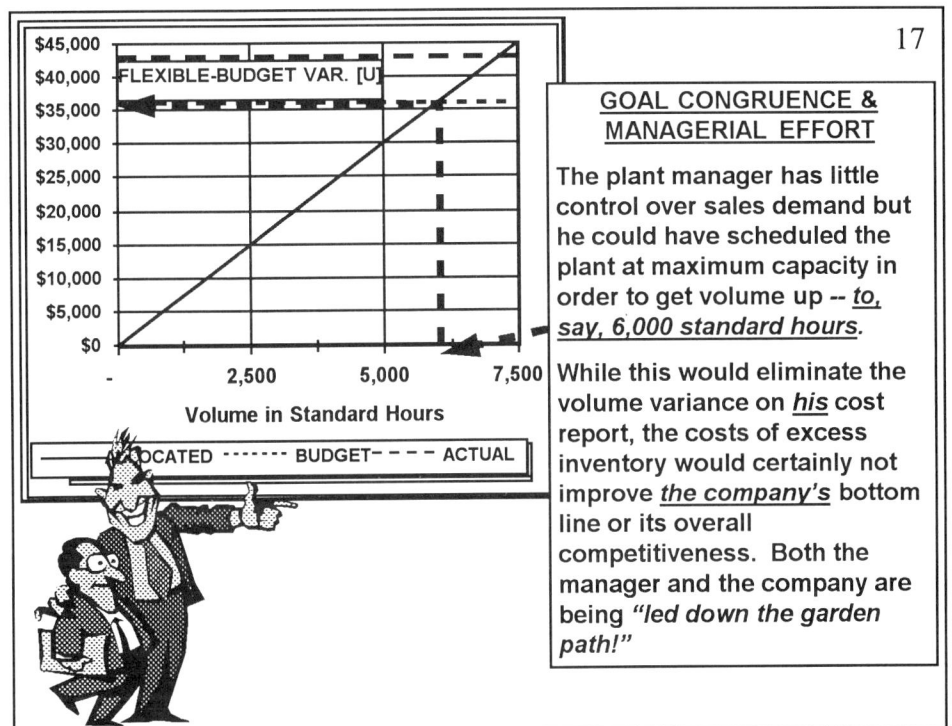

Case 8-2
ACTIVITY-BASED FLEXIBLE BUDGETS

The Billing Department of the Portland Power Company

Analysis of the Account Inquiry Activity Center

NOTES

Billing Department
Cost Behavior for Activity Centers

Activity Center	Traceable Costs Variable	Fixed	Cost-Driver Activity
Account Inquiry	$ 79,910	$ 155,270	3,300 Labor-Hours
Correspondence	9,800	25,584	2,800 Letters
Account Billing	154,377	81,400	2,440,000 Lines
Bill Verification	10,797	78,050	20,000 Accounts

NOTES

Determining the Flexible Budget Formula
Account Inquiry Activity Center

Fixed Costs + (*Variable Costs* ÷ *Driver Units*) × *Driver Units*
= $155,270 + ($79,910 ÷ 3,300 Lbr.-Hrs) × Lbr.-Hrs.
= $155,270 + $24.22 × Lbr.-Hrs.

Traceable Costs

Activity Center	Variable	Fixed	Cost-Driver Activity
Account Inquiry	$ 79,910	$155,270	3,300 Labor-Hours
Correspondence	9,800	25,584	2,800 Letters
Account Billing	154,377	81,400	2,440,000 Lines
Bill Verification	10,797	78,050	20,000 Accounts

Billing Department
Ranges of Cost-Driver Activity

Activity Center	Cost Driver	Relevant Range	
Account Inquiry	**Labor-Hours**	3,000	5,000
Correspondence	Letters	2,500	3,500
Account Billing	Lines	2,000,000	3,000,000
Bill Verification	Accounts	15,000	25,000

NOTES

Flexible Budget
Account Inquiry Activity Center

	Budget Formula	Cost Driver -- Number of Labor-Hours		
		3,000	4,000	5,000
Variable Costs	$24.22/Hr.	$ 72,660	$ 96,880	$ 121,100
Fixed Costs	$155,270	155,270	155,270	155,270
Total Flexible Budget		$227,930	$252,150	$276,370

NOTES

Billing Department
Actual Results

Activity Center	Cost-Driver Level (Actual)	Actual Cost
Account Inquiry	4,400 Labor-Hours	$229,890
Correspondence	3,250 Letters	38,020
Account Billing	2,900,000 Lines	285,000
Account Verification	22,500 Accounts	105,320

NOTES

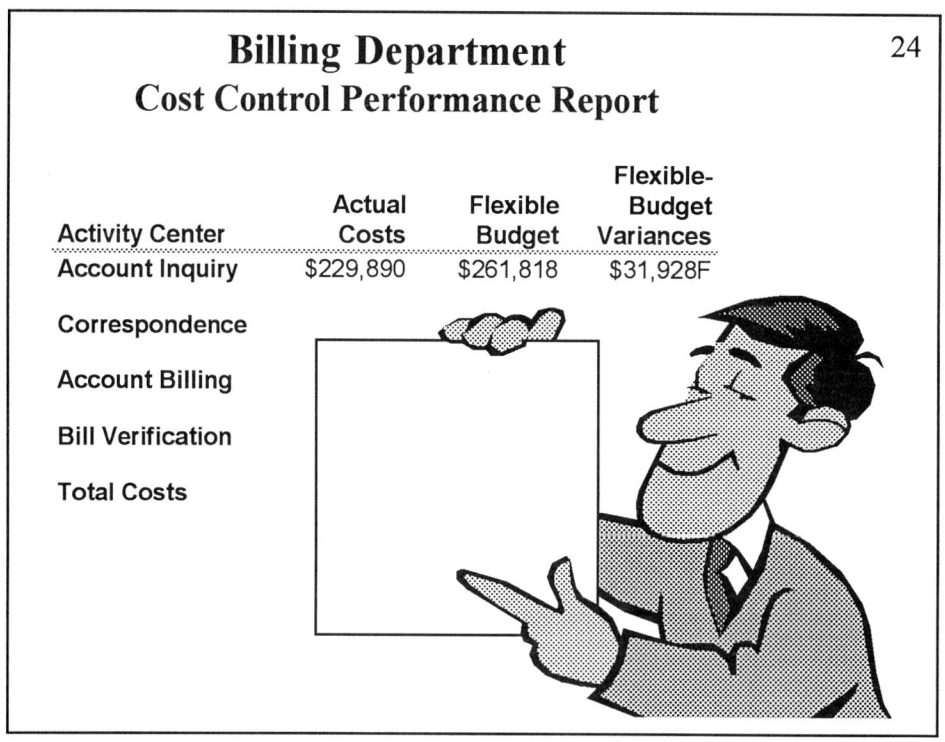

Billing Department
Cost Control Performance Report

Activity Center	Actual Costs	Flexible Budget	Flexible-Budget Variances
Account Inquiry	$229,890	$261,818	$31,928F
Correspondence			
Account Billing			
Bill Verification			
Total Costs			

$155,250 + ($24.22 × 4,400 Ltrs.) = $261,818

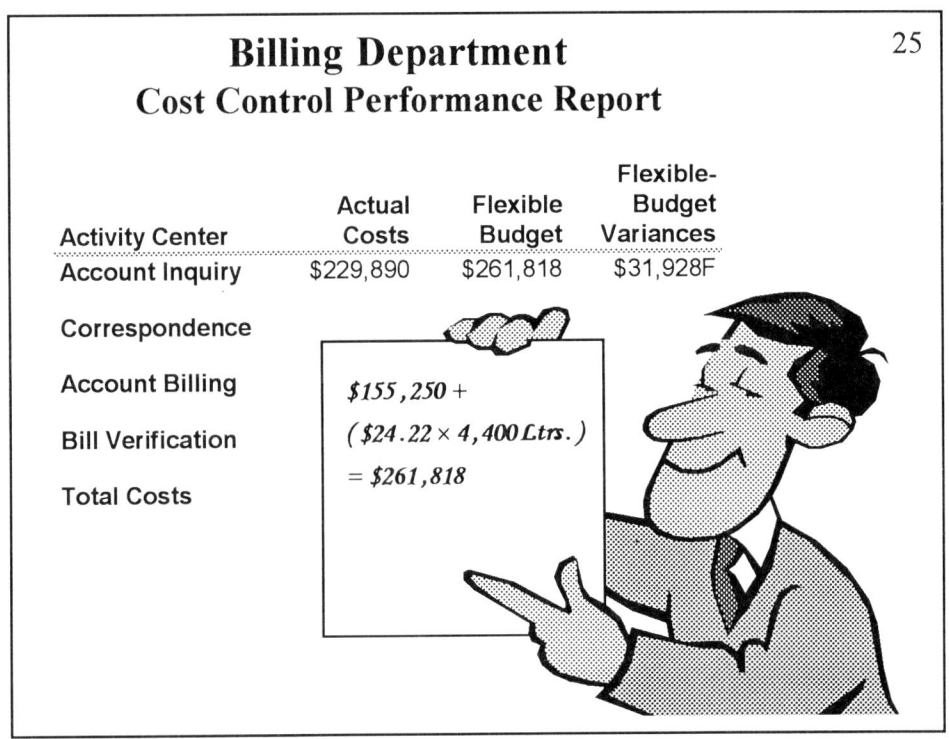

PowerNotes for Cost Accounting: A Managerial Emphasis, Ninth Edition

Income Effects of Alternative Inventory-Costing Methods

NOTES

Variable, Absorption Costing, and Break-even Analysis

NOTES

- **Under variable costing, fixed manufacturing overhead costs are excluded from inventoriable costs and are a cost of the period in which they are incurred.**
- **Under absorption costing, these costs are inventoriable and become expenses only when a sale occurs.**

NOTES

> **4**
>
> The Marple Company has built a massive water-desalting factory next to an ocean. The factory is completely automated. It has its own source of power, light, heat, etc. The salt water costs nothing. All producing and other operating costs are fixed - they do not vary since volume is controlled by adjusting a few dials on a control panel. The employees have flat annual salaries.
>
> The price of the desalted water, $.25 per gallon, is expected to remain unchanged for the foreseeable future.

NOTES

The following are data regarding the first two years of operations:

	In Gallons		Costs [All Fixed]	
	Sales	Production	Manufacturing	Other
19X6	3,000,000	6,000,000	$600,000	$200,000
19X7	3,000,000	0	600,000	200,000

Orders can be processed in four hours, so management decided, in early 19X6, to gear production strictly to sales.

MARPLE COMPANY
OPERATING INCOME
VARIABLE COSTING ($000s)

		19X6	19X7	BOTH
Sales		$750	$750	$1,500
Fixed Costs:				
Manufacturing	$600			
Other	200	800	800	1,600
Operating Loss		$(50)	$(50)	$ (100)

6

NOTES

MARPLE COMPANY
OPERATING INCOME
VARIABLE COSTING ($000s)

		19X6	19X7	BOTH
Sales		$750	$750	$1,500
Fixed Costs:				
Manufacturing	$600			
Other	200	800	800	1,600
Operating Loss		$(50)	$(50)	$(100)

Notice that operating income (loss) under *variable costing* follows sales and is not affected by inventory level. In this case, inventory was built up during 19X6 to 3,000,000 gallons with no impact on the operating loss.

NOTES

MARPLE COMPANY
OPERATING INCOME ($000s)
VARIABLE COSTING

		19X6	19X7	BOTH
Sales		$750	$750	$1,500
Fixed Costs:				
Manufacturing	$600			
Other	200	800	800	1,600
Operating Loss		$(50)	$(50)	$(100)

$$\text{Break - even point} = \frac{\text{Fixed Costs}}{\text{Contribution Margin}}$$

$$= \frac{\$800,000}{\$.25 \text{ per Gallon}}$$

$$= 3,200,000 \text{ gallon}$$

NOTES

NOTES

MARPLE COMPANY
OPERATING INCOME ($000s)
ABSORPTION COSTING

	19X6	19X7	Both
Sales	$750	$750	$1,500
Less cost of goods sold:			
Beginning inventory	-	300	-
Cost of goods manufactured	600	-	600
Cost of goods available	600	300	600
Ending inventory	300	-	-
Cost of goods sold	300	300	600
Underapplied overhead -- loss from idle capacity	-	600	600
Other expenses	200	200	400
Total charges	500	1,100	1,600
Net income (loss)	$250	$(350)	$(100)

NOTES

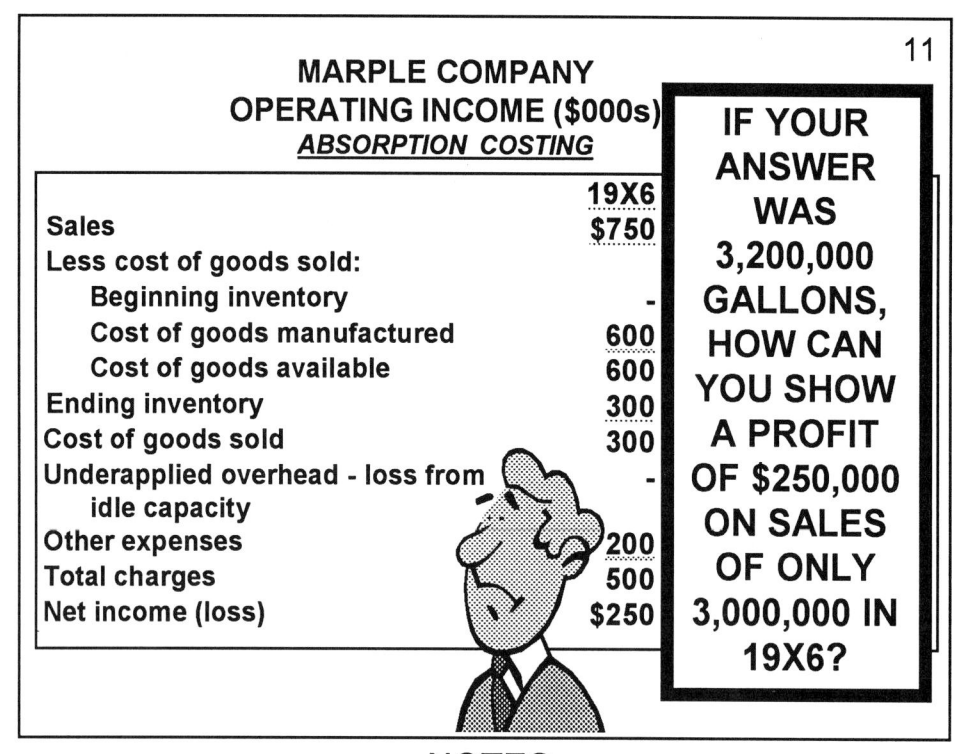

NOTES

Summary Comments

- The central issue is the timing of release of fixed factory overhead to expense.
- Variable costing dovetails exactly with general break-even analysis, while absorption costing does not.
- The difference between income reported under these two methods is entirely due to the treatment of fixed manufacturing costs. Under absorption costing, these costs are treated as assets (inventory) until the associated goods are sold.

NOTES

PowerNotes for Cost Accounting: A Managerial Emphasis, Ninth Edition

Determining How Costs Behave

NOTES

Quantitative Analysis of Cost Relationships

NOTES

Cost Estimation Approaches

- ☐ Industrial Engineering Method
- ☐ Conference Method
- ☐ Account Analysis Method
- ➲ *Quantitative Analysis of Current or Past Cost Relationships*

Steps in Estimating A Cost Function

- **Choose the dependent variable**
- **Identify the cost driver(s)**
- **Collect data on the dependent variable and the cost driver(s)**
- **Plot the data**
- **Estimate the cost function**
- **Evaluate the estimated cost function**

NOTES

Quality Implement Corporation (QIC) produces farm implements for large vehicles used for farming. QIC is refining its cost system and is currently studying the costs of the maintenance activity.

Activity analysis indicates that maintenance activity consists primarily of labor setting up machines using certain supplies. Costs include labor, supplies, and energy. QIC employs two full-time mechanics to perform maintenance. The annual salary of a maintenance mechanic is $25,000 (fixed cost). Two plausible cost drivers have been suggested: units produced and number of setups. QIC has performed the first four steps in the cost estimation process. *You are asked to estimate and evaluate the prospective cost functions.*

NOTES

PowerNotes for Cost Accounting: A Managerial Emphasis, Ninth Edition

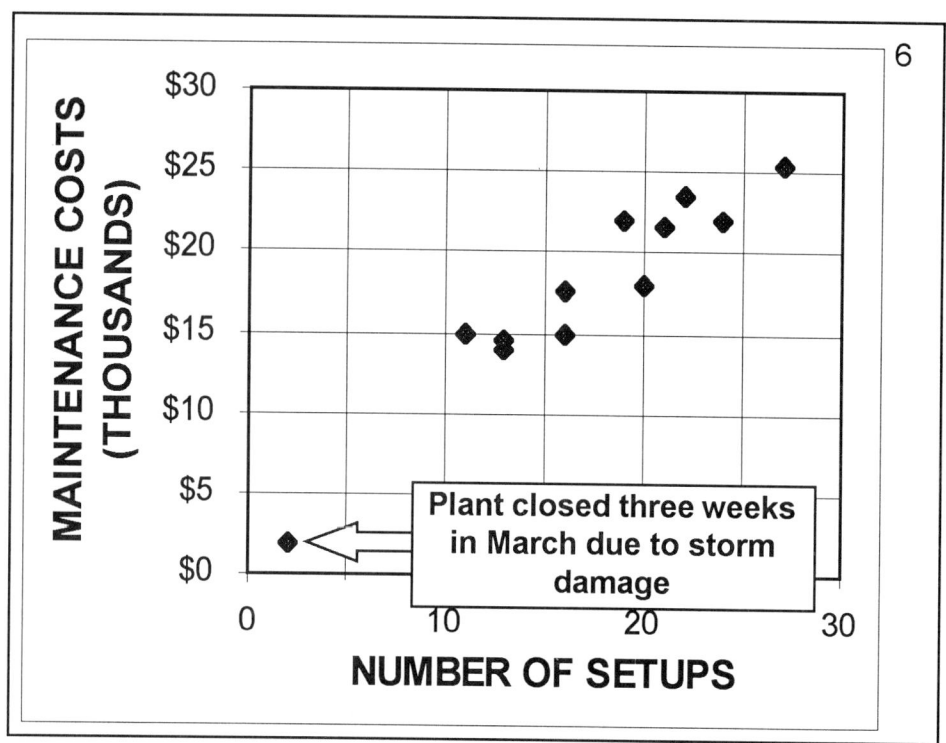

NOTES

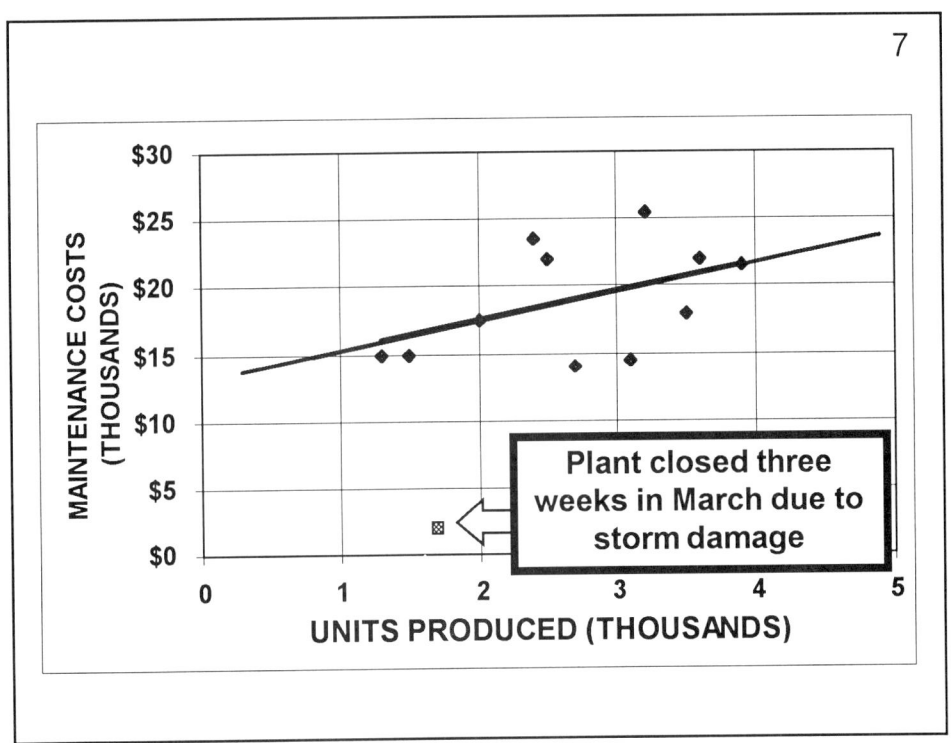

NOTES

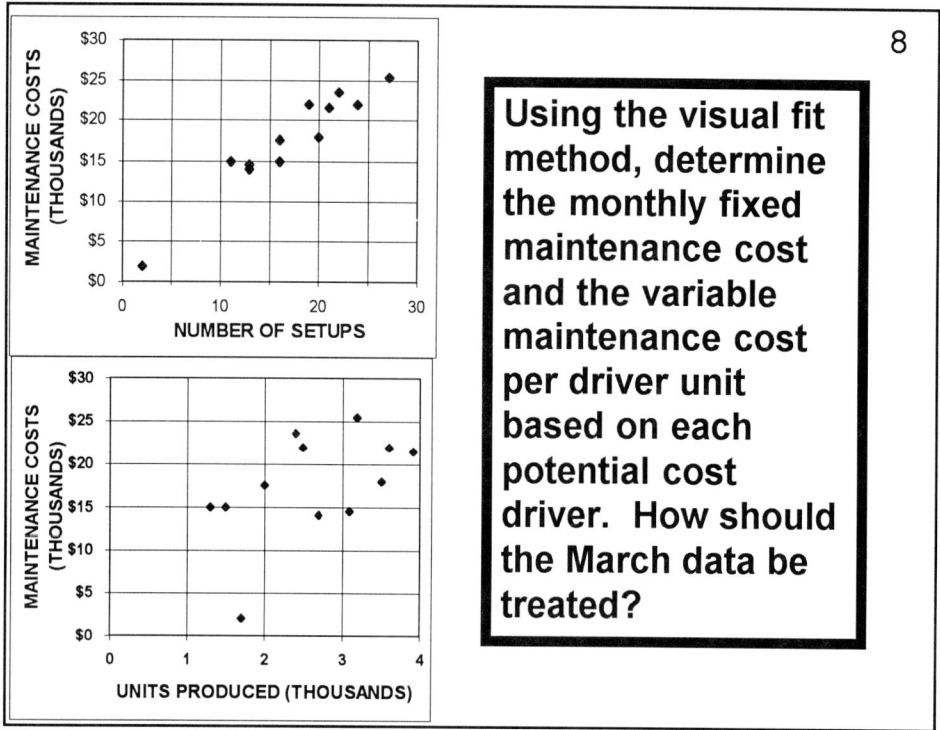

Using the visual fit method, determine the monthly fixed maintenance cost and the variable maintenance cost per driver unit based on each potential cost driver. How should the March data be treated?

NOTES

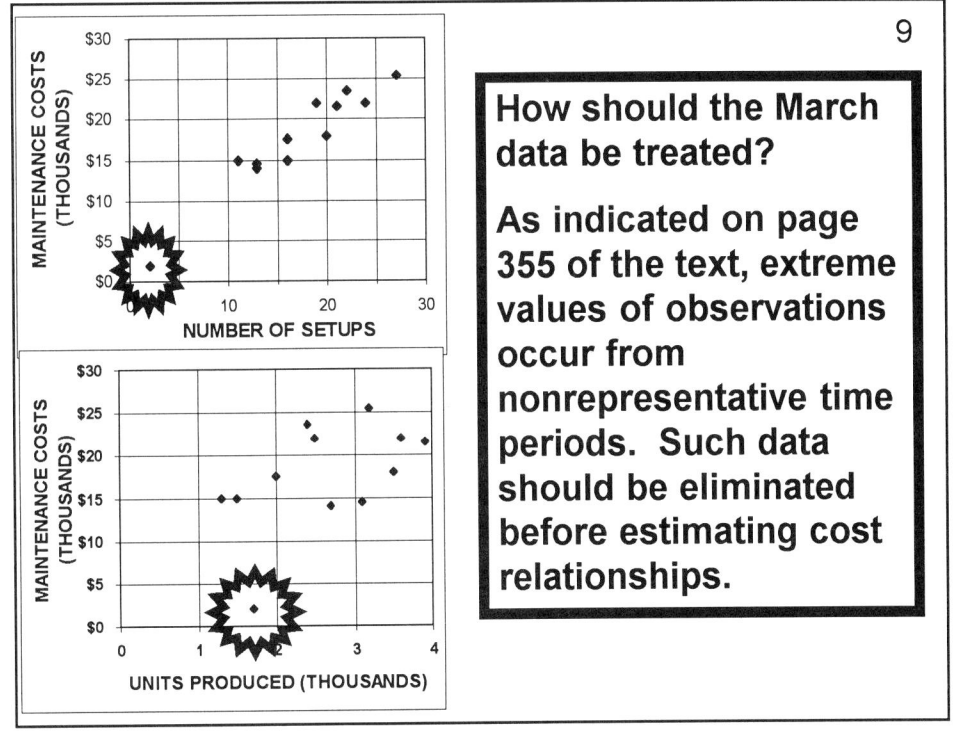

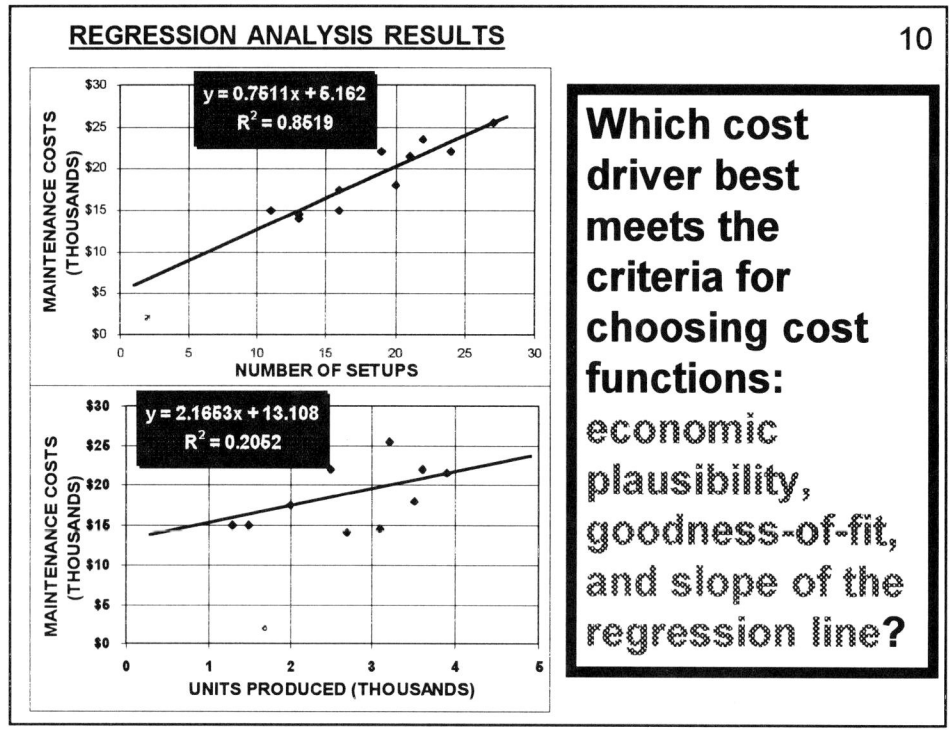

Both cost drivers appear to be *economically plausible*. However, if maintenance activity is primarily associated with a "batch-level" activity such as setups, the setup driver is preferred. Of the costs associated with maintenance activity, supplies and energy are primarily variable and salaries are fixed at a monthly amount of $4,167 [2 ·$25,000 ÷12]. The regression results indicate a fixed cost of $5,162 using setups, compared to $13,108 using units. Thus, number of setups is the preferred cost driver based on economic plausibility.

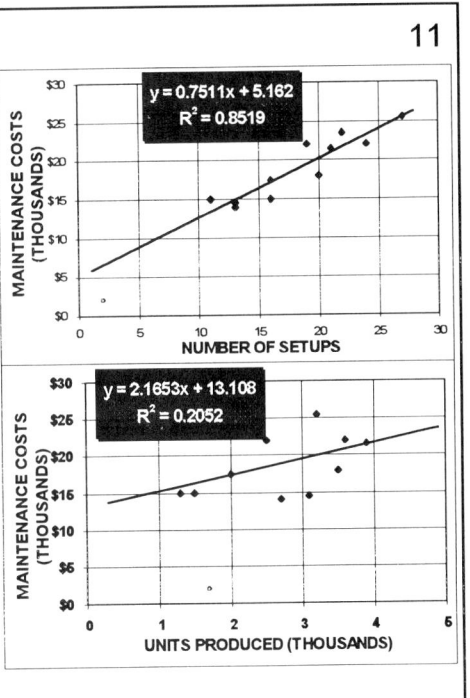

NOTES

The *coefficient of determination, R^2*, measures the percentage of variation in maintenance cost explained by number of setups or units produced. Generally, an R^2 of 0.30 or higher passes the *goodness-of-fit test* (text, page 360).

Units produced has an R^2 of only 0.2052 so it does not pass the goodness-of-fit test. Number of setups has an R^2 of 0.8519, passing the goodness-of-fit test.

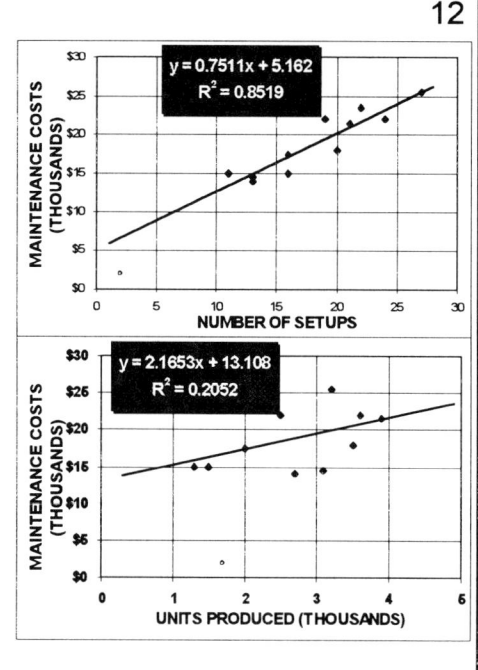

NOTES

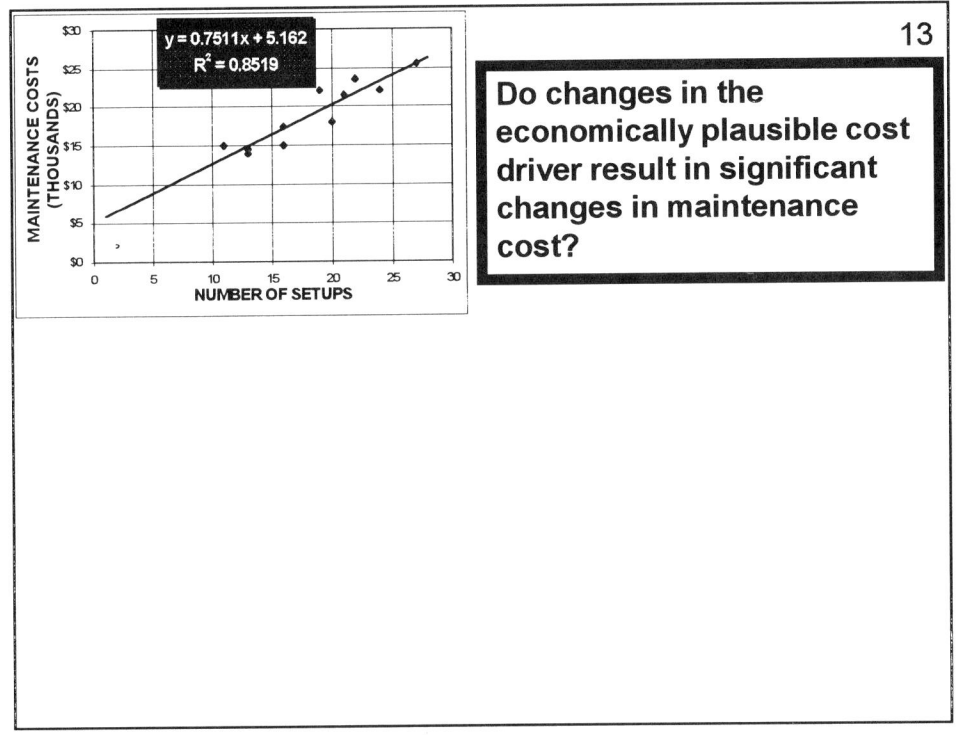

Do changes in the economically plausible cost driver result in significant changes in maintenance cost?

NOTES

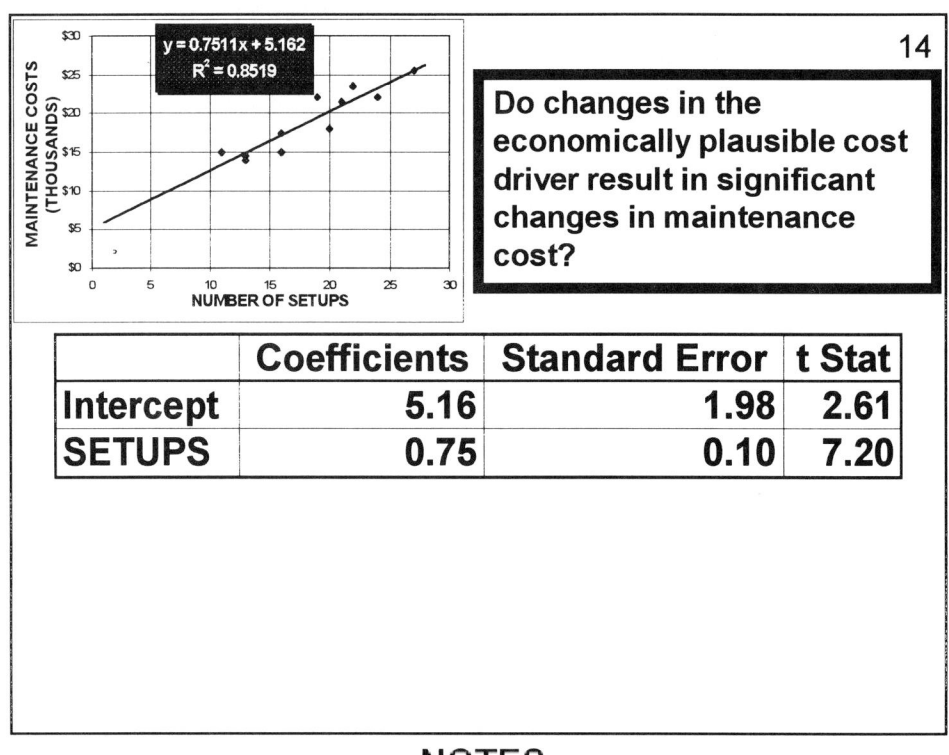

	Coefficients	Standard Error	t Stat
Intercept	5.16	1.98	2.61
SETUPS	0.75	0.10	7.20

Do changes in the economically plausible cost driver result in significant changes in maintenance cost?

NOTES

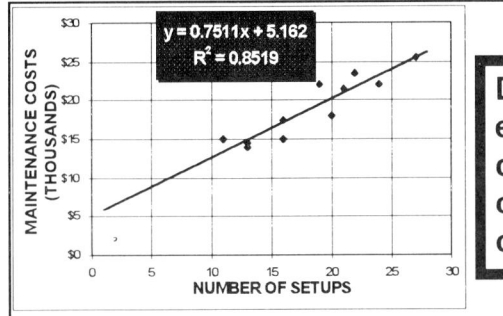

Do changes in the economically plausible cost driver result in significant changes in maintenance cost?

	Coefficients	Standard Error	t Stat
Intercept	5.16	1.98	2.61
SETUPS	0.75	0.10	7.20

The slope of the regression line is 0.75, meaning that each additional setup performed results in an average increase in maintenance costs of $750. The importance of setups in "driving" maintenance costs is measured by the t statistic. Both t statistics are greater than 2.23 (text page 360) implying a significant relationship exists.

NOTES

PowerNotes for Cost Accounting: A Managerial Emphasis, Ninth Edition

Relevant Revenues, Relevant Costs, and the Decision Process

RELEVANT INFORMATION AND DECISION MAKING

Production Decisions: Measuring the Cost of Quality

RELEVANT-COST ANALYSIS

- Chapter 11 covers various types of decisions using the fundamental principle that relevant costs are future costs that differ among alternatives.
- Examples of relevant-cost analysis include outsourcing and make-versus-buy, adding/dropping a customer, and equipment replacement.
- Another example is the decision by one company to keep or replace the raw material it uses in the production of several products.

NOTES

The Business Issue

- BAC Company uses a nylon raw material RM # 033 in producing four products. RM # 033 is a byproduct that contains some metal fragments that do not melt down during processing. This causes the die plates to become clogged, resulting in downtime for cleaning. Extra wear and gear damage to machines also occurs. RM # 033 also has a byproduct, a gassy oil that may be dangerous to exposed workers. Figure 1 on the following slide depicts a typical production run of 6 hours using RM # 033.
- The product manager says there has never been a complaint about the products made using RM # 033 and the cost is very low at $0.50 per pound. The closest alternative - regular nylon - costs $0.99 per pound but contains no metal impurities.
- Management has asked for an analysis of the alternative of using regular nylon compared to continuing the use of RM # 033.

NOTES

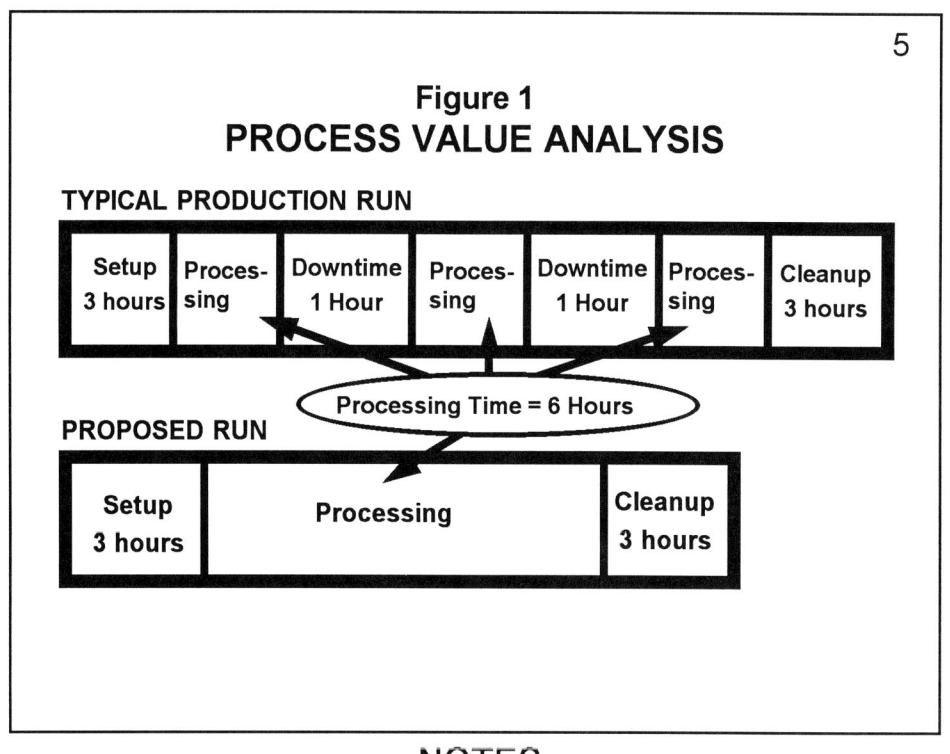

NOTES

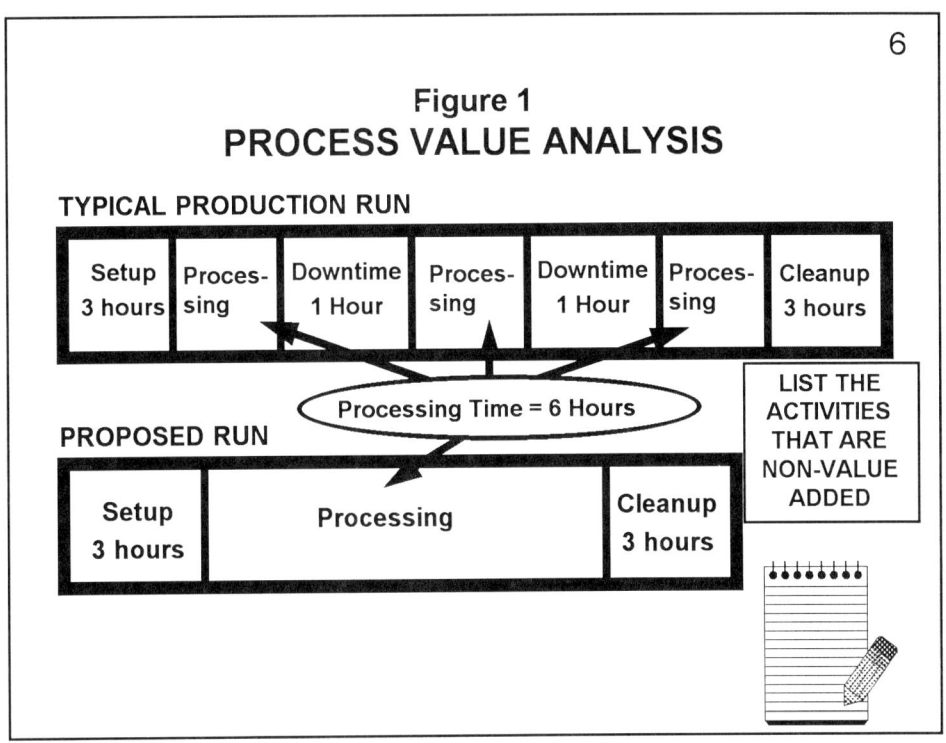

NOTES

PROCESS VALUE ANALYSIS

NON-VALUE-ADDED
- Setups - essential
- Downtime - discretionary
- Cleanup - essential

There are two categories of non-value-added activities - essential and discretionary. For BAC, setup and cleanup are essential activities - they should be part of a continuous improvement program. Downtime is discretionary - it can be eliminated by using the regular nylon.

NOTES

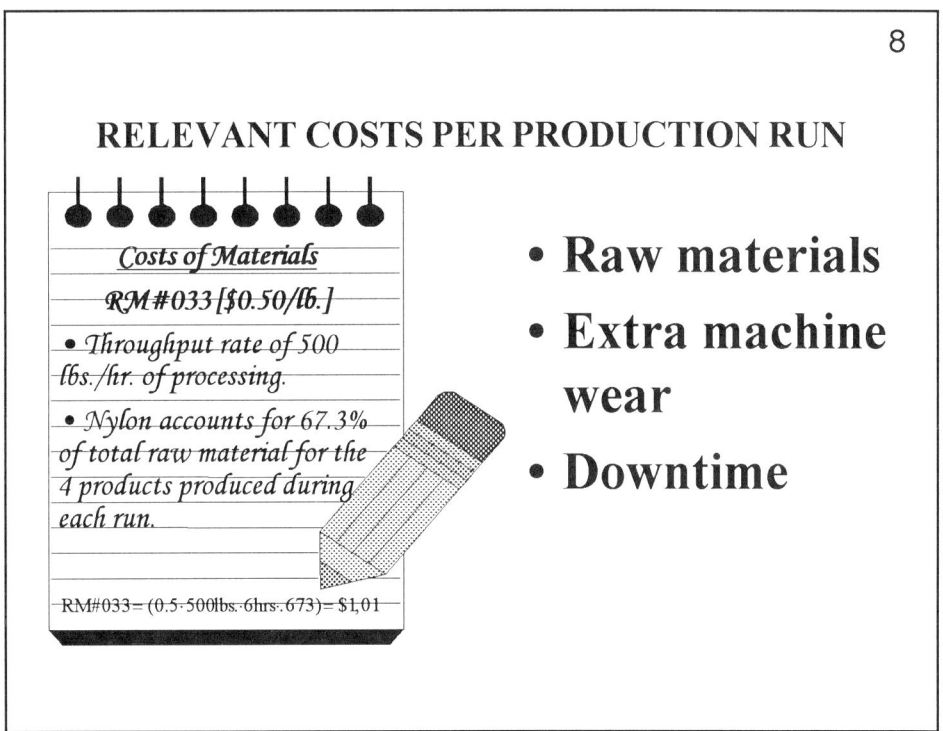

RELEVANT COSTS PER PRODUCTION RUN

Costs of Materials
Regular Nylon [$0.99/lb.]
- *Throughput rate of 500 lbs./hr. of processing.*
- *Nylon accounts for 67.3% of total raw material for the 4 products produced during each run.*

Regular = (0.99 · 500 lbs. · 6 hrs · .673)
         = $2,000

- **Raw materials**
- **Extra machine wear**
- **Downtime**

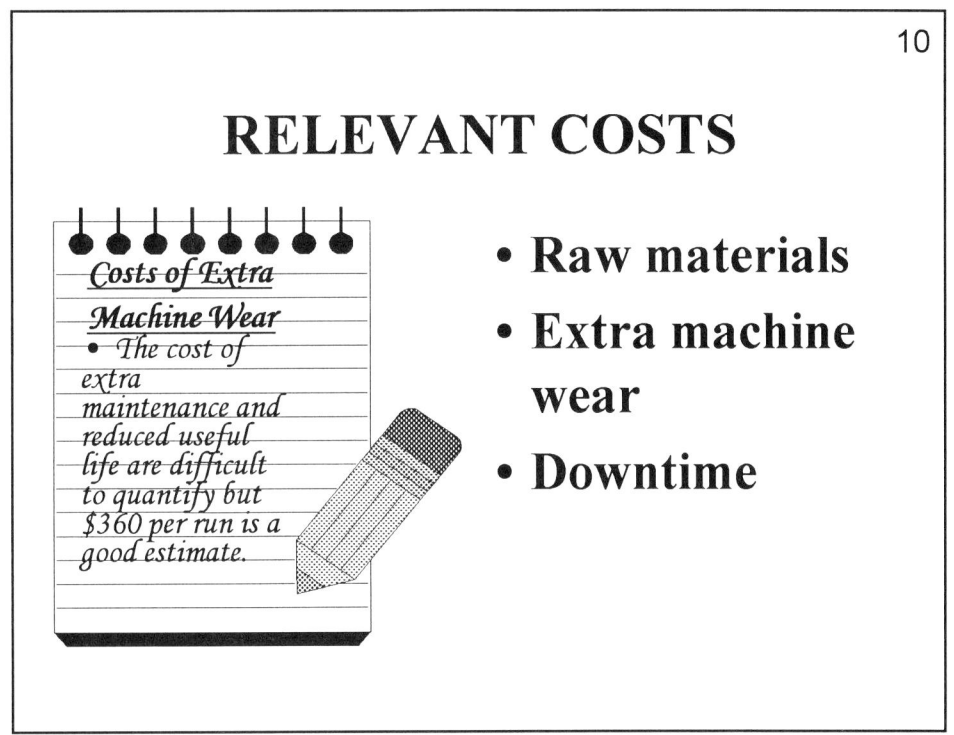

RELEVANT COSTS

Costs of Downtime
- Direct labor
- Overtime labor
- Inspection and analysis
- Lost contribution
- Management time discussing problem

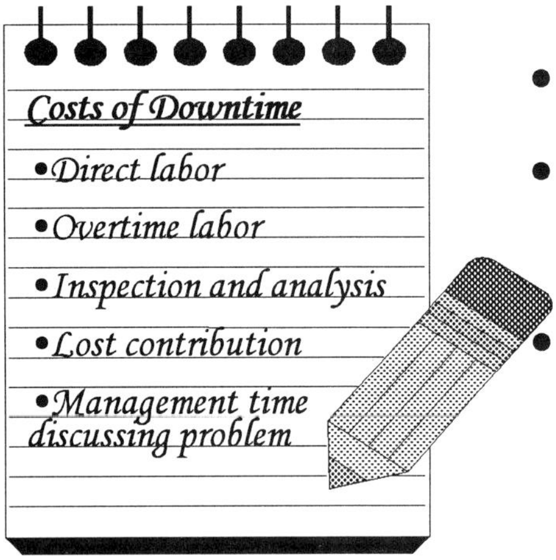

- Raw materials
- Extra machine wear
- Downtime

NOTES

	PRODUCT CONTRIBUTION			
Product	Sales Revenue/lb.	Standard Cost/lb.[1]	Contribution	Contribution/ One Hour[2]
A	$1.754	$0.891	$0.863	$ 431.50
B	2.850	0.958	1.892	946.00
C	1.714	0.964	0.750	375.00
D	2.106	0.914	1.192	596.00
				$2,348.50
Packing cost at a constant rate of $0.03/lb.[3]				60.00
				$2,288.50
Average Contribution (rounded)				$ 572.00

[1] *Standard cost includes: material cost, scrap at 10%, fixed costs of the machine.*
[2] *Throughput rate of 500 pounds per hour for each of the four products.*
[3] *Each of the four products has a throughput of 500 pounds per hour.*

NOTES

AVERAGE COST OF DOWNTIME DUE TO LOW-QUALITY RM # 033

Direct labor per hour [2 workers x $12.00]	$ 24
Overtime labor per hour [3 workers x 12.00 x 1.5]	54
Inspection and analysis	9
Lost contribution per hour	572
Management time	36
Cost of one hour of downtime	$ 695
Cost of downtime per run [$695 x 2 hours]	$1,390

NOTES

DIFFERENTIAL ANALYSIS COST PER RUN

Differential Costs	RM#033	Regular Nylon	Difference
Material	$1,010	$2,000	-$ 990
Extra Machine Wear	360	0	360
Downtime	1,390	0	1,390
Total	$2,760	$2,000	$ 760

NOTES

As a result of the analysis, the following memo (in part) was distributed.

memo:

FROM: Sales Manager

...Therefore, I request that we change the bills of material that call for RM # 033 to our current prime nylon raw material. Even though there will be a sizable increase in raw material price that will affect standard costs and profit margins negatively, the money we will save due to less machine wear and downtime from using higher quality nylon reduces our overall costs by an estimated $760 per run.

NOTES

HIDDEN COSTS OF QUALITY-DOWNTIME COSTS

Direct labor per hour [2 workers x $12.00]	$ 24
Overtime labor per hour [3 workers x 12.00 x 1.5]	54
Inspection and analysis	9
Lost contribution per hour	572
Management time	3
Cost of one hour of downtime	$ 695
Cost of downtime per run [$695 x 2 hours]	$1,390

- *What does the sales manager mean by "hidden costs?"*
- **The downtime costs above are indirect costs and thus are allocated to all products, becoming "hidden." These quality costs can now be directly traced to the nylon-based products A-D. Many companies do not measure quality costs because it is difficult to measure the various costs of quality.**

NOTES

PowerNotes for Cost Accounting: A Managerial Emphasis, Ninth Edition

Pricing Decisions, Product Profitability Decisions, and Cost Management

NOTES

COST-PRICE PARADIGMS AND MARKETING DECISIONS

NOTES

COST-PRICE PARADIGMS AND MARKETING DECISIONS

ABSORPTION APPROACH
[MATERIALS + LABOR + FUNCTIONAL COSTS] + DESIRED PROFIT = PRICE
External Reporting Focus

NOTES

ABSORPTION APPROACH

[MATERIALS + LABOR + FUNCTIONAL COSTS] + DESIRED PROFIT = PRICE

External Reporting Focus

ABSORPTION APPROACH TO PRICING

Manufacturing Costs:	
Direct Materials	$200,000
Direct Labor	250,000
Overhead	450,000
Marketing and Administrative Costs	500,000
Total	$1,400,000
Production in Units	200,000
Unit Cost	$7.00

Assume that production & sales this year are 200,000 units with cost data as given in the table to the left. Orders for an additional 20,000 units can be generated by distributing them in a new market area during the last quarter. Marketing these 20,000 units will be handled in the normal manner. These units will be produced using otherwise idle capacity.

QUESTIONS

- What unit price should be charged for the 20,000 units if the desired profit margin *(markup)* is 20%?

- What new information is needed?

NOTES

ABSORPTION APPROACH

[MATERIALS + LABOR + FUNCTIONAL COSTS] + DESIRED PROFIT = PRICE

External Reporting Focus

ABSORPTION APPROACH TO PRICING

Manufacturing Costs:	
Direct Materials	$200,000
Direct Labor	250,000
Overhead	450,000
Marketing and Administrative Costs	500,000
Total	$1,400,000
Production in Units	200,000
Unit Cost	$7.00

ANSWERS

- The unit cost of $7.00 would be the basis for pricing. The unit price would be 1.2 x $7.00 or *$8.40*. The fallacy in this approach to pricing is treating all costs as if they were variable. Unit costs are useful for predicting variable costs but can be misleading when used to predict fixed costs. Since the absorption approach does not differentiate between variable and fixed cost it is not useful for marketing decisions.

- Cost behavior information and the contribution approach is the information needed.

NOTES

COST-PRICE PARADIGMS AND MARKETING DECISIONS

ABSORPTION APPROACH
[MATERIALS + LABOR + FUNCTIONAL COSTS] + DESIRED PROFIT = PRICE
External Reporting Focus

CONTRIBUTION APPROACH
[VARIABLE COSTS + FIXED COSTS] + DESIRED PROFIT = PRICE
Cost Behavior Focus

7

ABSORPTION APPROACH
[MATERIALS + LABOR + FUNCTIONAL COSTS] + DESIRED PROFIT = PRICE
External Reporting Focus

CONTRIBUTION APPROACH
[VARIABLE COSTS + FIXED COSTS] + DESIRED PROFIT = PRICE
Cost Behavior Focus

CONTRIBUTION APPROACH

Variable Costs:	
Direct Materials	$1.00 per unit
Direct Labor	1.25 per unit
Overhead	0.50 per unit
Marketing and Administrative	0.25 per unit
Total Variable Costs	$3.00 per unit
Fixed Costs:	
Manufacturing	$350,000
Marketing and Administrative	450,000
Total Fixed Costs	$800,000

QUESTIONS
- What unit price should be used for the 20,000 units under this approach?
- Under what conditions would this approach not yield accurate unit cost estimates?
- If these conditions exist, what information is needed to refine the cost estimates?

NOTES

ABSORPTION APPROACH	CONTRIBUTION APPROACH
[MATERIALS + LABOR + FUNCTIONAL COSTS] + DESIRED PROFIT = PRICE	[VARIABLE COSTS + FIXED COSTS] + DESIRED PROFIT = PRICE
External Reporting Focus	Cost Behavior Focus

CONTRIBUTION APPROACH

Variable Costs:	
Direct Materials	$1.00 per unit
Direct Labor	1.25 per unit
Overhead	0.50 per unit
Marketing and Administrative	0.25 per unit
Total Variable Costs	$3.00 per unit
Fixed Costs:	
Manufacturing	$350,000
Marketing and Administrative	450,000
Total Fixed Costs	$800,000

ANSWERS

- The unit cost = 3.00 + (800,000/220,000) = $6.64 so the unit price is 1.2 x 6.64 = **$7.97**.

- Product or process diversity causes the consumption of resources to vary across products and processes.

- What are the key activities, resources, and cost drivers for indirect costs?

NOTES

COST-PRICE PARADIGMS AND MARKETING DECISIONS

ABSORPTION APPROACH
[MATERIALS + LABOR + FUNCTIONAL COSTS] + DESIRED PROFIT = PRICE
External Reporting Focus

CONTRIBUTION APPROACH
[VARIABLE COSTS + FIXED COSTS] + DESIRED PROFIT = PRICE
Cost Behavior Focus

ACTIVITY APPROACH
[DIRECTLY TRACED COSTS + ACTIVITY-BASED COSTS] + DESIRED PROFIT = PRICE
Process Focus

NOTES

ACTIVITY APPROACH

ACTIVITY/RESOURCE [Cost Driver]	TRACEABLE COST	FLOW OF DRIVER UNITS	COST PER DRIVER UNIT
Direct Material	$200,000		
Direct Labor	250,000		
Processing [Machine Hrs.]			
Variable	110,000	2,000 MHrs	$55.00
Fixed	250,000		
Setup [Setups]:			
Variable	30,000	10 setups	$3,000
Fixed	60,000		
Mrktg & Admin. [Orders]:			
Variable	160,000	40 orders	$4,000
Fixed	340,000		

ACTIVITY APPROACH
[DIRECTLY TRACED COSTS
+ACTIVITY-BASED COSTS]
+ DESIRED PROFIT = PRICE
Process Focus

The product and process characteristics of the 20,000 units are more complex than the average for the 200,000 units. It will take 560 machine hours, 4 setups, and 18 orders.

QUESTIONS

• What unit price should be used?

• The minimum price (short run) is the avoidable cost of the 20,000 units. What is the minimum price to "break-even" on the 20,000 units under the first three approaches?

NOTES

ACTIVITY APPROACH

ACTIVITY/RESOURCE [Cost Driver]	TRACEABLE COST	FLOW OF DRIVER UNITS	COST PER DRIVER UNIT	EXPECTED DRIVER UNITS	ACTIVITY-BASED COST
Direct Material	$200,000	200,000 units	$1.00	220,000	$220,000
Direct Labor	250,000	200,000 units	$1.25	220,000	275,000
Processing [MHrs.]:					
Variable	110,000	2,000 MHrs	$55.00	2,560	140,800
Fixed	250,000				250,000
Setup [Setups]:					
Variable	30,000	10 setups	$3,000	14	42,000
Fixed	60,000				60,000
Mrktg & Admin. [Orders]:					
Variable	160,000	40 orders	$4,000	58	232,000
Fixed	340,000				340,000
Total					$1,559,800
Cost per Unit					$7.09

ACTIVITY APPROACH
[DIRECTLY TRACED COSTS +ACTIVITY-BASED COSTS] + DESIRED PROFIT = PRICE
Process Focus

ANSWERS

• The unit price = 1.2 x 7.09 = **$8.51**.

• The minimum price is the variable costs. Under the absorption approach, this information is not available. Under the contribution and activity approaches, the minimum price is $3.00 and $7.99, respectively.

NOTES

ACTIVITY APPROACH

ACTIVITY/RESOURCE [Cost Driver]	TRACEABLE COST	FLOW OF DRIVER UNITS	COST PER DRIVER UNIT	EXPECTED DRIVER UNITS	ACTIVITY-BASED COST
Direct Material	$200,000	200,000 units	$1.00	220,000	$220,000
Direct Labor	250,000	200,000 units	$1.25	220,000	275,000
Processing [MHrs.]:					
Variable	110,000	2,000 MHrs	$55.00	2,560	140,800
Fixed	250,000				250,000
Setup [Setups]:					
Variable	30,000	10 setups	$3,000	14	42,000
Fixed	60,000				60,000
Mrktg & Admin. [Orders]:					
Variable	160,000	40 orders	$4,000	58	232,000
Fixed	340,000				340,000
Total					$1,559,800
Cost per Unit					$7.09

ACTIVITY APPROACH
[DIRECTLY TRACED COSTS +ACTIVITY-BASED COSTS] + DESIRED PROFIT = PRICE
Process Focus

AVOIDABLE COST--ACTIVITY APPROACH	
DIRECT MATERIAL	$1.00
DIRECT LABOR	1.25
PROCESSING [560x55/20,000]	1.54
SETUP [4x3,000/20,000]	.60
ORDERS [18x4,000/20,000]	3.60
TOTAL UNIT COST	$7.99

NOTES

COST-PRICE PARADIGMS AND MARKETING DECISIONS

ABSORPTION APPROACH
[MATERIALS + LABOR + FUNCTIONAL COSTS] + DESIRED PROFIT = PRICE
External Reporting Focus

CONTRIBUTION APPROACH
[VARIABLE COSTS + FIXED COSTS] + DESIRED PROFIT = PRICE
Cost Behavior Focus

ACTIVITY APPROACH
[DIRECTLY TRACED COSTS + ACTIVITY-BASED COSTS] + DESIRED PROFIT = PRICE
Process Focus

MARKET APPROACH
SELLING PRICE LESS DESIRED PROFIT = TARGET COST
Customer Focus

NOTES

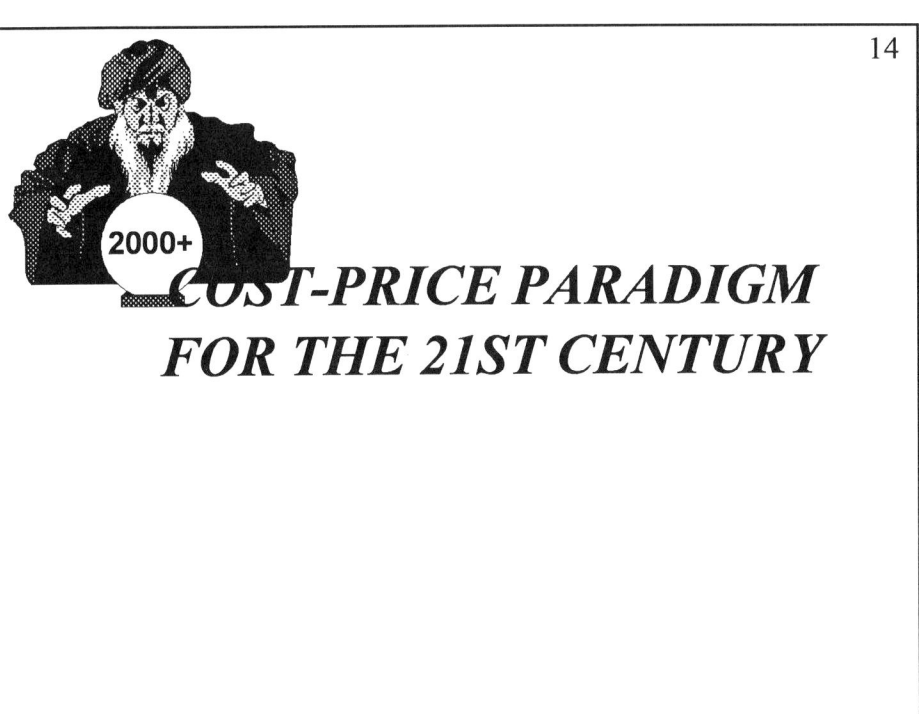

COST-PRICE PARADIGM FOR THE 21ST CENTURY

NOTES

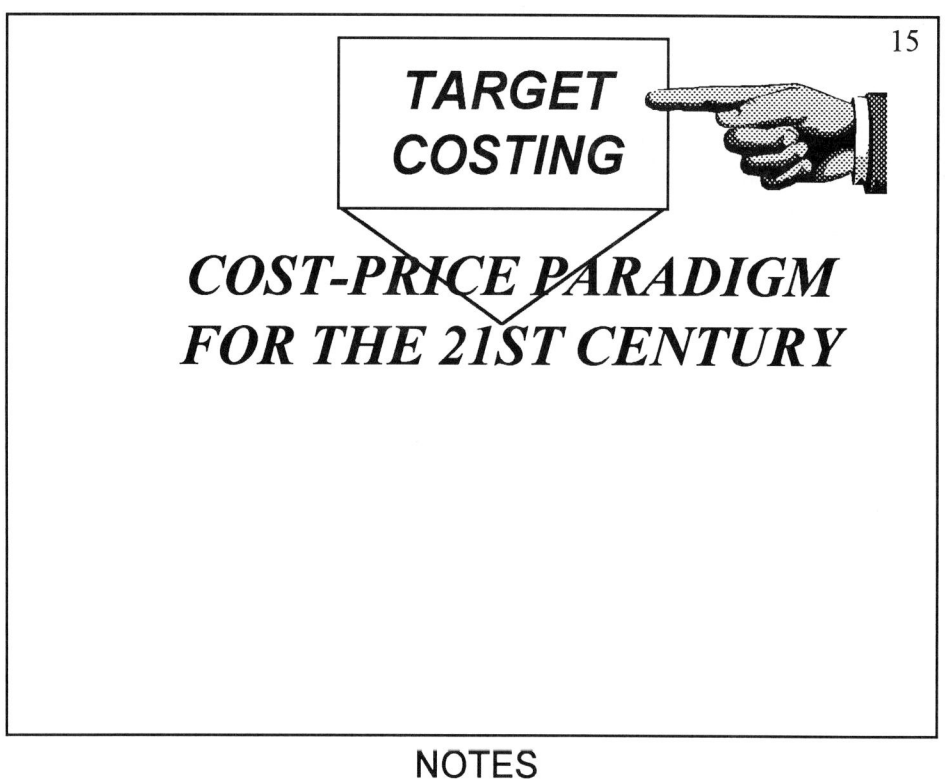

NOTES

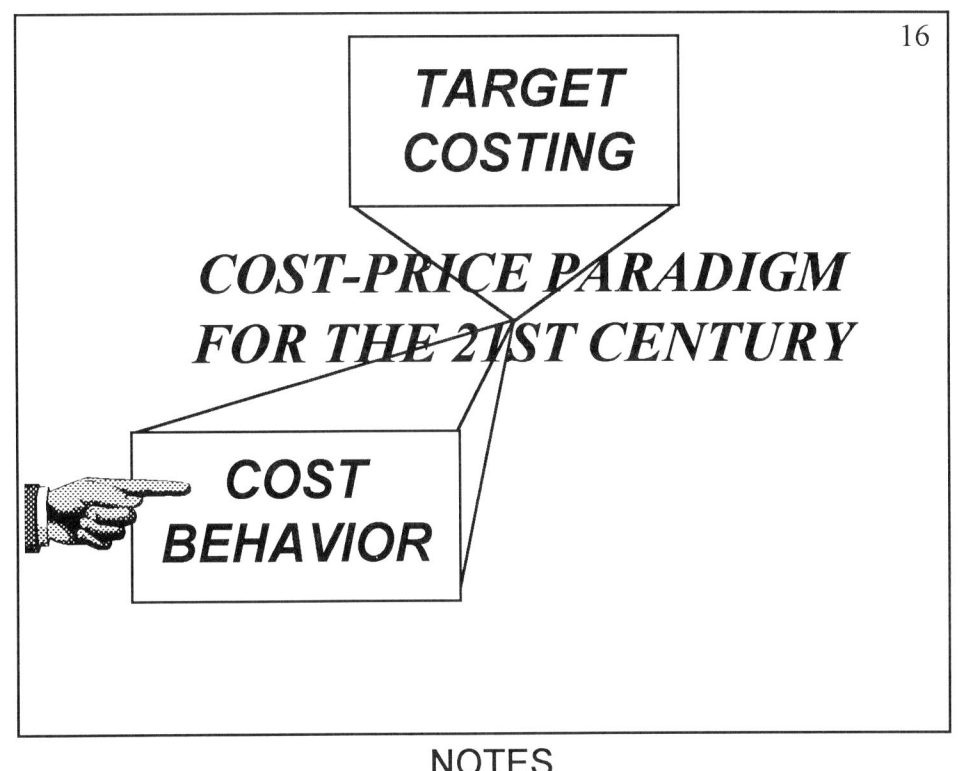

NOTES

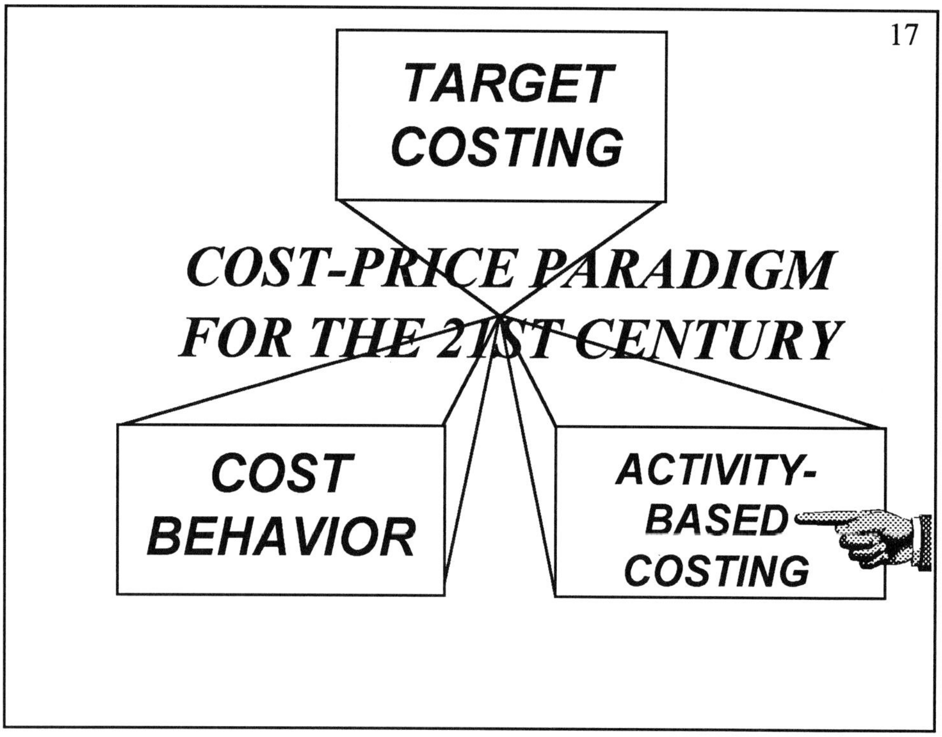

COST-PRICE PARADIGM FOR THE 21ST CENTURY

- TARGET COSTING
- COST BEHAVIOR
- ACTIVITY-BASED COSTING

NOTES

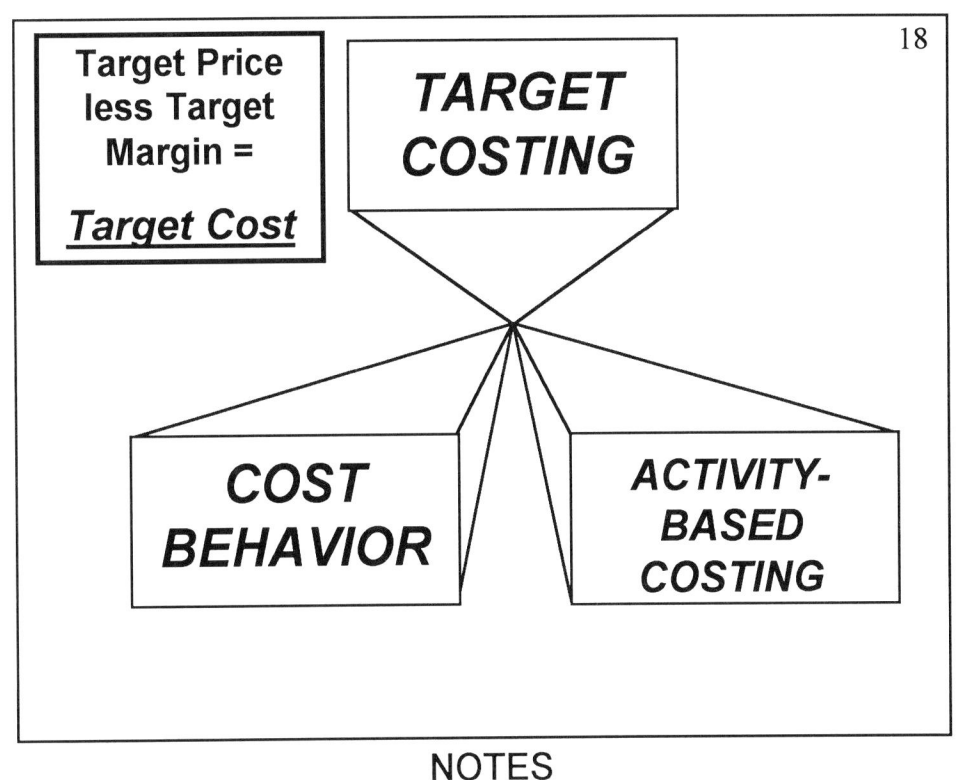

NOTES

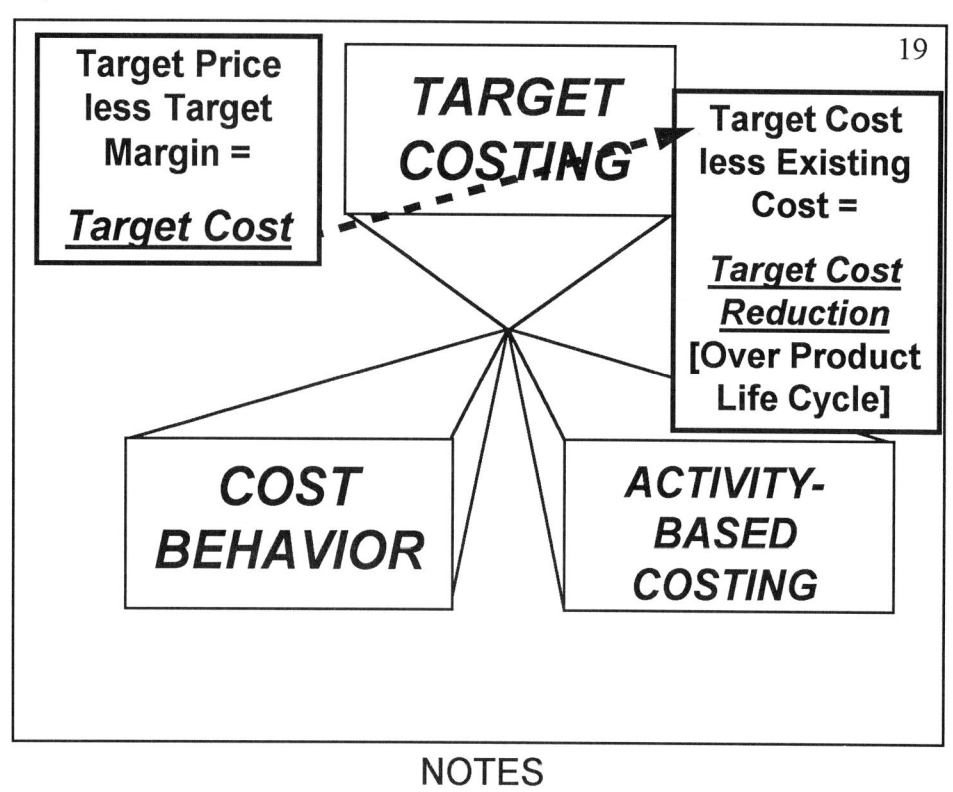

NOTES

TARGET COSTING

Target Cost less Existing Cost = *Target Cost Reduction* [Over Product Life Cycle]

Cost reduction is achieved by applying understanding of *cost behavior and key business activities.*

- COST BEHAVIOR
- ACTIVITY-BASED COSTING

TARGET COSTING

COST-PRICE PARADIGM FOR THE 21ST CENTURY

Suppose that the company is considering entering a new market region with a product mix similar to the current mix represented by the entire 220,000 units. Assume the product life cycle for the 220,000 units is short - one year. This implies that prices may not be adjusted over time using feedback from customers. Market research indicates that customers value the company's products at an average unit price of $7.40. Management is willing to accept a lower 10% margin in order to penetrate this new market region.

What is the required (target) unit cost and unit cost reduction over the product life cycle?

NOTES

Methods to Allocate Support Departments' Costs

- Direct allocation method

- Step-down allocation method

- Reciprocal allocation method

Information for the month of August, 19X7 for Pierce Corporation is as follows:

	SUPPORT DEPARTMENTS	
	Personnel	Legal
Overhead costs incurred	$20,000	$10,000
Service provided to:		
Personnel		10%
Legal	20%	
Operating - X	40%	30%
Operating - Y	40%	60%

NOTES

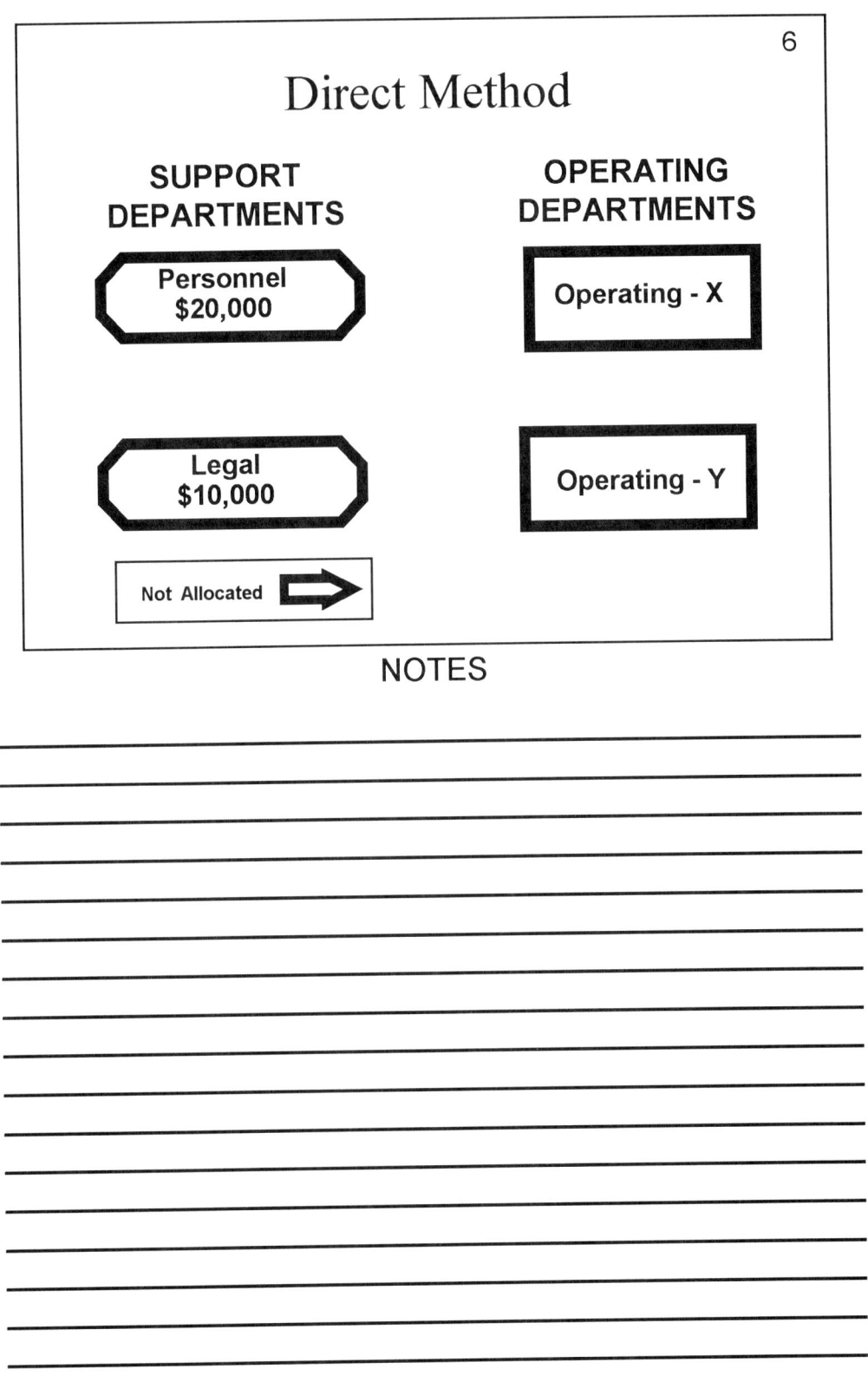

NOTES

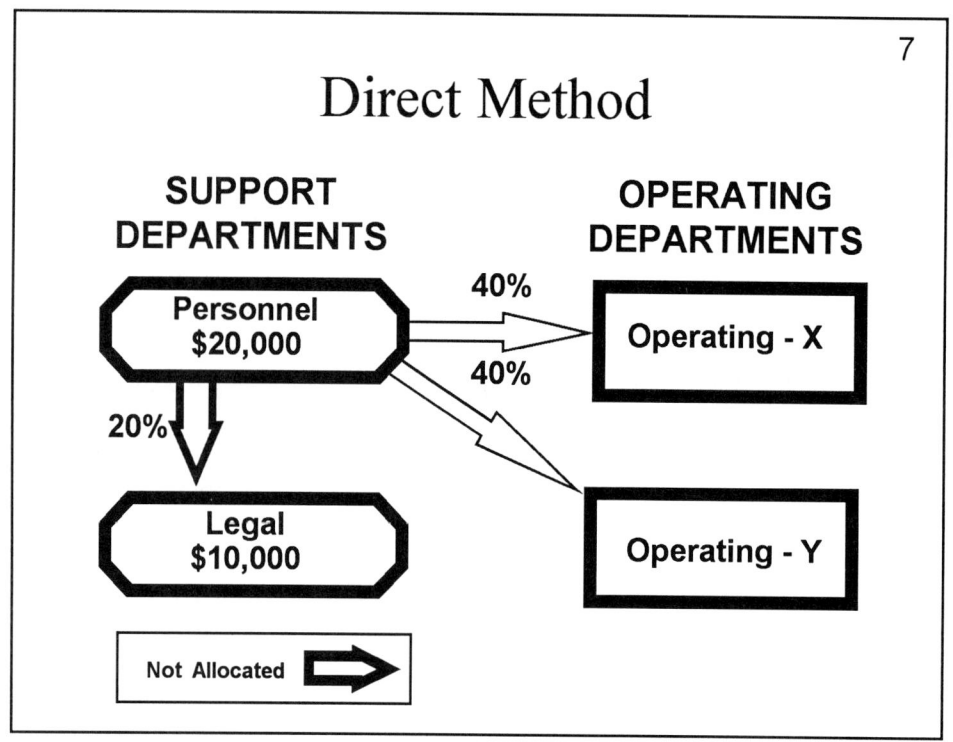

NOTES

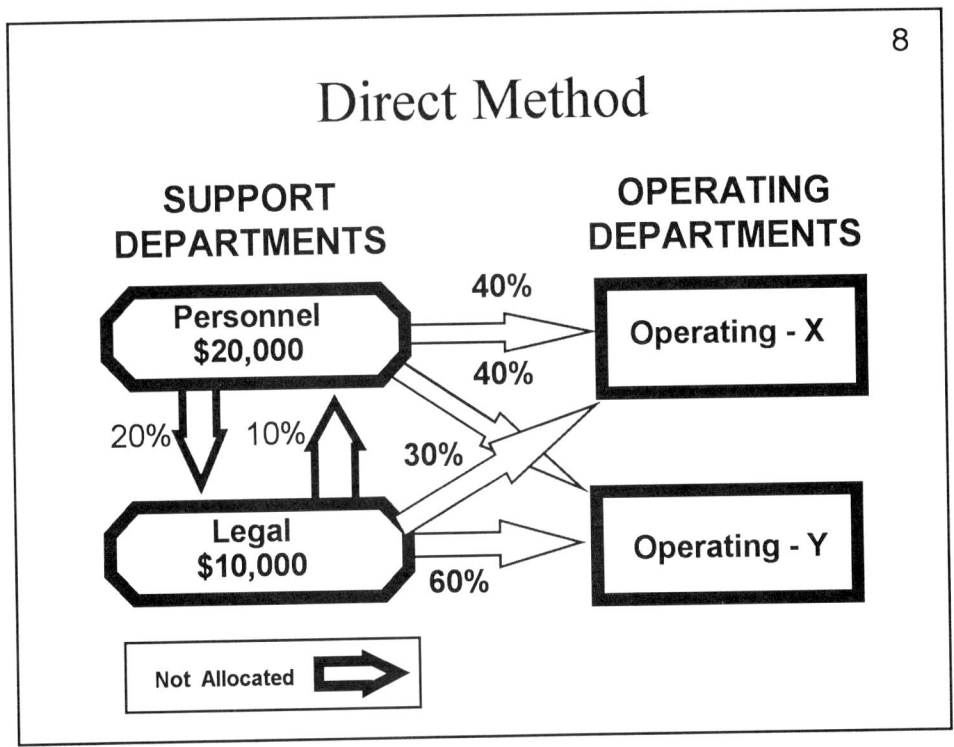

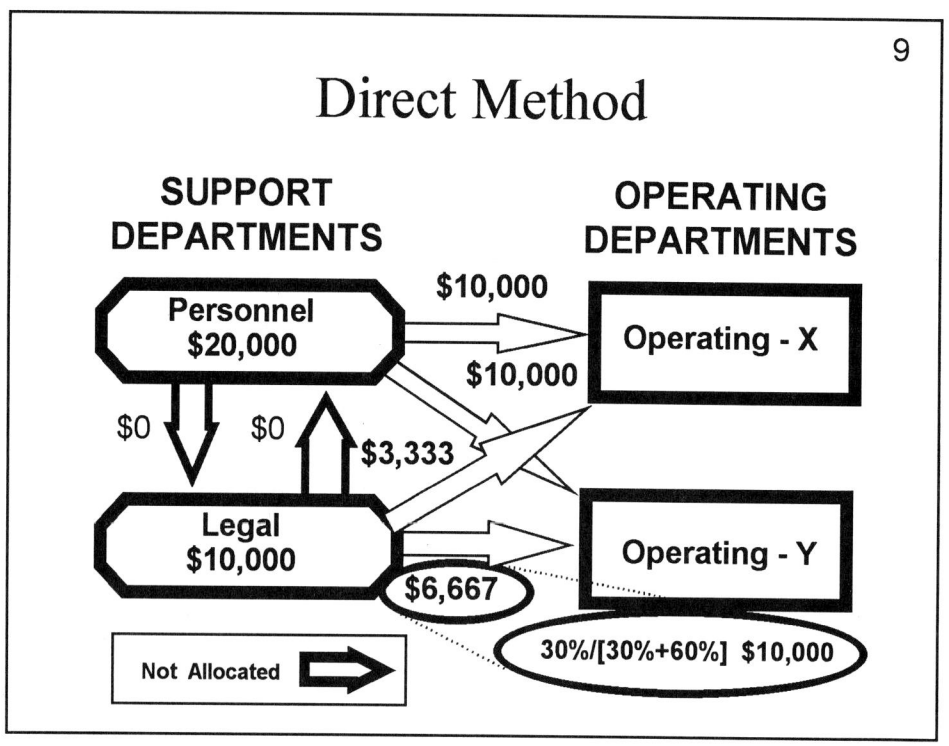

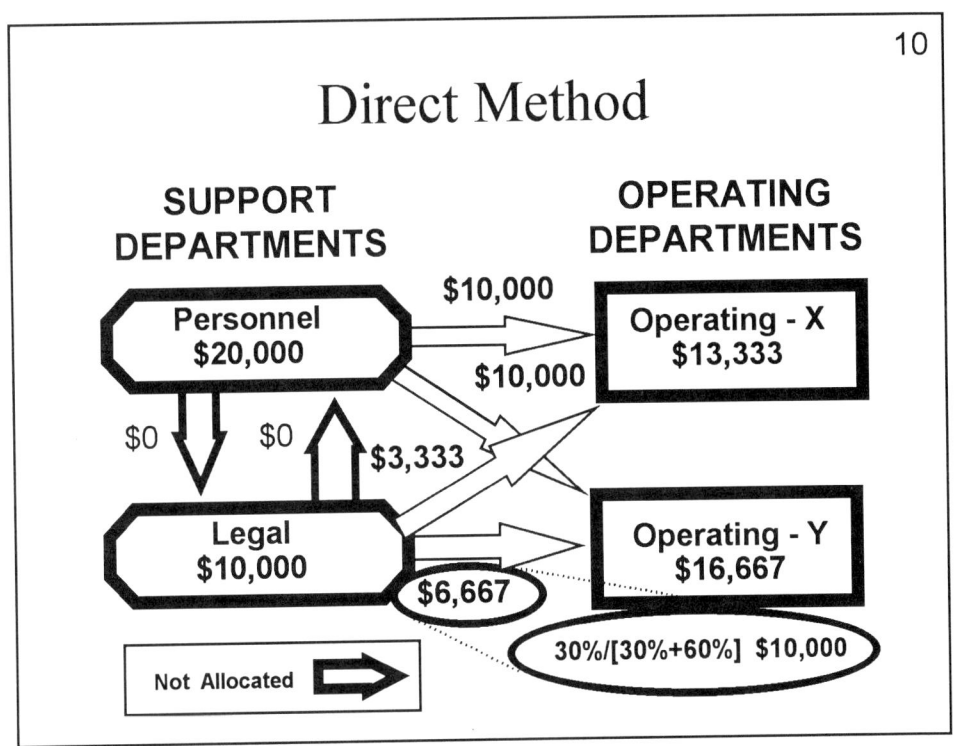

NOTES

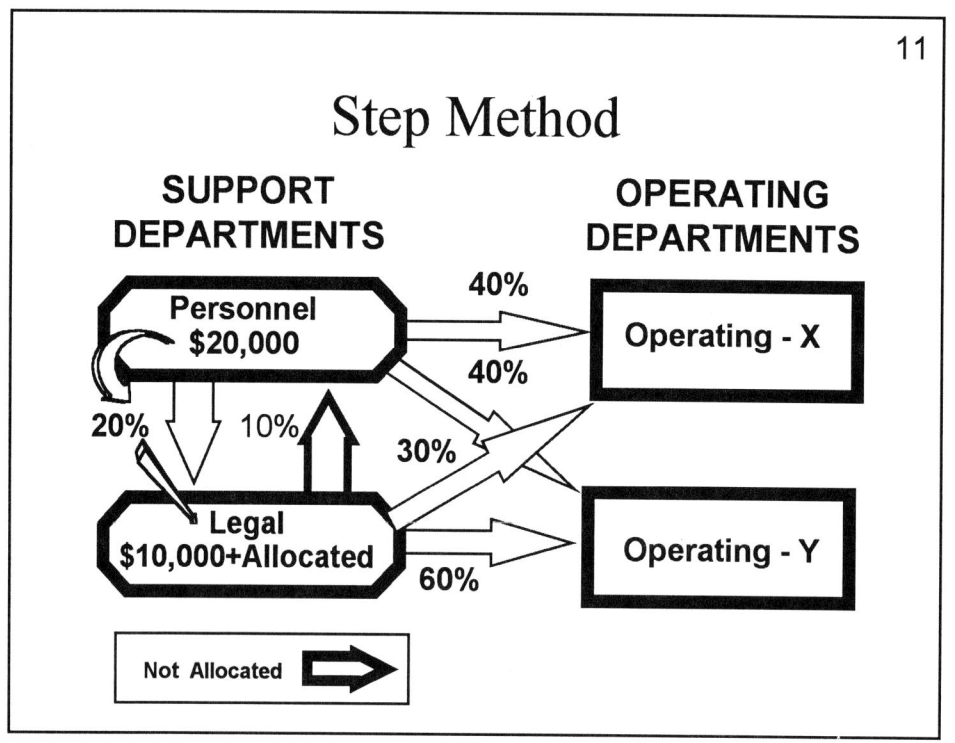

NOTES

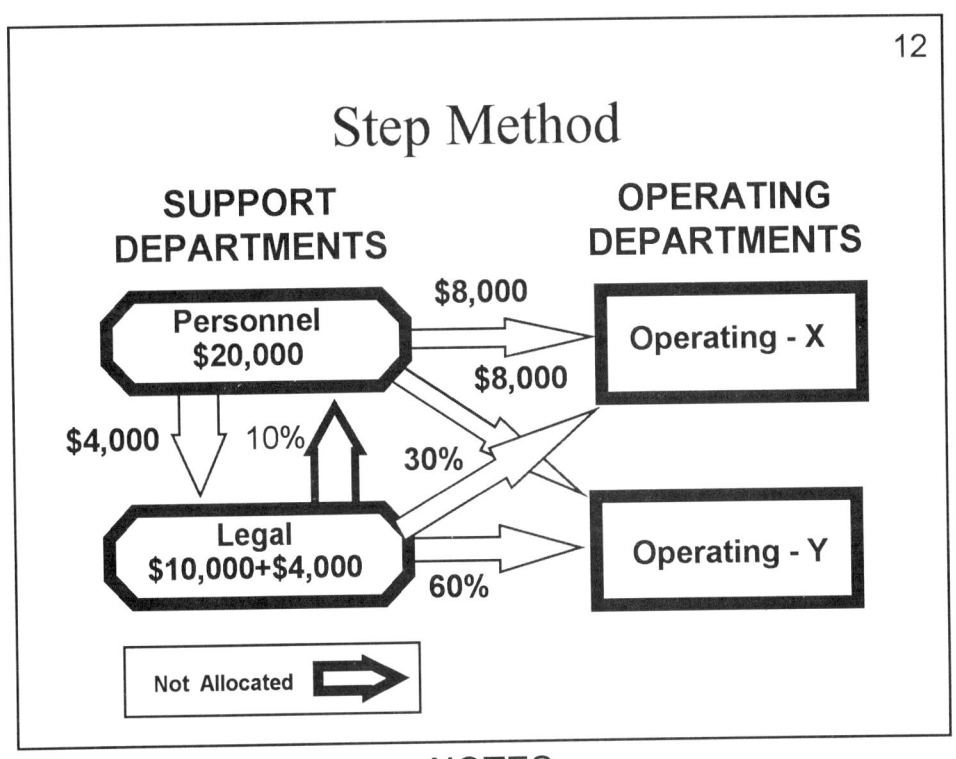

NOTES

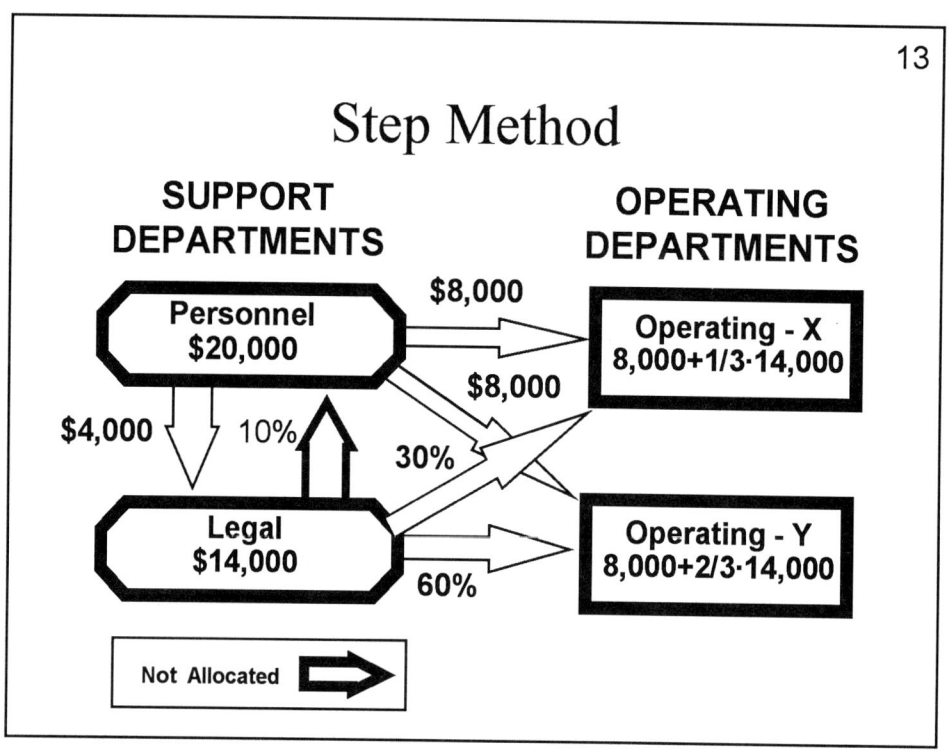

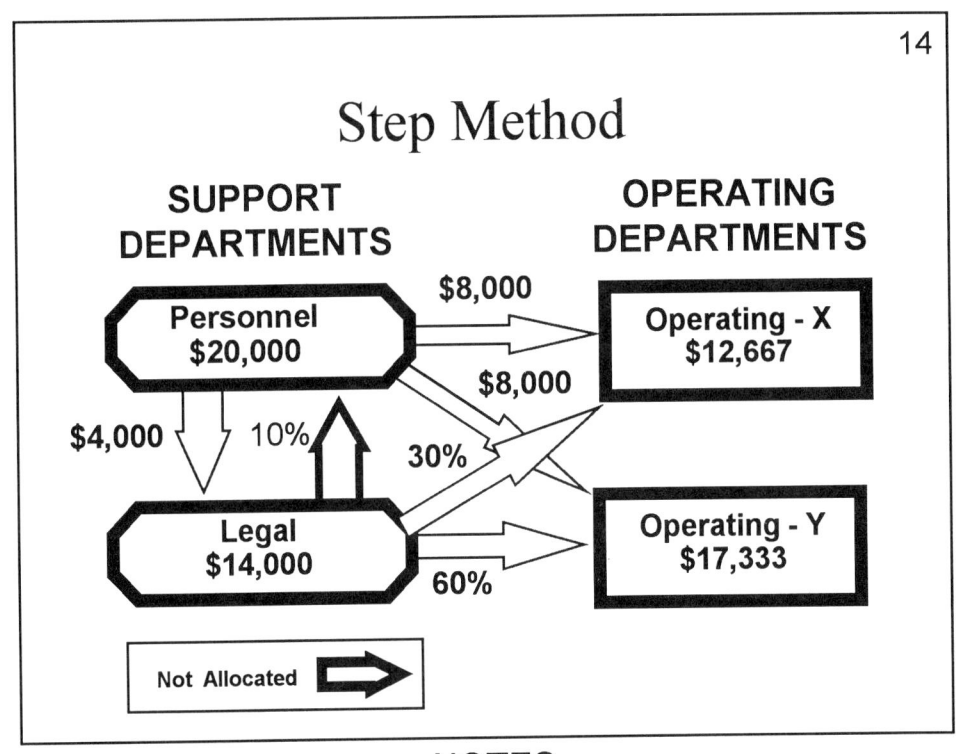

NOTES

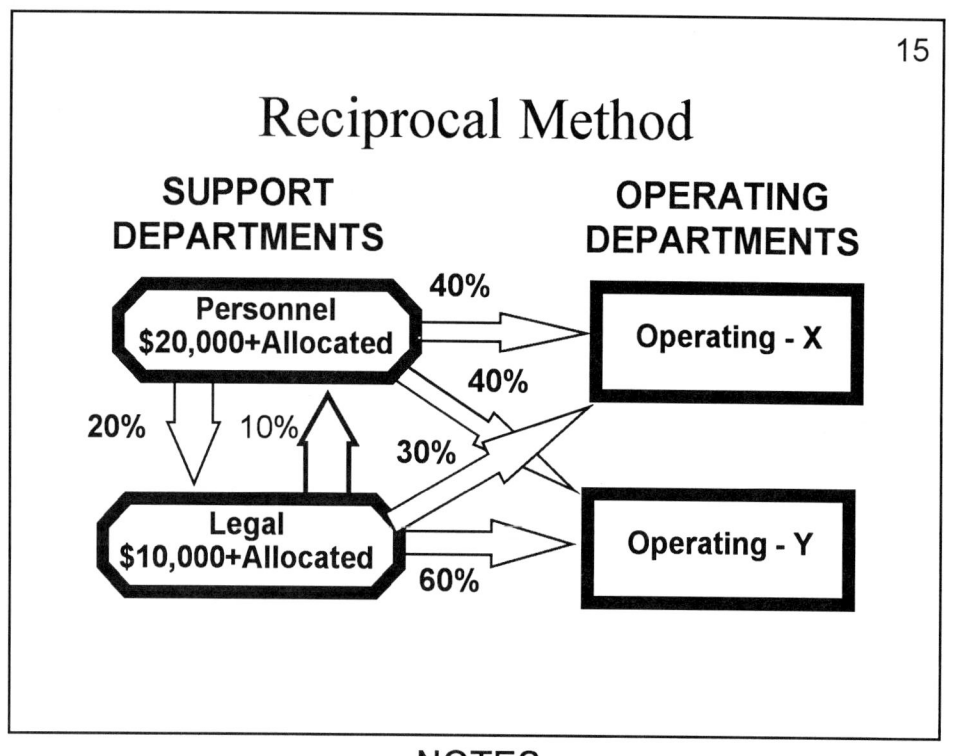

NOTES

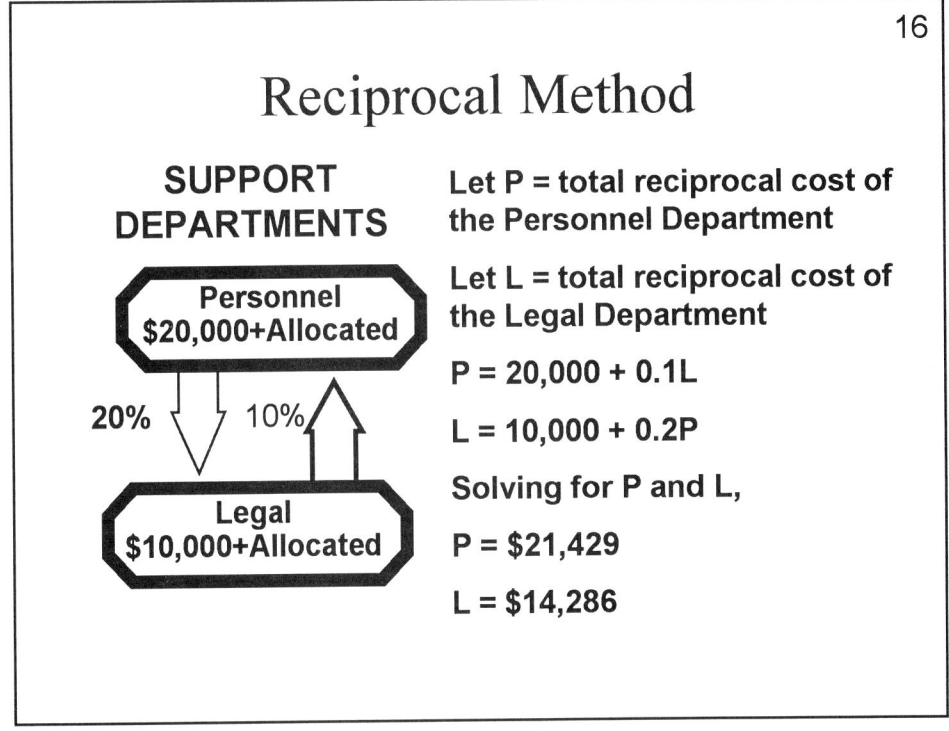

Reciprocal Method

SUPPORT DEPARTMENTS

- Personnel $21,429
- Legal $14,286

Let P = total reciprocal cost of the Personnel Department

Let L = total reciprocal cost of the Legal Department

$P = 20{,}000 + 0.1L$

$L = 10{,}000 + 0.2P$

Solving for P and L,

$P = \$21{,}429$

$L = \$14{,}286$

NOTES

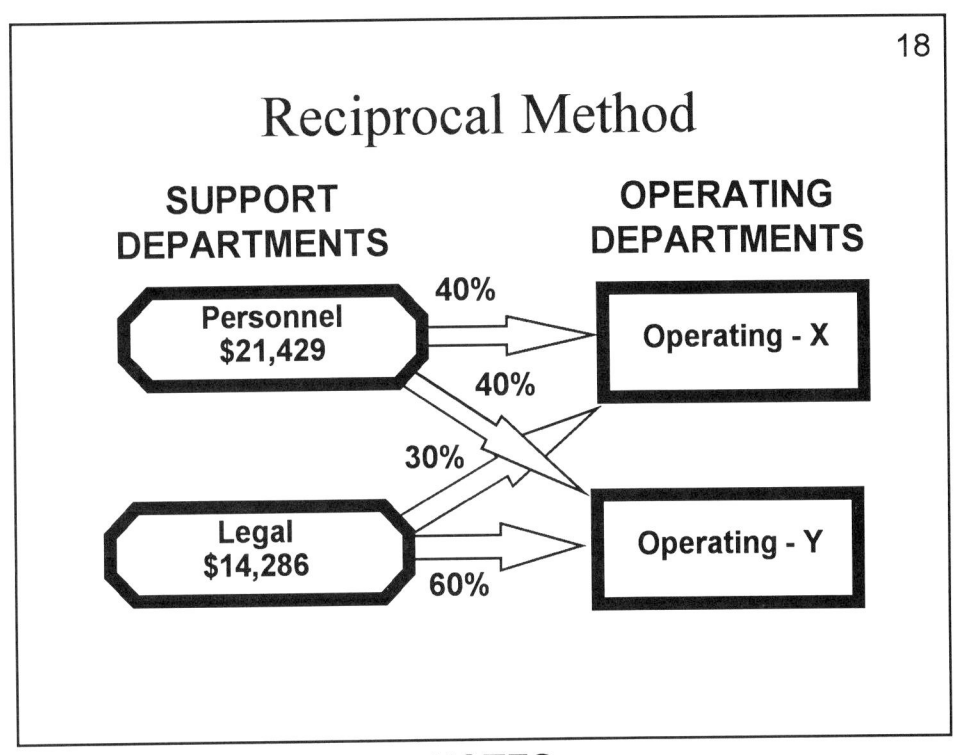

NOTES

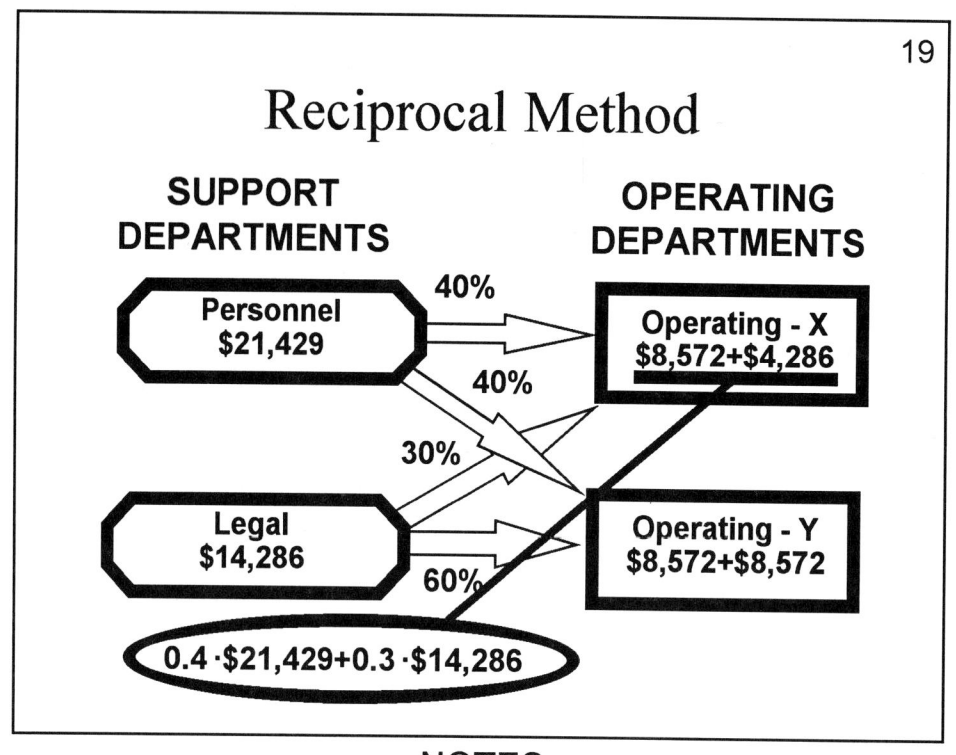

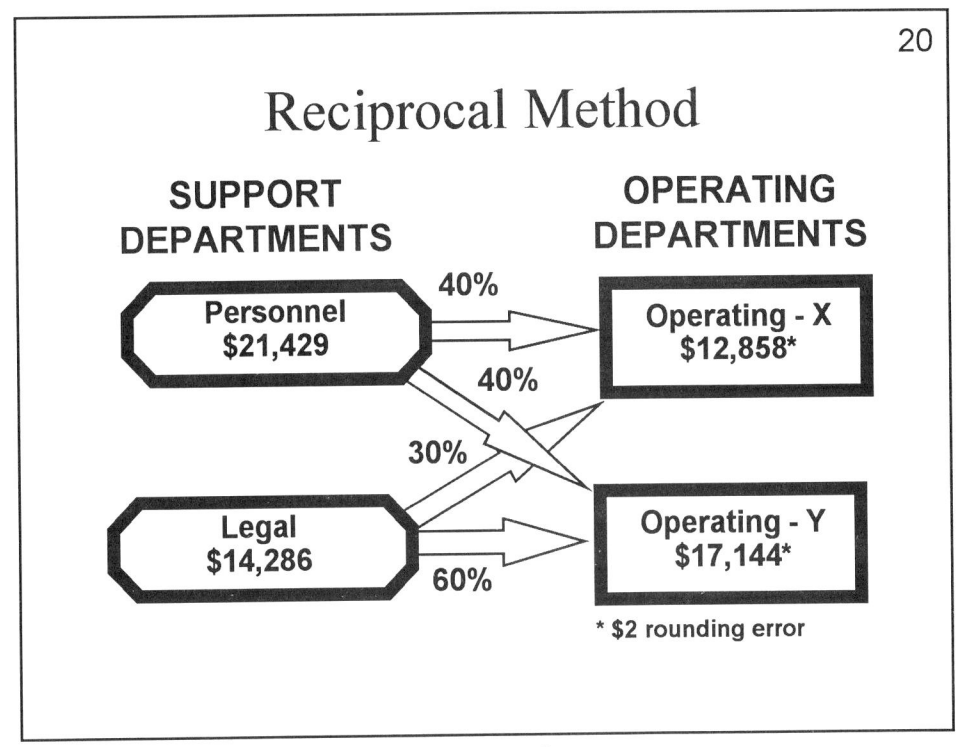

NOTES

Comparison of Methods

METHOD	ALLOCATED SERVICE DEPARTMENT COST		
	Operating -X	Operating - Y	Total
DIRECT	$13,333	$16,667	$30,000
STEP	$12,667	$17,333	$30,000
RECIPROCAL	$12,858	$17,144	$30,002

Differences among the 3 methods' allocations increase

- as the magnitude of the reciprocal services increases, and
- as the differences across operating departments' usage of each support service increase.

NOTES

PowerNotes for Cost Accounting: A Managerial Emphasis, Ninth Edition

14

Cost Allocation: II

NOTES

PowerNotes for Cost Accounting: A Managerial Emphasis, Ninth Edition

Choosing Indirect-Cost Pools and Determining Cost Rates

Plantwide Rates versus Department Rates

- Indirect costs allocated to individual products, services, customers, or other cost objects are a function of
  - Cost pool choices
  - Cost allocation base choices
- A cost pool is *homogeneous* if the cause-effect relationship between the cost allocator (driver) and the costs of related pool activities is the same or similar.

NOTES

Guidelines for Refining the Costing System

- Expand the number of indirect-cost pools until each pool is homogeneous.
- Identify an appropriate cost allocation base for each indirect-cost pool.

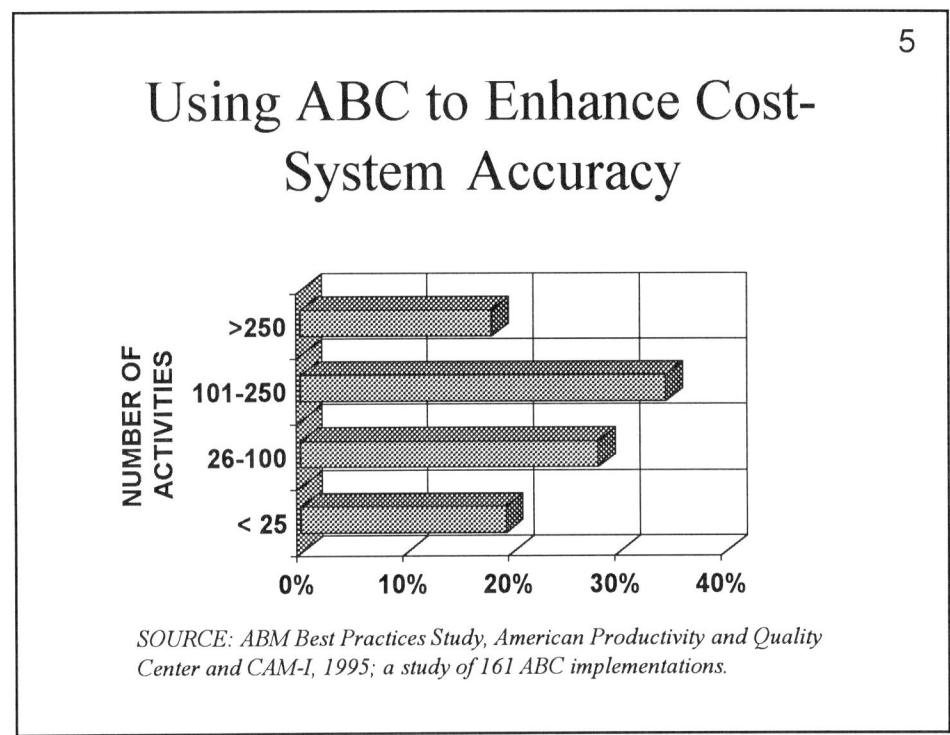

NOTES

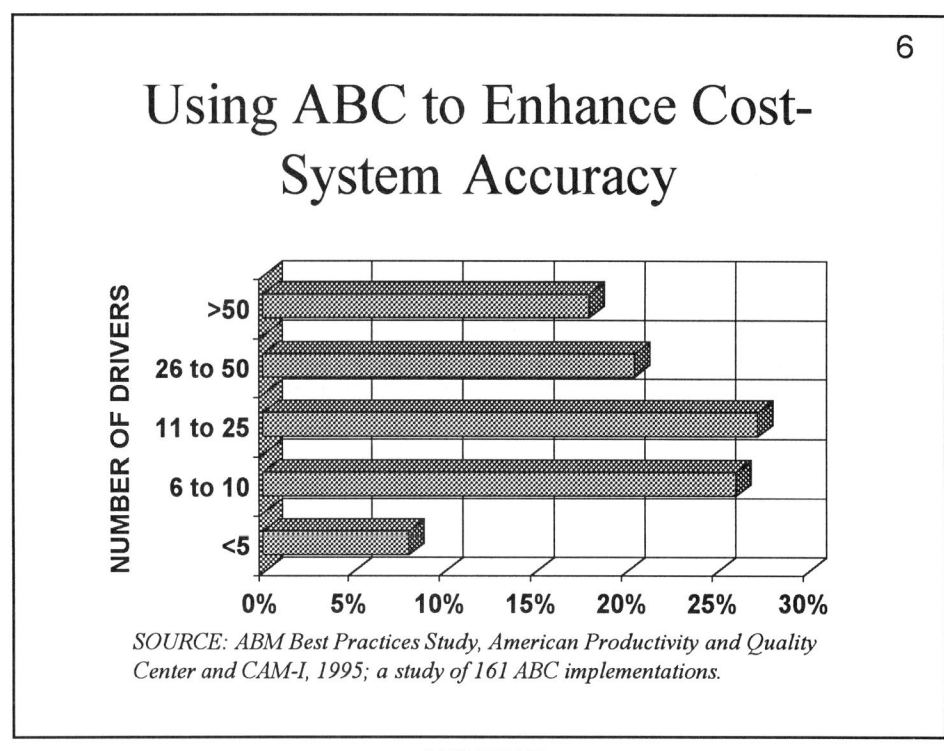

NOTES

Plantwide Rates versus Departmental Rates

- In a multiproduct environment, should the company use a single plantwide manufacturing overhead rate or separate departmental rates?
  - Do individual departments differ in the cause-effect or benefits-received relationship between manufacturing overhead costs and the cost driver?
  - Do individual products differ in the way they are processed by departments?

NOTES

The Cordova Manufacturing Company [CMC] has two producing departments, machining and assembly. A recent automation of CMC's machining operations [CAM system and robotic workstations] drastically reduced the amount of direct labor needed in the machining operations.

CMC is considering switching from a plantwide rate based on direct-labor hours to a department rate system with machine hours for the machining department and direct-labor hours in assembly. Budgeted data for 19X7 are:

	MACHINING	ASSEMBLY	TOTAL
Total overhead costs*	$525,000	$420,000	$945,000
Machine hours	105,000		105,000
Direct-labor hours	15,000	30,000	45,000

* *After allocating service department costs*

NOTES

To evaluate the proposed department-based allocation system, CMC has chosen two representative products. These products use the following machine hours and direct-labor hours:

	Machine Hours in Machining	Direct-Labor Hours in Machining	Direct-Labor Hours in Assembly
Product A	10.0	1.0	14.0
Product B	17.0	1.5	3.0

Management needs a manufacturing overhead cost comparison of the proposed departmental costing system to the existing system based on a plantwide rate.

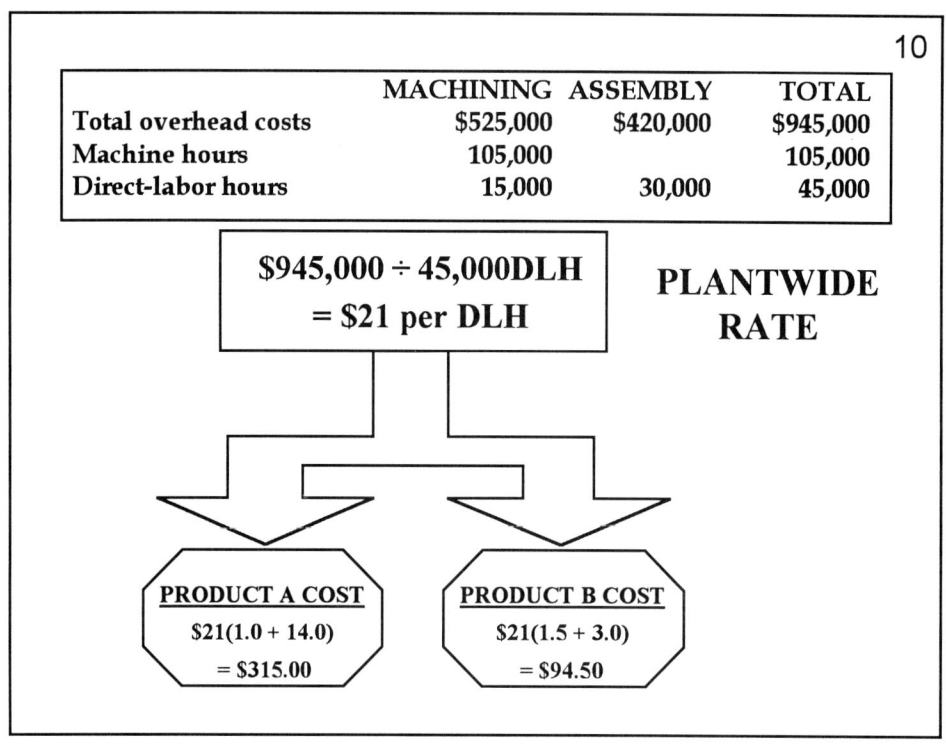

NOTES

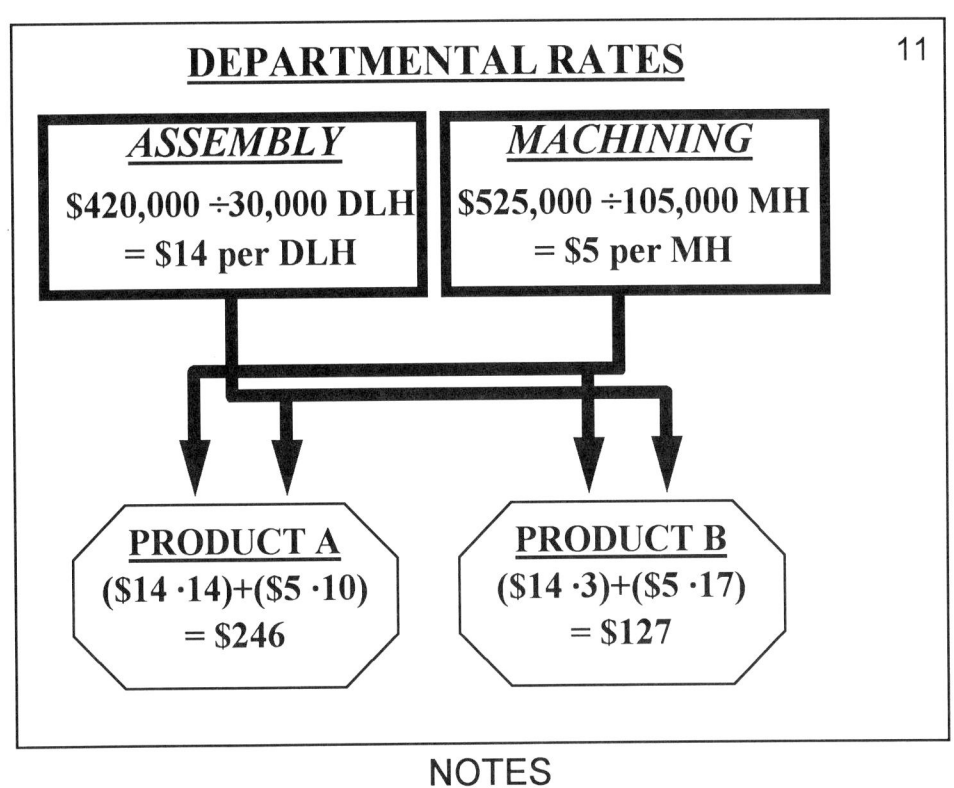

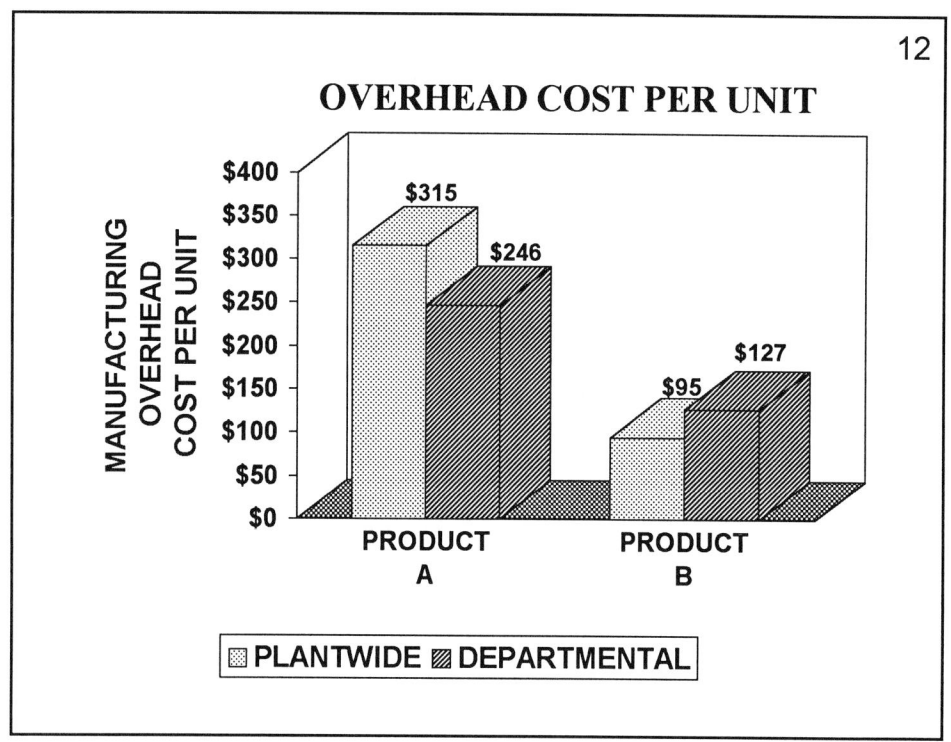

NOTES

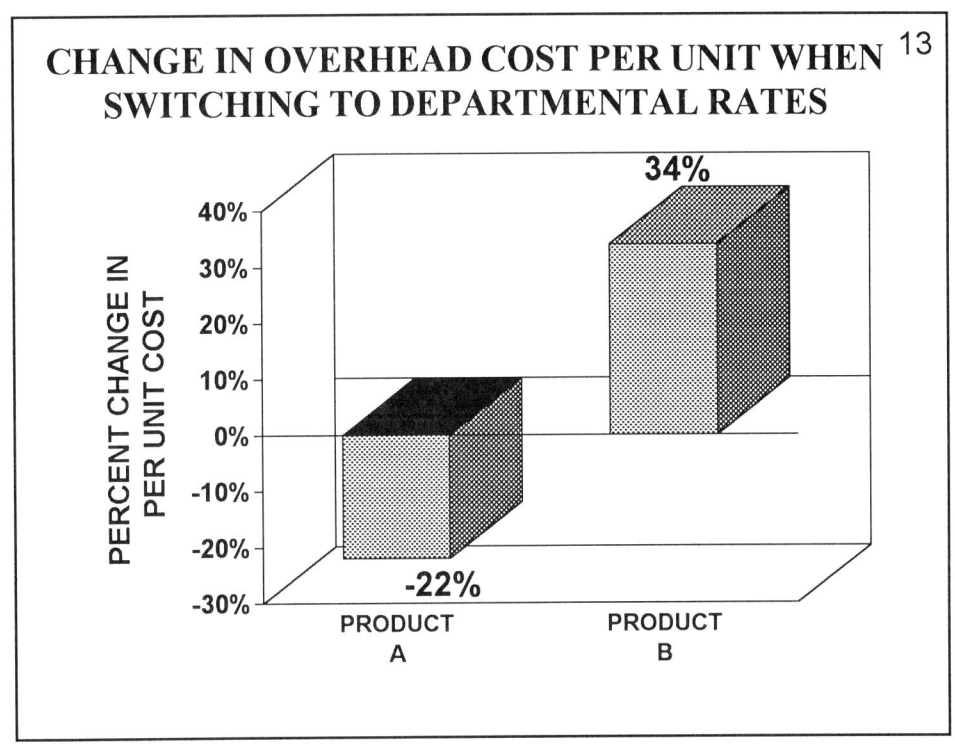

NOTES

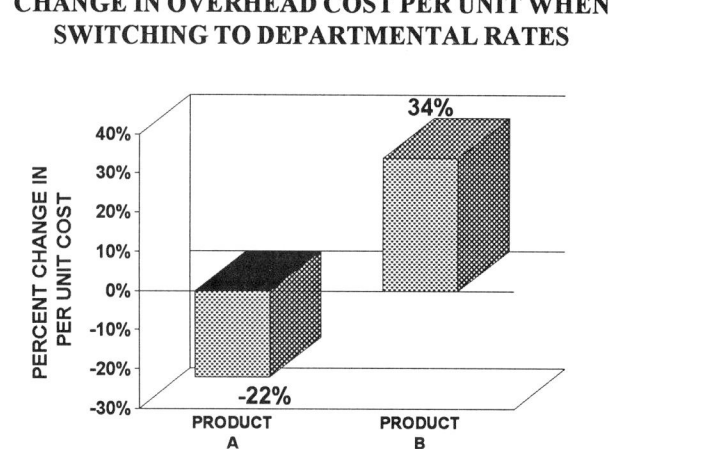

CHANGE IN OVERHEAD COST PER UNIT WHEN SWITCHING TO DEPARTMENTAL RATES

A major change in costs results from using departmental instead of plantwide rates. Product A is very labor intensive, whereas Product B is machine intensive. This leads to a substantial increase in the cost allocated to B when machine hours are used and a decrease in allocation to A.

NOTES

PowerNotes for Cost Accounting: A Managerial Emphasis, Ninth Edition

15

Cost Allocation: Joint Products and Byproducts

Joint Costs and Decision Making

A petrochemical company has a batch process whereby 1,000 gallons of a raw material are transformed into 100 pounds of Z-1 and 400 pounds of Z-2. Although the joint costs of their production are $900, both products are worthless at their split-off point.

Additional separable costs of $300 are necessary to give Z-1 a sales value of $800 as Product A. Similarly, additional separable costs of $150 are necessary to give Z-2 a sales value of $800 as Product B.

NOTES

Physical-Units Method

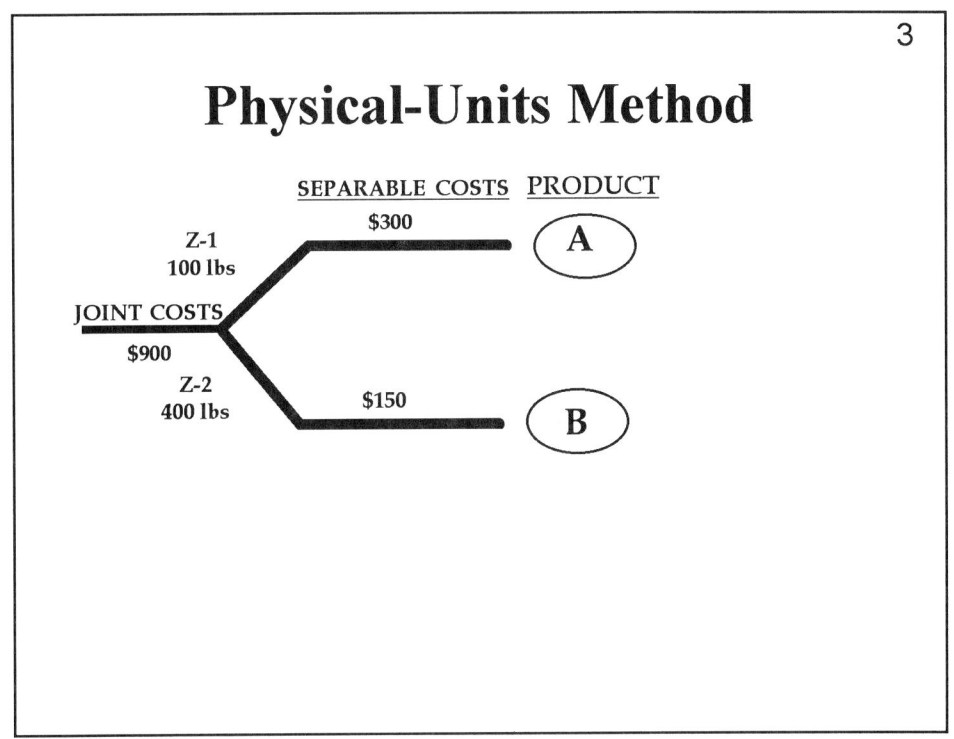

NOTES

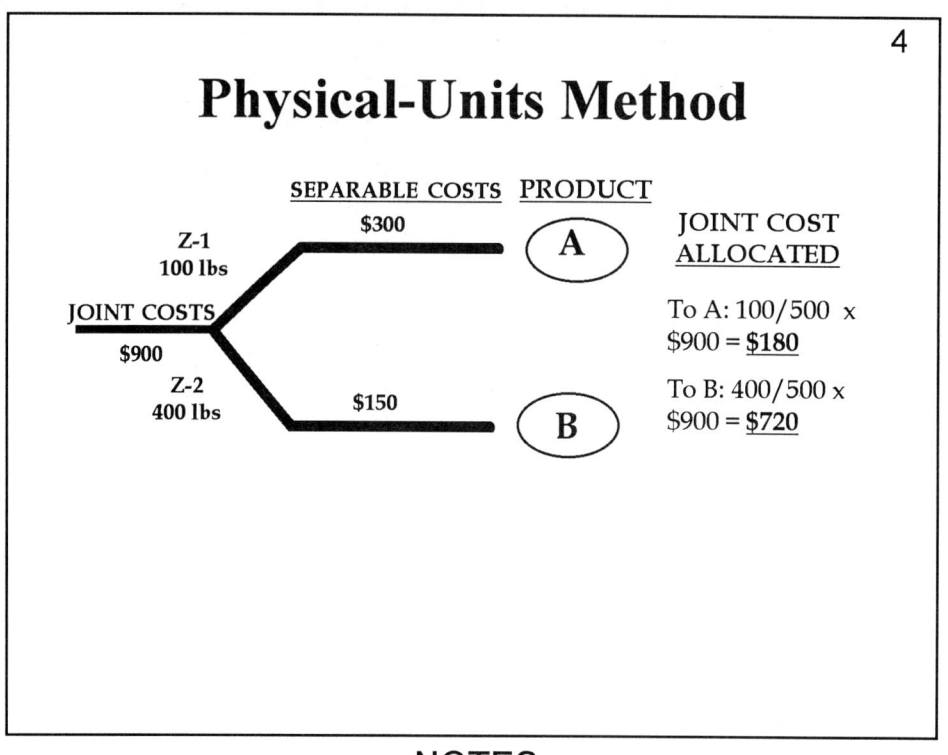

NOTES

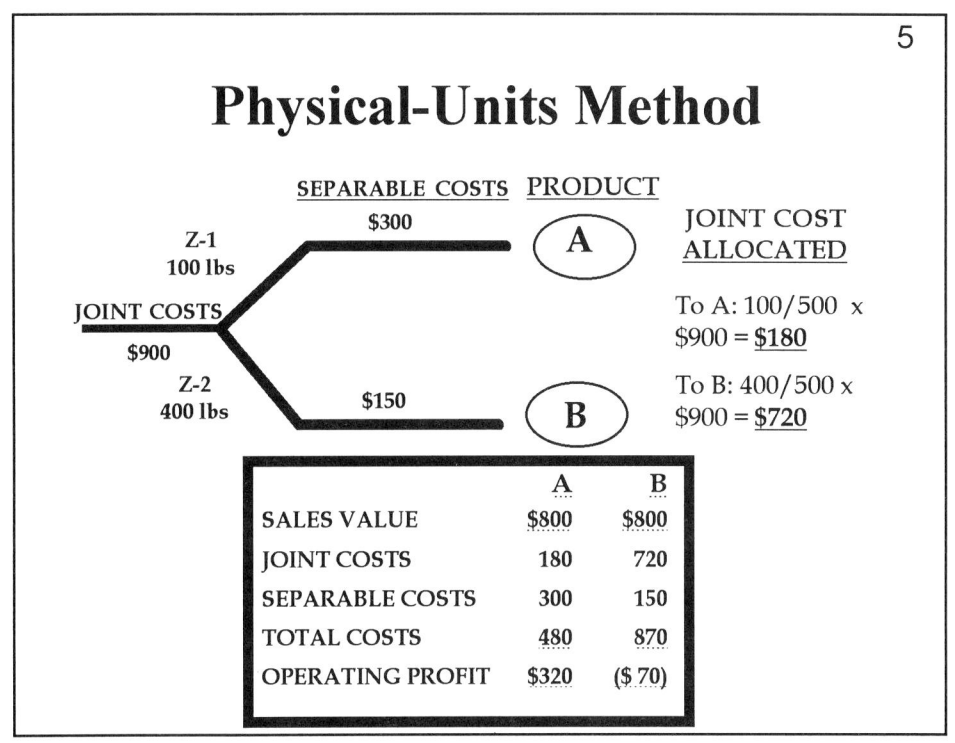

NOTES

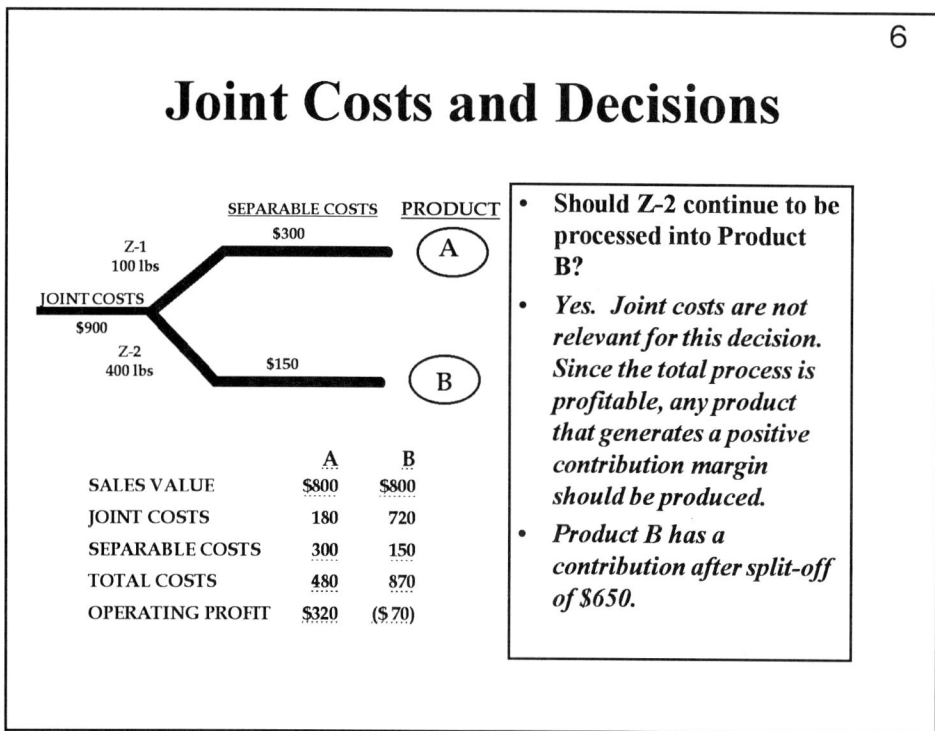

Relative-Sales-Value Method

- Assume that there is no market for Z-1 or Z-2 at the split-off point. Determine the profitability of Products A and B using the relative-sales-value method.

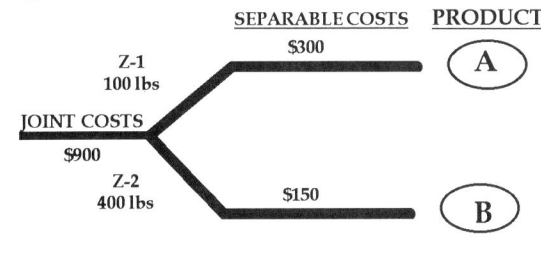

Relative-Sales-Value Method

	A	B	TOTAL
Sales Value	$800	$800	$1,600
Separable Costs	300	150	450
Sales Value Imputed at Split-off Point	500	650	1,150
Allocation of Joint Cost, 500/1,150 and 650/1,150, Respectively	391	509	900
Operating Profit (Loss)	$109	$141	$250

NOTES

Joint Costs and Decisions

	A	B	TOTAL
Sales Value	$800	$800	$1,600
Separable Costs	300	150	450
Sales Value Imputed at Split-off Point	500	650	1,150
Allocation of Joint Cost, 500/1,150 and 650/1,150, Respectively	391	509	900
Operating Profit (Loss)	$109	$141	$250

- Based on the above figures, engineering has proposed a method that will increase the production of Product B by 50 pounds with a corresponding decrease in A without changing the per pound cost factors. Compute the impact on overall profit if this proposal is accepted.

Engineering Proposal

	A	B	Total
Pounds	50	450	500
Sales Value	$400	$900	$1,300
Separable Costs			
Contribution to Joint Costs		(450/400) x $800	
Joint Costs			
Operating Profit			

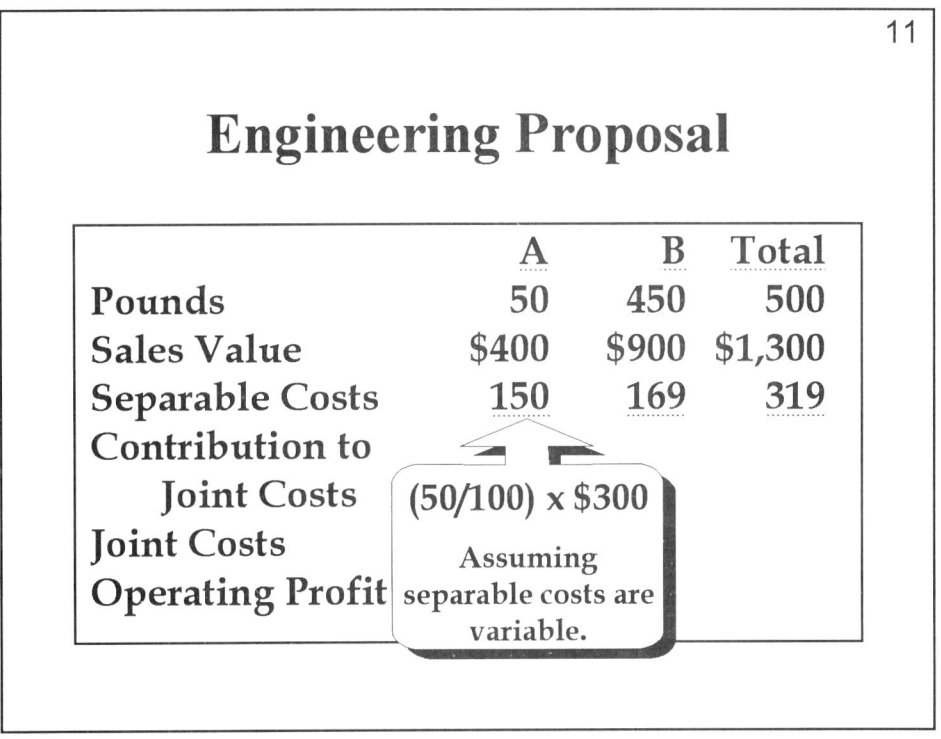

Engineering Proposal

	A	B	Total
Pounds	50	450	500
Sales Value	$400	$900	$1,300
Separable Costs	150	169	319
Contribution to Joint Costs	$250	$731	981
Joint Costs			900
Operating Profit			$81

NOTES

Choose Product with Maximum Contribution per Unit of Constraining Resource

- ***The proposal should not be accepted.*** Product B does have the greater book profit and contribution after the split-off point, but Product A has the greatest contribution per pound, which is the scarce resource.

	A	B	Total
Pounds	50	450	500
Sales Value	$400	$900	$1,300
Separable Costs	150	169	319
Contribution to Joint Costs	$250	$731	981
Joint Costs			900
Operating Profit			$81

VERSUS $250 IF 100 LB. OF A & 300 LB. OF B

PowerNotes for Cost Accounting: A Managerial Emphasis, Ninth Edition

16

Revenues, Revenue Variances, and Customer-Profitability Analysis

NOTES

Customer Profitability Analysis

Customer-profitability analysis examines how individual customers, or groupings of customers, differ in their profitability.

Profit Planning at Bliss & Laughlin Industries, Inc.

- **Bliss & Laughlin Industries, Inc. [B&L] is a steel-finishing company based in Illinois.**
- **B&L produces 800 steel products plus many products produced to customer specifications. B&L products are used by original equipment manufacturers, automotive companies, and service centers.**

SOURCE: "Using ABC for Process Analysis, Customer Profitability, and Manufacturing Flexibility," C. Marx and J. Balogh, Activity-Based Management:: Lessons from the ABM Battlefield, Edited by S. Player and D. Keys, MasterMedia Ltd., New York, 1995.

NOTES

The Key Business Issue at B&L

- **The key business issue B&L faced in 1991 was declining earnings. During the period from 1988 to 1991, net income went from over $2 million to a net loss of more than $3.6 million.**
- **Activity-based costing was implemented.**
- **The goal: to determine the company's problems and opportunities, and support the profit planning process by focusing attention on profitable customer classes, customer accounts, and products.**

NOTES

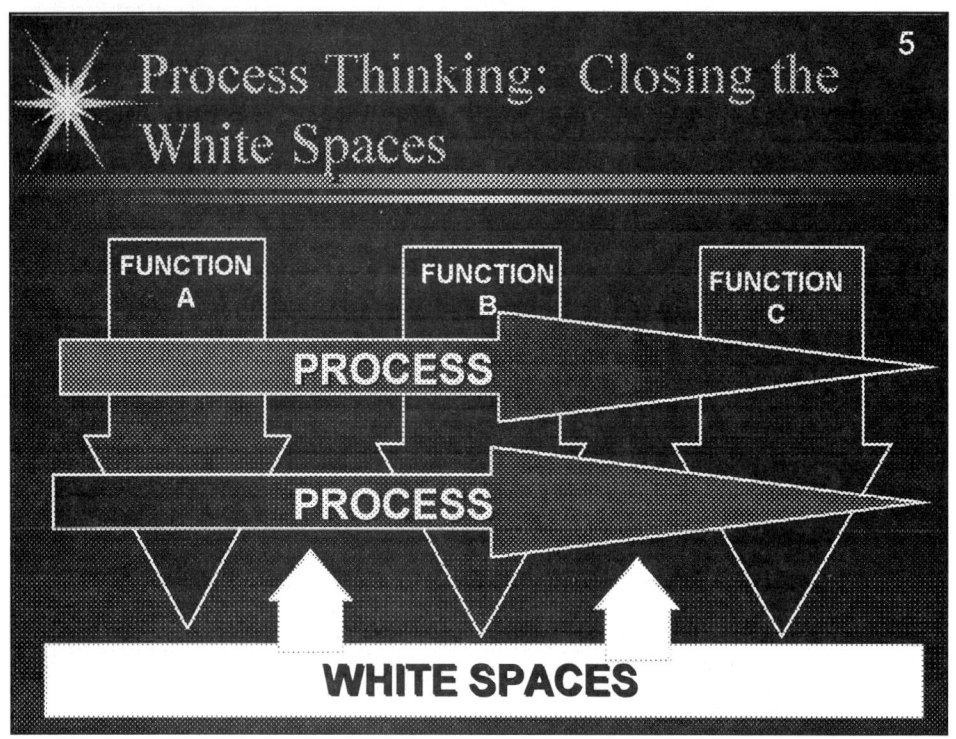

NOTES

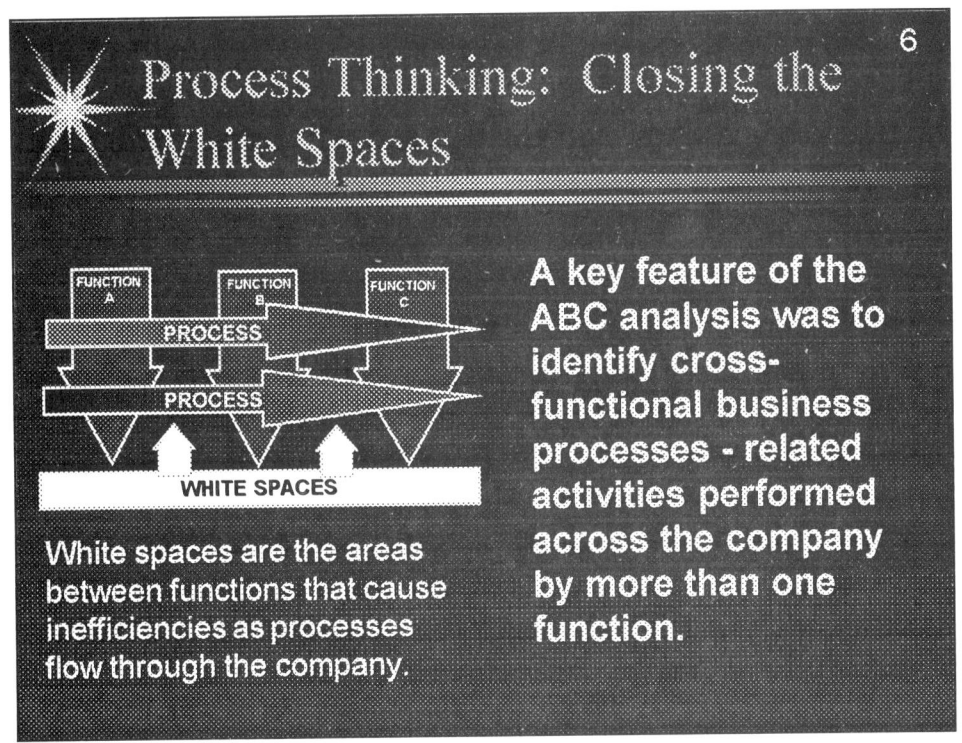

NOTES

Processes and Activity Drivers

Business Process	Driver
Determine Customer Needs	# Customers
Prepare and Deliver Quotes	# Line Items Quoted
Schedule the Mill	# Shop Orders
Acquire Resources	# Line Items Received
Make the Product	# Plant #1 Tons
Deliver the Product	# Line Items Shipped
Service the Product	# Customer Claims
Interplant Sustaining	# Interplant Tons
Corporate Sustaining	# Corporate Tons
Customer Specific	# Plant #1 Tons

NOTES

Profit Planning at Bliss & Laughlin Industries, Inc.

- **B&L used ABC analysis to develop a strategic view of costs of processes, products, and *customers*.**
- **Customer analysis revealed that 80% of sales came from only 10% of B&L customers!**

Actions Taken by B&L

- **B&L used ABC results to develop customer profitability profiles and goals. Actions taken based on these profiles included:**
  - **Customers with high costs (purchasing less than one truckload of steel per year) were reevaluated.**
  - **Customer segmenting by profitability resulted in changes to service levels and inventory items.**

Actions Taken by B&L

- **A large original equipment manufacturer was generating a net loss of $700,000 on annual shipments of 5,000 tons. A policy of "improve or remove" was adopted.**
  - **Negotiations with the customer resulted in a series of changes, including modifications to material source and pricing, process manufacturing, product testing, and pricing.**

The Results

- **The result (for this customer) was an increase in profitability to more than $1.1 million per year with a doubling of volume!**
- **The exhibit below depicts B&L's overall dramatic turnaround (amounts in thousands)!**

	1991		1994	
NET SALES	$114,528	100%	$152,435	100%
COST OF SALES	107,545	93%	136,173	89%
GROSS PROFIT	6,983	6%	16,262	11%
S, G, & A	10,645	9%	12,631	8%
PRETAX INCOME (LOSS)	$(3,662)	(3.2%)	$3,661	2.4%

PowerNotes for Cost Accounting: A Managerial Emphasis, Ninth Edition

17

Process-Costing Systems

NOTES

Process-Costing Systems

- A process-costing system is a costing system in which the cost of a product or service is obtained by assigning costs to masses of like or similar units and then computing unit costs on an average basis.

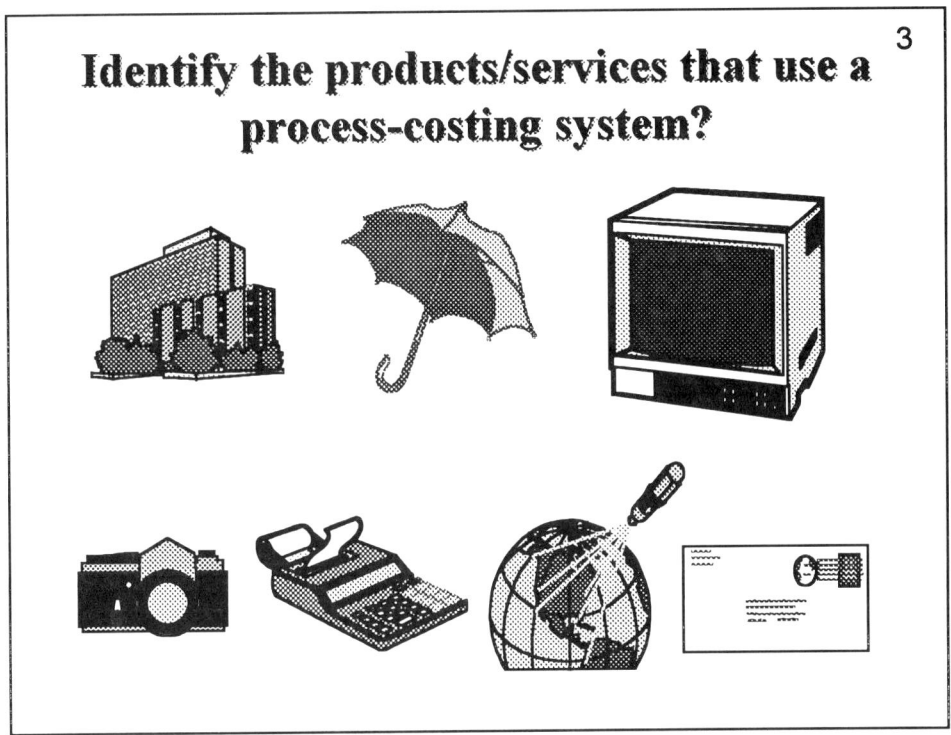

NOTES

Identify the products/services that use a process-costing system?

NOTES

Procedure for Process Costing

① Summarize the flow of physical units of output.

② Compute output in terms of equivalent units.

③ Compute equivalent unit costs.

④ Summarize total costs to account for and assign these costs to units completed and to units in ending work-in-process.

Consider the Cooking Department of Woodland Foods, a food-processing company. Compute the cost of work completed and the cost of ending work-in-process using the weighted-average method.

Units

Beginning work-in-process: 5,000 units; 100% completed for materials, 40% completed for conversion costs

Started during the month: 28,000 units

Ending work-in-process: 2,000 units; 100% completed for materials, 50% for conversion costs

NOTES

STEPS 1 AND 2 ARE PERFORMED USING THIS INFORMATION

Units

Beginning work-in-process: 5,000 units; 100% completed for materials, 40% completed for conversion costs

Started during the month: 28,000 units

Ending work-in-process: 2,000 units; 100% completed for materials, 50% for conversion costs

NOTES

① Summarize the flow of physical units of output.

Flow of Production	(Step 1) Physical Units
Completed and transferred out	31,000
Ending work-in-process	<u>2,000</u>
	33,000

NOTES

② Compute output in terms of equivalent units.

	(Step 1) Physical Units	(Step 2) Equivalent Units	
Flow of Production		Material	Conversion
Completed and transferred out	31,000	31,000	31,000
Ending work-in-process	2,000	2,000	1,000
	33,000	33,000	32,000

NOTES

Costs

Beginning work-in-process:
- Direct materials $8,060
- Conversion   1,300 $ 9,360

Direct materials added in current month   41,440

Conversion costs added in current month   14,700

Total costs to account for $65,500

NOTES

Costs

Beginning work-in-process:
- Direct materials $8,060
- Conversion   1,300 $ 9,360

Direct materials added in current month   41,440

Conversion costs added in current month   14,700

Total costs to account for $65,500

THIS INFORMATION IS USED FOR STEPS 3-4

NOTES

③ Compute equivalent unit costs.

	(Step 1) Physical Units	(Step 2) Equivalent Units	
		Material	Conversion
Flow of Production			
Completed and transferred out	31,000	31,000	31,000
Ending work in process	2,000	2,000	1,000
	33,000	33,000	32,000

Beginning work in process	$ 9,360	$ 8,060	$ 1,300
Costs added currently	56,140	41,440	14,700
Total costs to account for	$65,500	$49,500	$16,000
Equivalent units		÷ 33,000	÷ 32,000
Equivalent unit costs		$ 1.50	$ 0.50

NOTES

④ Summarize total costs to account for and assign these costs to units completed and to units in ending work-in-process.

Transferred out, 31,000·$2.00	$62,000	
Ending work-in-process		
Direct materials	$ 3,000	$1.50·2,000
Conversion	500	$0.50·1,000
Total costs accounted for	$65,500	

NOTES

PowerNotes for Cost Accounting: A Managerial Emphasis, Ninth Edition

18

Spoilage, Reworked Units, and Scrap

NOTES

Accounting for Spoilage

- *Spoilage* refers to unacceptable units of production that are discarded or are sold for net disposal proceeds.
- Objectives of accounting for spoilage:
  - Determine the magnitude of the costs
  - Distinguish between normal and abnormal spoilage

Accounting for Spoilage

- *Normal spoilage* is spoilage that arises under efficient operating conditions.
  - Costs of normal spoilage are usually viewed as a part of the costs of *good units* manufactured.
  - Normal spoilage rates should be computed using the total good units completed as the base.

NOTES

Accounting for Spoilage

- *Abnormal spoilage* is spoilage that is not expected to arise under efficient operating conditions.
  - Abnormal spoilage is regarded as avoidable and controllable.
  - Abnormal spoilage costs are written off as losses.

NOTES

Process Costing and Spoilage Assumptions

- **All spoilage occurs at the inspection point.**
- **Normal spoilage is a percent of *good units* passing the inspection point.**
- **Normal spoilage is allocated to ending WIP only if ending WIP has passed the inspection point.**

Process Costing and Spoilage

① *Summarize the flow of physical units of output.*
② *Compute output in terms of equivalent units.*
③ *Compute equivalent unit costs.*
④ *Summarize total costs to account for and assign these costs to units completed, spoiled units, and to units in ending work-in-process*

NOTES

Adams Company

The Adams Company manufactures a plastic casing for electronic devices in its processing department. All direct material is added at the beginning of processing in large injection-molding machines. Conversion costs consisting of operator wages, energy, supplies and other manufacturing overhead are used evenly during the processing cycle. Spoilage is detected only after the casing is removed from the molding machine and inspected. Normally, the spoiled units are 10% of good output.

NOTES

Production Data for May 19_7
Physical Units

Work-in-process, beginning inventory (May 1)	2,000
Direct materials (100% complete)	
Conversion costs (70% complete)	
Started during May	9,000
Completed and transferred out in May (good units)	8,500
Work-in-process, ending inventory (May 31)	1,500
Direct materials (100% complete)	
Conversion costs (50% complete)	

NOTES

Production Data for May 19_7
Total Costs

Work-in-process, beginning inventory
    Direct materials $15,000
    Conversion costs   <u>11,200</u> $ 26,200
Direct materials costs added
    during May   72,000
Conversion costs added
    during May   <u>79,650</u>
Total costs to account for   <u>$177,850</u>

NOTES

Computing Spoiled Units

Total spoiled units = (Beginning units + Units started) - (Good units transferred out + Ending units)

= (2,000 + 9,000) - (8,500 + 1,500)

= 1,000 units

Abnormal spoilage = Total spoilage - Normal spoilage

= 1,000 - 0.10 • 8,500

= 150 units

Step 1: Summarize Output in Physical Units

Flow of Production	Physical Units
Good units completed and transferred out	8,500
Normal spoilage	850
Abnormal spoilage	150
Work-in-process, ending	1,500
Total	11,000

NOTES

Step 2: Compute Equivalent Units

Flow of Production	Physical Units	Equivalent Units Direct Materials	Equivalent Units Conversion Costs
Good units completed and transferred out	8,500	8,500	8,500
Normal spoilage	850	850	850
Abnormal spoilage	150	150	150
Work-in-process, ending	1,500	1,500	750
Total	11,000	11,000	10,250
Deduct Work-in-process, beginning	2,000	2,000	1,400
Started during current period	9,000		
Work done in current period		9,000	8,850

NOTES

Step 3: Compute Equivalent Unit Costs

	Direct Materials	Conversion Costs
Work-in-process, beginning	$15,000	$11,200
Equivalent units of beginning Work-in-process	÷ 2,000	÷ 1,400
Cost per equivalent unit	$7.50	$8.00
Costs added in current period	$72,000	$79,650
Equivalent units of work done in current period	÷ 9,000	÷ 8,850
Cost per equivalent unit	$8.00	$9.00

NOTES

Step 4: Summarize and Assign Total Costs - Direct Materials

	Equivalent Units	Cost per Equivalent Unit	Total Costs
Total costs to account for			
Work-in-process, beginning	2,000	$7.50	$15,000
Work done in current period	9,000	$8.00	$72,000
To account for	11,000	$7.91	$87,000
Good units completed and transferred out (8,500)			
Costs before normal spoilage	8,500	$7.91	$67,235
Normal spoilage	850	$7.91	$ 6,724
Costs of goods units transferred out			$73,959
Abnormal spoilage	150	$7.91	$ 1,187
Work-in-process, ending	1,500	$7.91	$11,865
Accounted for	11,000		$87,011*

* Rounding error

NOTES

Step 4: Summarize and Assign Total Costs - Conversion Costs

	Equivalent Units	Cost per Equivalent Unit	Total Costs
Total costs to account for			
Work-in-process, beginning	1,400	$8.000	$11,200
Work done in current period	8,850	$9.000	$79,650
To account for	10,250	$8.863	$90,850
Good units completed and transferred out (8,500)			
Costs before normal spoilage	8,500	$8.863	$75,336
Normal spoilage	850	$8.863	$ 7,534
Costs of goods units transferred out			$82,870
Abnormal spoilage	150	$8.863	$ 1,329
Work-in-process, ending	750	$8.863	$ 6,647
Accounted for	10,250		$90,846*

* Rounding error

NOTES

Step 4: Summarize Total Costs - Total Production Costs

	Direct Materials	Conversion	Total
Total costs to account for			
Work-in-process, beginning	$15,000	$11,200	$ 26,200
Work done in current period	$72,000	$79,650	$151,650
To account for	$87,000	$90,850	$177,850
Good units completed and transferred out (8,500)			
Costs before normal spoilage	$67,235	$75,336	$142,571
Normal spoilage	$ 6,724	$ 7,534	$ 14,258
Costs of goods units transferred out	$73,959	$82,870	$156,829
Abnormal spoilage	$ 1,187	$ 1,329	$ 2,516
Work-in-process, ending	$11,865	$ 6,647	$ 18,512
Accounted for	$87,011*	$90,846*	$177,857*

* Rounding error

NOTES

PowerNotes for Cost Accounting: A Managerial Emphasis, Ninth Edition

Cost Management: Quality, Time, and the Theory of Constraints

NOTES

Theory of Constraints and Throughput Contribution Analysis

NOTES

Definition and Objective

- The theory of constraints [TOC] describes methods to maximize operating income when faced with some bottleneck and some nonbottleneck operations (see page 698).

- The objective of TOC is to increase throughput contribution while decreasing investments in operating costs.

Applying TOC

- Recognize that the bottleneck resource determines throughput contribution for the plant as a whole
- Find the bottleneck resource
- Keep the bottleneck resource busy and subordinate all nonbottleneck resources
- Increase bottleneck efficiency and capacity

NOTES

Throughput Accounting at Bertch Cabinet Mfg., Inc.

- **Bertch is a fully integrated manufacturer of wood cabinets and accessories (mirrors).**
- **Annual sales in top 10% of U.S. domestic cabinet manufacturers.**
- **Manufacturing process is complicated - over 20 different machining operations are required for a raised panel door.**

SOURCE: *"From Activity-Based Costing to Throughput Accounting,"* J. MacArthur, Management Accounting *(April 1996), pp. 30-38.*

NOTES

Production Changes Resulting from Implementing TOC

- **Reduced lead time (from order to delivery) - from four weeks to two weeks**
- **Batch sizes reduced from weekly requirements to daily requirements**
- **Inventory placed in front of bottleneck resources**

NOTES

Bertch Accountants' Response: Throughput Accounting

- **Three operational measures replace current costing system:**
  - Throughput
  - Inventory [investments]
  - Other Operating Costs
- **Emphasize products with the largest throughput per bottleneck constraint unit**

NOTES

If a product X generates throughput of $100 and requires 10 minutes at a bottleneck machine, the throughput per machine minute is $10. If another product, Y, generates higher throughput of $150 but requires 20 minutes at the bottleneck machine, it has only $7.50 throughput contribution per minute. Emphasis should be placed on production of product X as long a market demand exists.

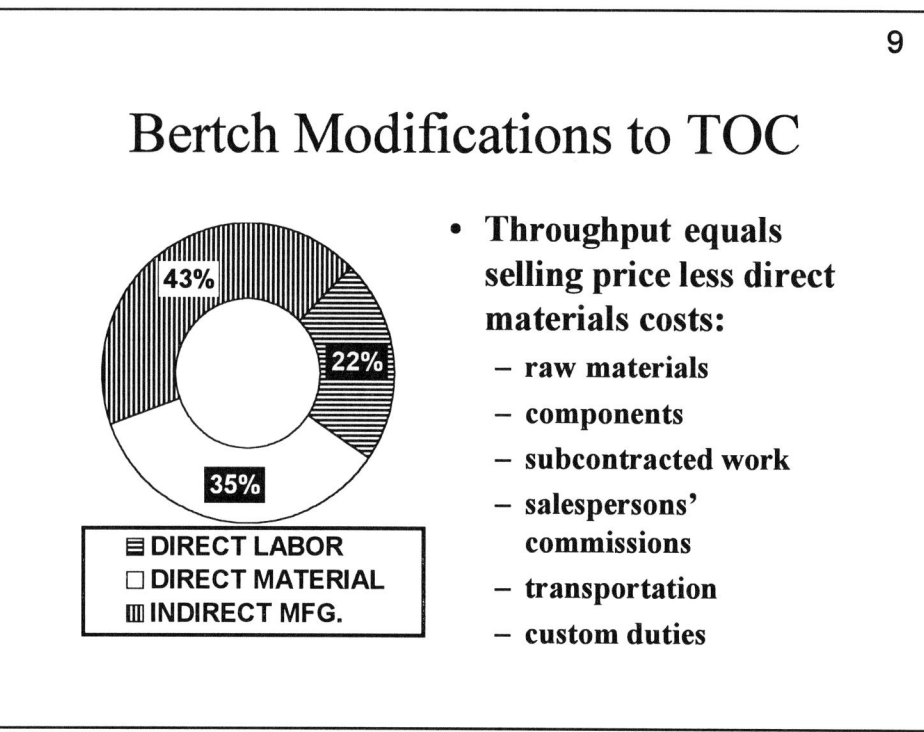

Bertch Modifications to TOC

- **Throughput equals selling price less direct materials costs:**
  - raw materials
  - components
  - subcontracted work
  - salespersons' commissions
  - transportation
  - custom duties

NOTES

Bertch Modifications to TOC

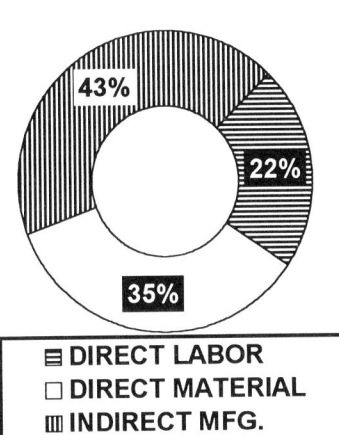

- DIRECT LABOR
- DIRECT MATERIAL
- INDIRECT MFG.

- 70% of direct labor is variable with units produced so...
- Throughput was modified to be sales less direct material and variable direct labor

Uses of TOC at Bertch

- **Divisional Profitability Performance Measure**
- **Ongoing Pricing Decisions**
- **New Contract Pricing (Customer Profitability)**
- **Product Mix Decisions**

Results: The *QCT* Impact

- ○ Lead time reduced [from 4 to 2 weeks for Bath Cabinet Division products]
- ➡ Reduced batch sizes and increased runs
  - ✓ reduces spoilage of wood products
  - ○ reduces delay for rework
  - ☐ reduces inventory levels

✓ **Higher** *Quality*

☐ **Lower** *Cost*

○ **Improved** *Timing*

Results: The *QCT* Impact

➡ **Reduced setup times [longest setup is now only 30 minutes]**
  ○ Freed-up capacity used to do more runs - reduces lead time
➡ **Smoother materials flow**
  ◻ Plant emergencies are fewer, requiring less expediting
➡ **Improved morale**
  ○ Productivity increases result in faster delivery to customers

✓ **Higher**
*Q*uality
◻ **Lower**
*C*ost
○ **Improved**
*T*iming

NOTES

Overall Results at Bertch

→ Sales revenues and profits increased in the Bath Cabinet and Semi-Custom Divisions

→ Increased sales volume has led to the addition of two shifts and construction of new capacity in resources that are constraining throughput

PowerNotes for Cost Accounting: A Managerial Emphasis, Ninth Edition

20

Operation Costing, Just-In-Time Systems, and Backflush Costing

Process Costing in a JIT System: Backflush Costing

- In just-in-time production systems, inventory of work-in-process is typically small compared to the costs of goods produced and sold.
- The cost of tracking work-in-process exceeds the benefits for many companies.
- *Backflush costing* is an accounting system that applies costs to products only when production is complete (text, page 726).

Backflush Costing Example: Rainier Devices

- Rainier Devices manufactures a variety of meters and other measuring devices. One product is an altimeter used by hikers and mountain climbers.
- Rainier adopted a JIT philosophy with an automated, computer-controlled, robotic production system.

NOTES

Rainier Devices

- Production is scheduled after an order is received, materials and parts arrive just as they are needed, the production cycle time for altimeters is less than 1 day, and completed units are packaged and shipped as part of the production cycle.

NOTES

Rainier Devices

- Rainier's backflush costing system has only three accounts related to production of altimeters: materials and parts inventory, conversion costs, and finished goods inventory.
- At the beginning of April (as at the beginning of every month), each of the three accounts had a balance of zero.

Rainier Devices

- Following are the April transactions related to the production of altimeters:
- Materials and parts purchased - $264,000
- Conversion costs incurred - $92,000
- Altimeters produced - 11,000 units
- The budgeted (or standard) cost for one altimeter is $24 for materials and parts and $8 of conversion costs.

Rainier Devices
Journal Entries for April to Record Production of Altimeters

Materials and parts inventory	264,000	
Accounts payable or cash		264,000
Conversion costs	92,000	
Accrued payroll, accounts payable, accumulated depreciation, etc.		92,000
Finished goods inventory	352,000	
Materials and parts inventory		264,000
Conversion costs		88,000

NOTES

To Record the Cost of Goods Sold for April

Cost of goods sold   352,000
    Finished goods inv.   352,000

(Assuming all altimeters are sold and shipped immediately upon production)

NOTES

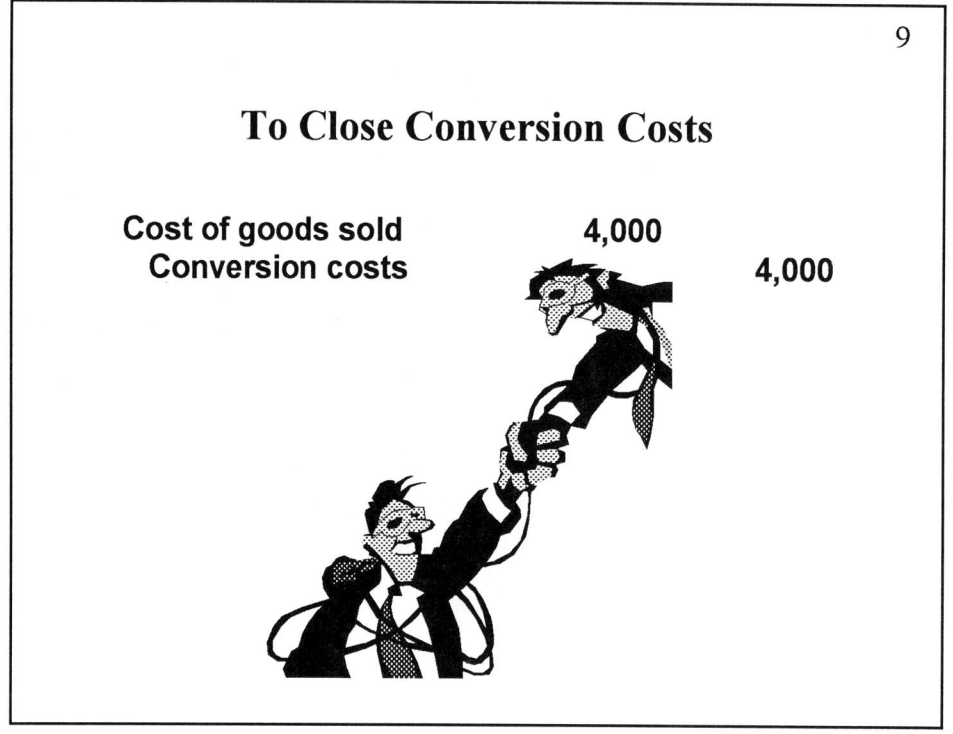

To Close Conversion Costs

Cost of goods sold   4,000
Conversion costs   4,000

NOTES

Survey of Company Practice:
Effects of Adopting JIT Production Systems

- Eight of 22 companies that recently implemented JIT adopted backflush costing
- Vendors reduced by 67%
- Rework and scrap reduced by 44%
- Setup times reduced by 47%
- Total inventory reduced by 46%

Source: Adapted from Swenson and Cassidy, "The Effect of JIT," Full citation is in Appendix A of the text.

NOTES

PowerNotes for Cost Accounting: A Managerial Emphasis, Ninth Edition

Inventory Management and Just-In-Time

Purchase Order Size for Retailer, EOQ, Just-In-Time Purchasing

Categories of Costs Associated with Goods for Sale

- ☐ Purchasing costs
- ☐ Ordering costs
- ☐ Carrying costs
- ☐ Stockout costs
- ☐ Quality costs

NOTES

Costs not recorded in the accounting system:

- Lost contribution margin due to poor-quality products
- Lost contribution margin due to use of capacity for rework or spoiled units
- Imputed interest on inventory

The Family Discount Store (FDS) operates a chain of retail discount stores. Its best-selling brand of baby diapers is Baby Care. Demand (D) in October 19_7 for Baby Care at its Quebec City store is 800 cases. In October 19_7, the Quebec City store estimated the ordering costs per purchase order (P) for Baby Care to be $40. The carrying costs (C) of each case of Baby Care diapers in inventory for a month were estimated to be $6.

NOTES

Determine the economic order quantity in October 19_7 for Baby Care using the equation method and verify by using an Excel spreadsheet:

Determine the economic order quantity in October 19_7 for Baby Care using the equation method and verify by using an Excel spreadsheet:

$$EOQ = \sqrt{\frac{2DP}{C}}$$

$$= \sqrt{\frac{2(800)(\$40)}{\$6}}$$

$$= \underline{103} \text{ CASES}$$

NOTES

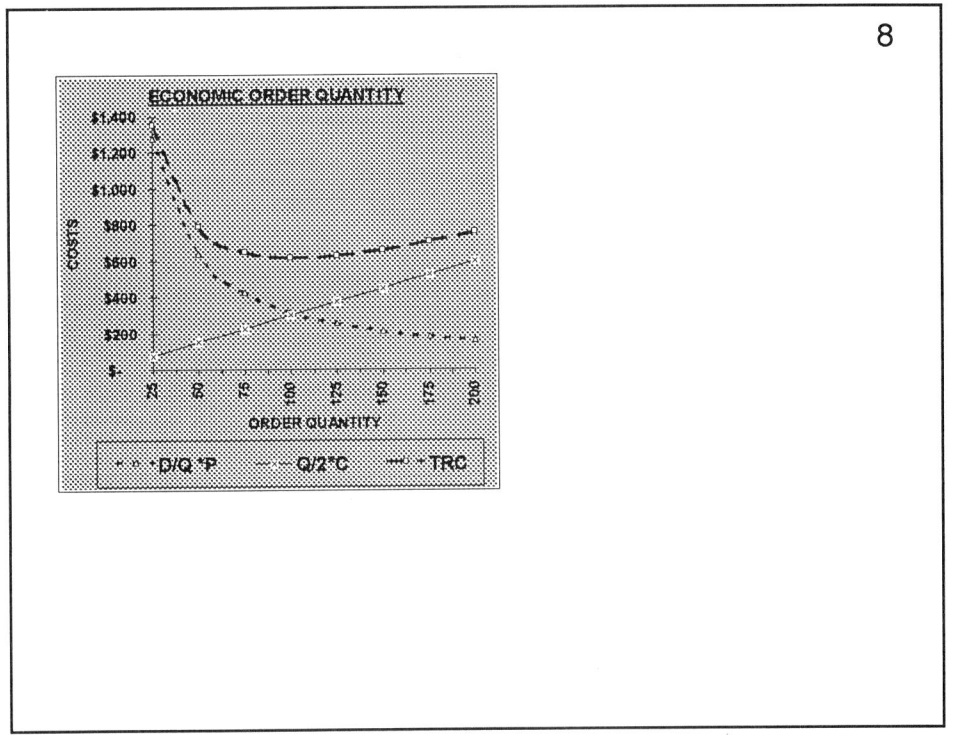

NOTES

9

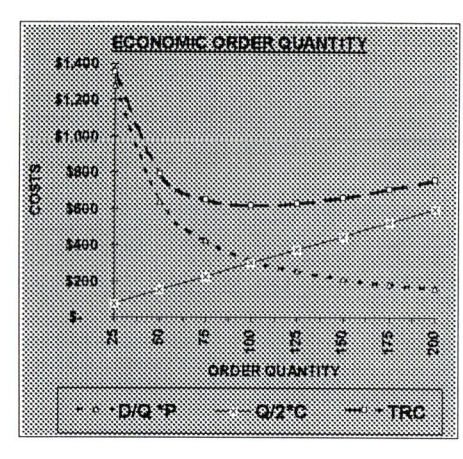

- What would be the impact on total costs of ordering 125 cases instead of the EOQ of 103 cases?
- From the graph, the total costs would increase very little.
- Costs of ordering and carrying inventory are *not* sensitive to minor errors in order quantity in this case.

Suppose that the carrying costs are re-estimated to be $10 per case to take into account an increase in warehouse-related costs. Determine the economic order quantity in October 19_7 using the equation method and verify using an Excel spreadsheet.

10

NOTES

Suppose that the carrying costs are re-estimated to be $10 per case to take into account an increase in warehouse-related costs. Determine the economic order quantity in October 19_7 using the equation method and verify using an Excel spreadsheet.

$$EOQ = \sqrt{\frac{2DP}{C}}$$

$$= \sqrt{\frac{2(800)(\$40)}{\$10}}$$

$$= \underline{\underline{80}} \text{ CASES}$$

NOTES

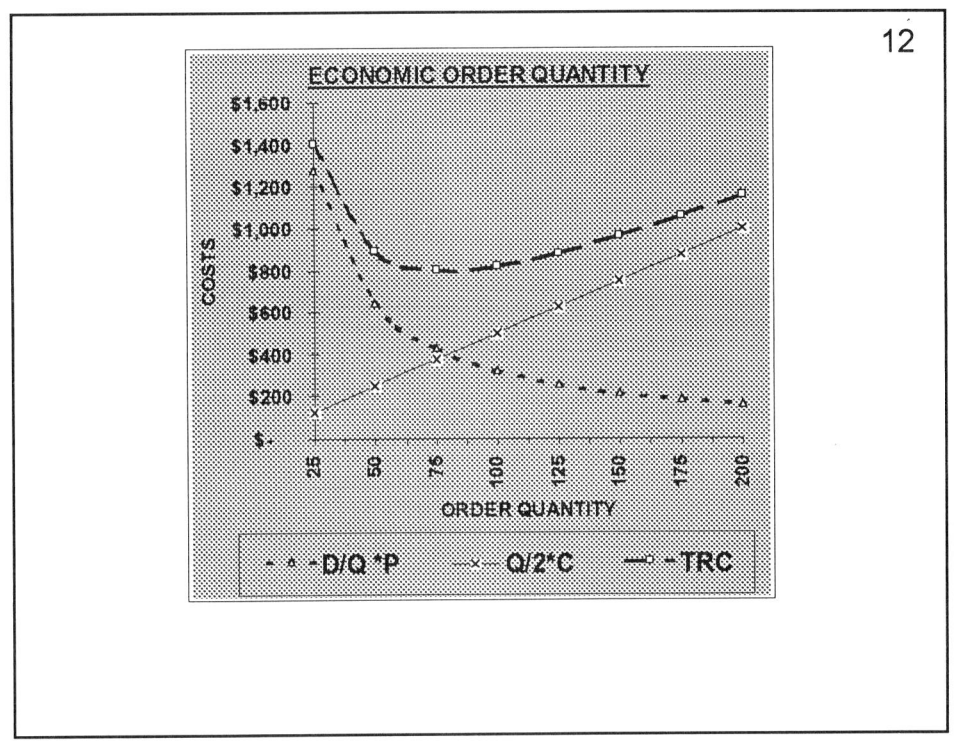

NOTES

How frequently should FDS place orders, based on the original and revised October EOQ results?

How frequently should FDS place orders, based on the October EOQ results?

$$\frac{D}{EOQ} = \frac{800}{103} = 7.77 \text{ Orders per Month}$$

or ≈ 1 every 4 days.

How frequently should FDS place orders, based on the October EOQ results?

$$\frac{D}{EOQ} = \frac{800}{103} = 7.77 \text{ Orders per Month}$$

or ≈ 1 every 4 days.

$$\frac{D}{EOQ} = \frac{800}{80} = 10 \text{ Orders per Month}$$

or ≈ 1 every 3 days.

NOTES

During September, FDS restructured its relationship with suppliers. It reduced the number of suppliers from 950 to 370. Only those suppliers that agreed to ship the exact quantities ordered, and with quality-control checks made before shipment, were given long-term supply contracts. Each individual purchase order involved minimal paperwork, and FDS was to make no quality checks of deliveries. The Quebec City store estimated its ordering costs per purchase order to be $4.20 after these changes were made.

Determine the EOQ and associated number of orders per month (and day) and verify using an Excel spreadsheet.

NOTES

Determine the EOQ and associated number of orders per month (and day) and verify using an Excel spreadsheet.

$$EOQ = \sqrt{\frac{2(800)(\$4.20)}{\$10}}$$

$$= \underline{\underline{25.92}} \text{ cases}$$

$$\frac{D}{EOQ} = \frac{800}{25.92}$$

$$\approx \underline{31} \text{ orders per month}$$

or $\underline{1}$ order per day

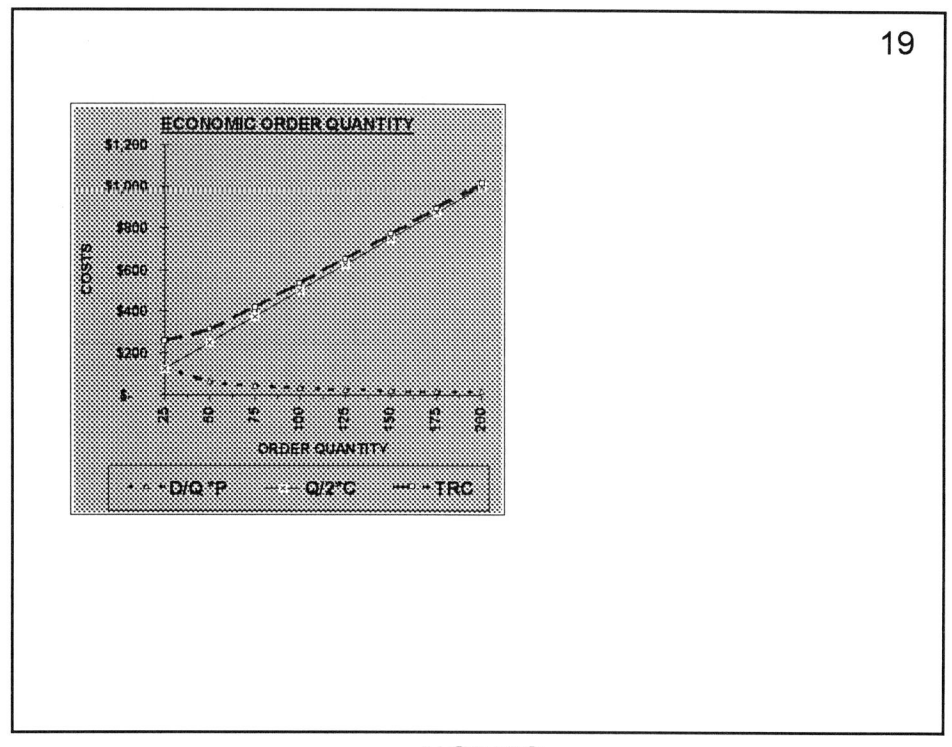

NOTES

20

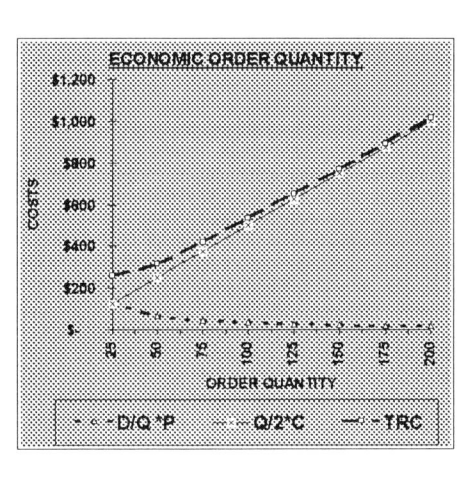

- Assume that the order quantity was set to 103 cases based on the original conditions. What is the impact on costs if the order quantity is not changed and remains at the original quantity of 103 cases?
- From the graph, the total costs would be about $270 above the EOQ cost.

Impact of Just-In-Time Purchasing Policy

A just-in-time purchasing policy involves the purchase of goods such that their delivery immediately precedes their demand.

An increase in the carrying cost coupled with a decrease in the cost of processing a purchase order led to increases in the optimal frequency of orders. FDS has increased the frequency of delivery from every fourth day to delivery every day. There is a reduction of 38.5 (103/2 - 26/2) cases in average inventory.

PowerNotes for Cost Accounting: A Managerial Emphasis, Ninth Edition

Capital Budgeting and Cost Analysis

PowerNotes for Cost Accounting: A Managerial Emphasis, Ninth Edition

Stages of Capital Budgeting and the Accountant's Role

- Identification
- Search
- **Information-acquisition**
- **Selection**
- Financing
- Implementation and **control**

- Operating personnel
- Accountants
- Treasurer

NOTES

Investment Analysis Models
A Graphical Approach to the Selection Stage

3

- Consider a new integrated circuit (IC-320) developed by Analog Instruments Company (AIC). AIC's development team was formed at the end of 1996 but, due to other commitments, did not begin work until the end of 1997.
- The initial investment in IC-320 of $200,000 is made at the end of 1997. The project has an expected life cycle of 8 years (end of 1996 through 2004).
- Predicted cash flows for IC-320 are as follows (assuming that all cash flows occur at the end of the year):

NOTES

Investment Analysis Models
A Graphical Approach to the Selection Stage

- Consider a new integrated circuit (IC-320) developed by Analog Instruments Company (AIC). AIC's development team was formed at the end of 1996 but, due to other commitments, did not begin work until the end of 1997.
- The initial investment in IC-320 of $200,000 is made at the end of 1997. The project has an expected life cycle of 8 years (end of 1996 through 2004).
- Predicted cash flows for IC-320 are as follows (assuming that all cash flows occur at the end of the year):

YEAR ENDED 19XX	CASH INFLOW [0000'S]	CASH OUTFLOW [0000'S]	NET CASH FLOW
96	$0	$0	$0
97	$0	$20	($20)
98	$4	$10	($6)
99	$10	$18	($8)
00	$35	$26	$9
01	$55	$32	$23
02	$45	$28	$17
03	$30	$20	$10
04	$15	$12	$3

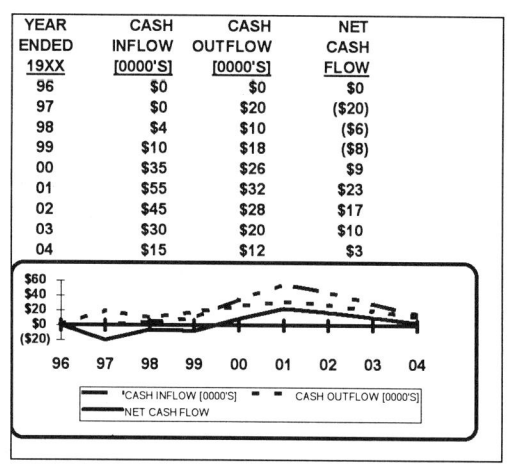

The Payback Time 5

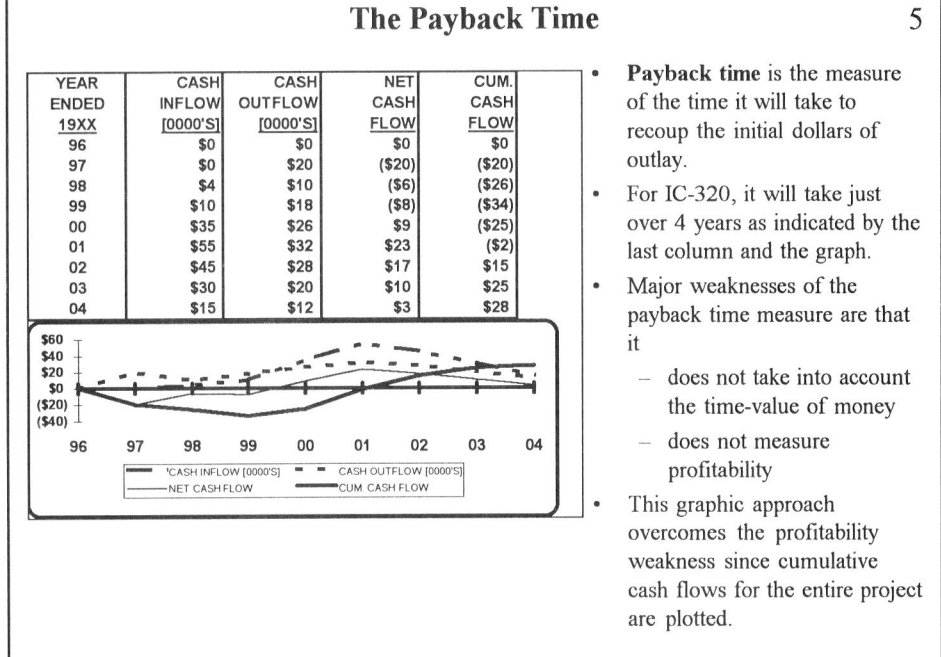

YEAR ENDED 19XX	CASH INFLOW [0000'S]	CASH OUTFLOW [0000'S]	NET CASH FLOW	CUM. CASH FLOW
96	$0	$0	$0	$0
97	$0	$20	($20)	($20)
98	$4	$10	($6)	($26)
99	$10	$18	($8)	($34)
00	$35	$26	$9	($25)
01	$55	$32	$23	($2)
02	$45	$28	$17	$15
03	$30	$20	$10	$25
04	$15	$12	$3	$28

- **Payback time** is the measure of the time it will take to recoup the initial dollars of outlay.
- For IC-320, it will take just over 4 years as indicated by the last column and the graph.
- Major weaknesses of the payback time measure are that it
  - does not take into account the time-value of money
  - does not measure profitability
- This graphic approach overcomes the profitability weakness since cumulative cash flows for the entire project are plotted.

NOTES

Break-even Time for New Products

- Some companies are using a profitability measure that combines the focus on time with consideration of the time-value of money.
- **Break-even time (BET)** is the amount of time from when the initial concept for a new product is approved by management until the time when the cumulative present value of the net cash inflows from the project equals the cumulative present value of the net investment outflows.
- Assume that AIC has a 14% required return on investments in new products such as IC-320.
- The computation of the BET and a graph of cumulative present value of net cash flows are given on the next slide. Compare the break-even time to the payback time for product IC-320.

NOTES

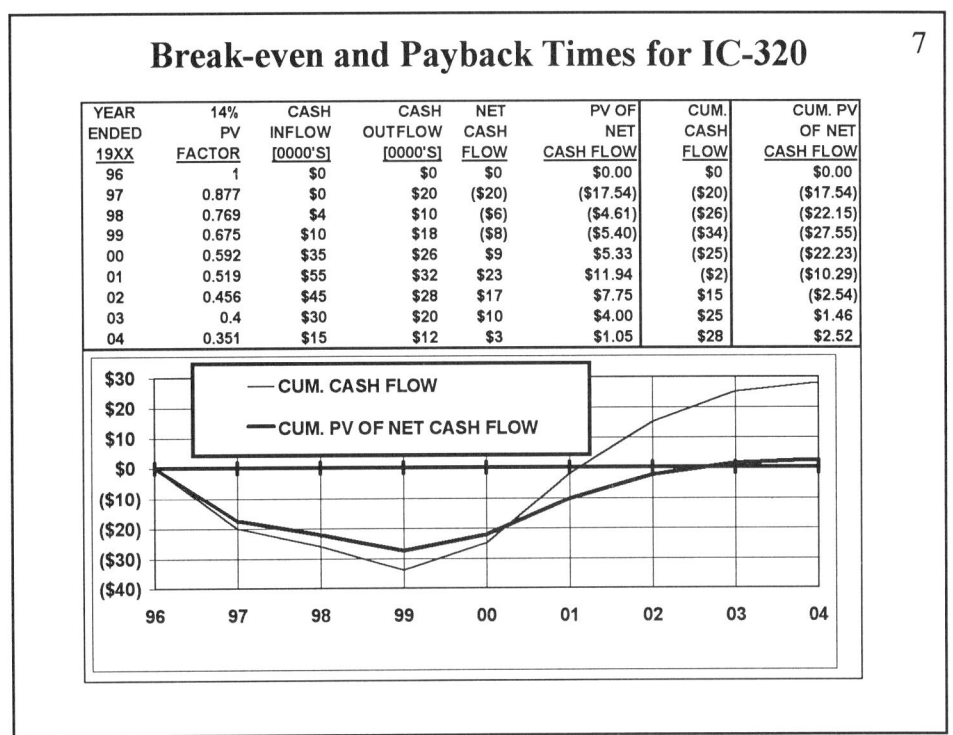

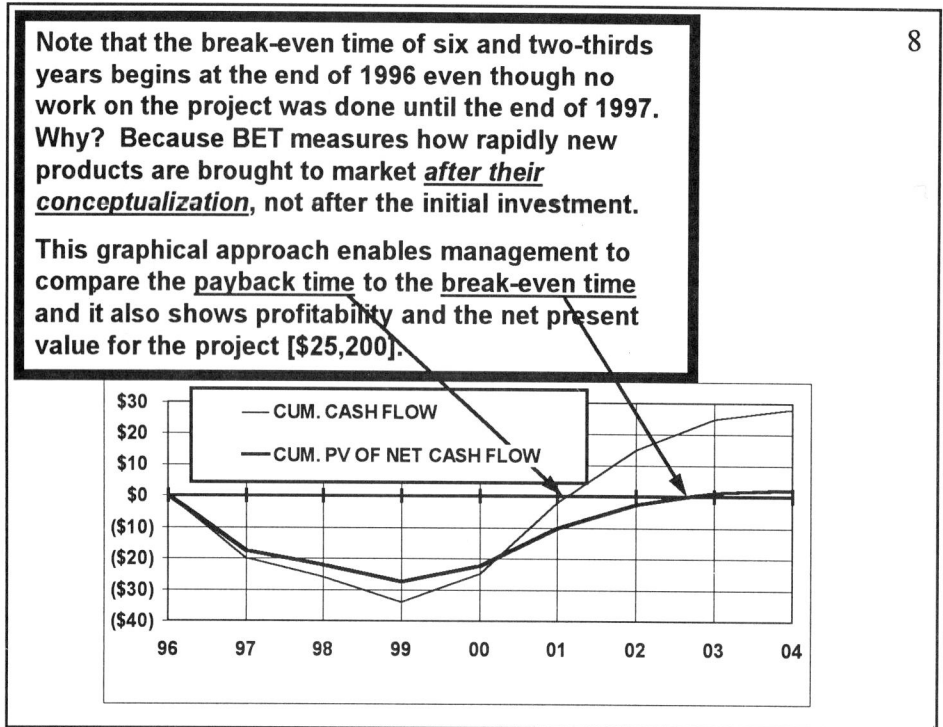

NOTES

Sensitivity Analysis

- AIC management is concerned about the uncertainty of estimated project cash inflows in the later years -- the estimates used thus far are "most likely." You have gathered both pessimistic and optimistic cash inflow data.
- Perform sensitivity analysis using these new estimates. Interpret the results.

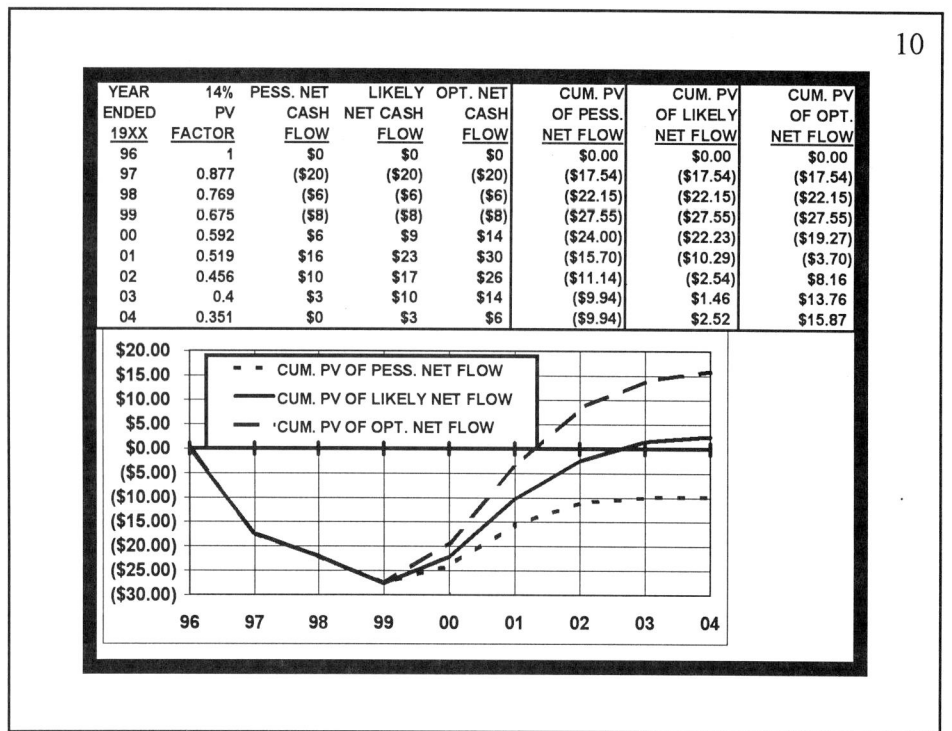

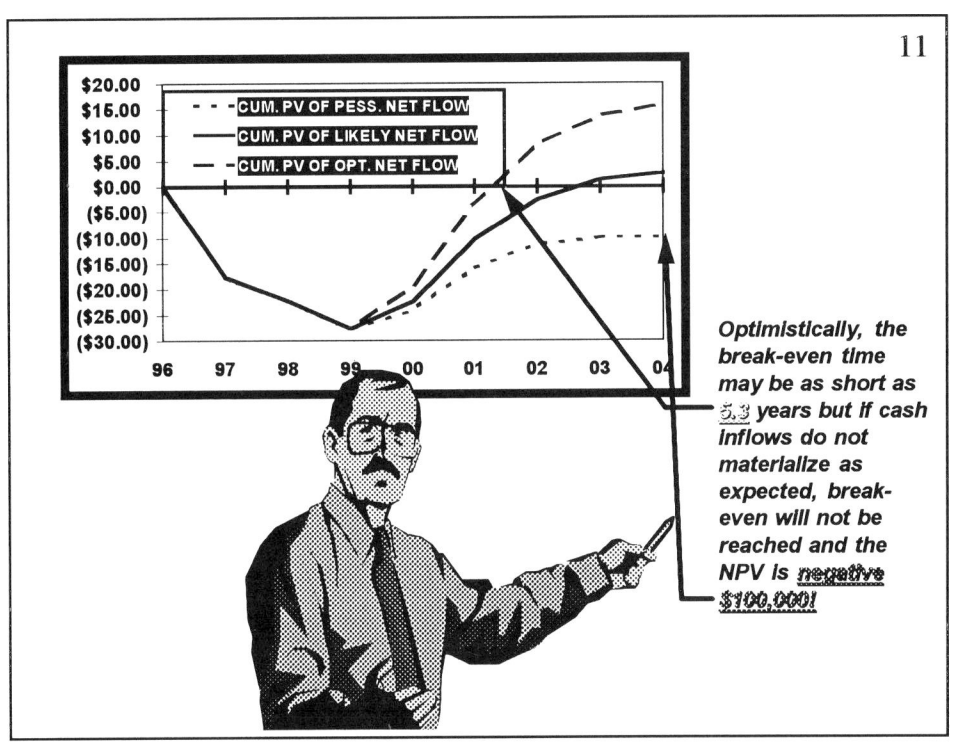

NOTES

PowerNotes for Cost Accounting: A Managerial Emphasis, Ninth Edition

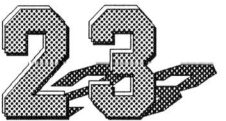

Capital Budgeting: A Closer Look

Note: The PowerPoint presentation uses various colors to depict lines on the graphs. These Power Notes use other legend codes such as dashed lines.

NOTES

Project Evaluation Criteria

- Consider a new integrated circuit (IC-320) developed by Analog Instruments Company (AIC). AIC's development team was formed at the end of 1996 but, due to other commitments, did not begin work until the end of 1997.
- AIC has seven evaluation criteria. Financial performance is only one of the seven. The financial analysis involves computing the payback time, break-even time, and net present value.
- The initial investment in IC-320 of $200,000 is made at the end of 1997. The project has an expected life cycle of 8 years (end of 1996 through 2004).
- Predicted cash flows for IC-320 are shown on the next slide (assuming that all cash flows occur at the end of the year).

This presentation is based, in part, on the article "Analyzing Capital Investments in New Products," by Suresh Kalagnanam and Suzanne K. Schmidt, *Management Accounting* (January 1996), pp. 31-36.

NOTES

PowerNotes for Cost Accounting: A Managerial Emphasis, Ninth Edition

Income Tax Effects on Profitability

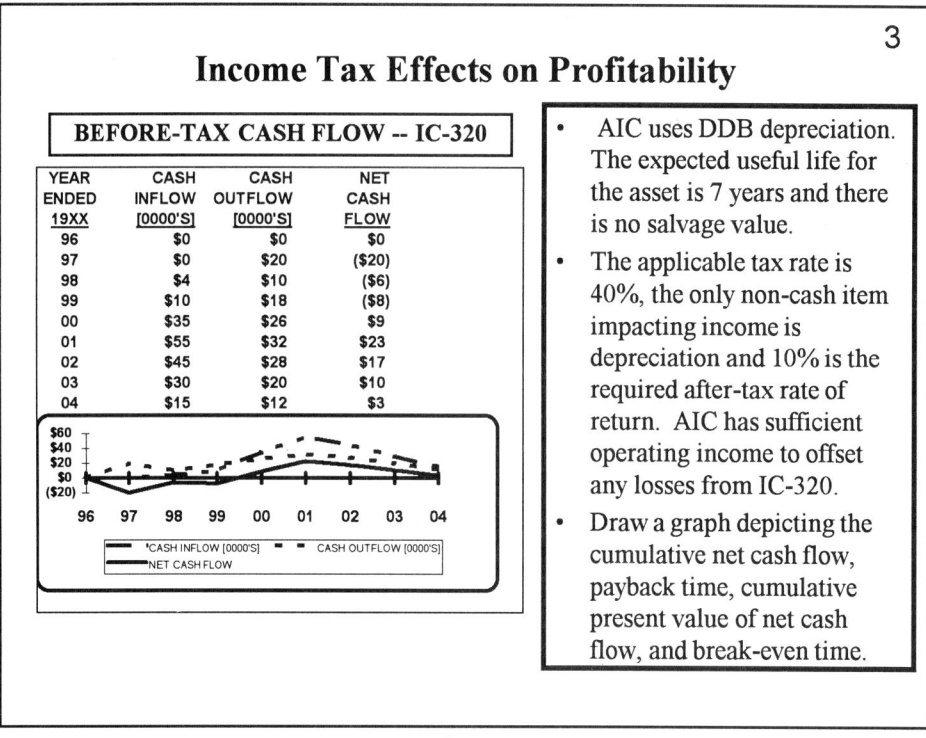

- AIC uses DDB depreciation. The expected useful life for the asset is 7 years and there is no salvage value.
- The applicable tax rate is 40%, the only non-cash item impacting income is depreciation and 10% is the required after-tax rate of return. AIC has sufficient operating income to offset any losses from IC-320.
- Draw a graph depicting the cumulative net cash flow, payback time, cumulative present value of net cash flow, and break-even time.

NOTES

PowerNotes for Cost Accounting: A Managerial Emphasis, Ninth Edition

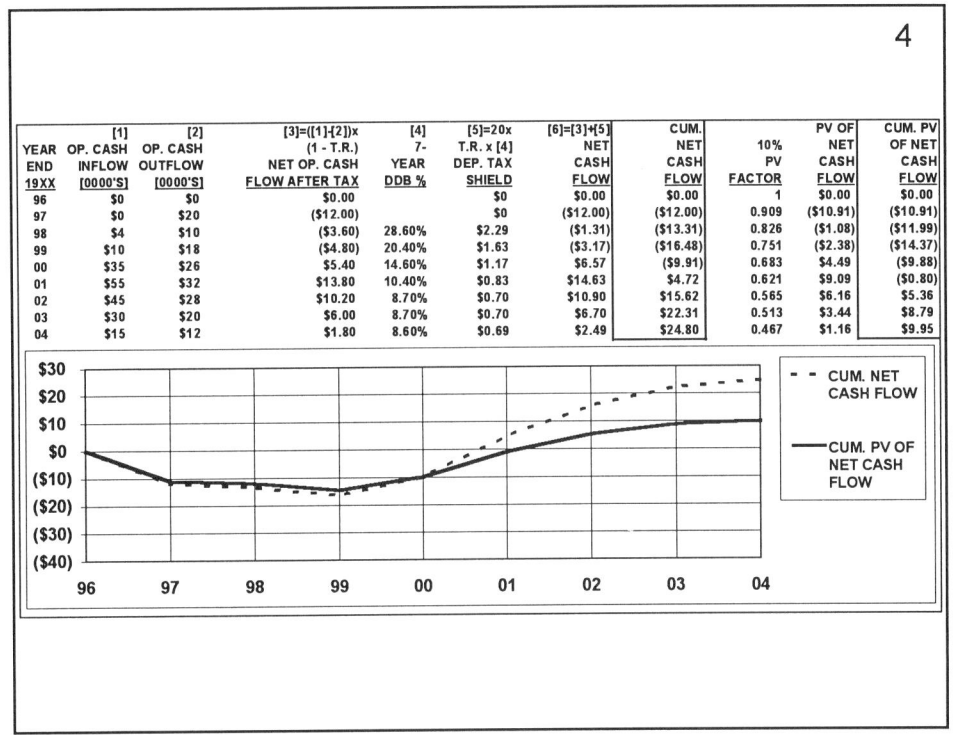

NOTES

23-4

TAX EFFECTS ON INVESTMENT CRITERIA

- The next slide shows two charts for AIC's proposed investment in IC-320. One chart gives cash flows and present value of cash flows on a before-tax basis. The second chart shows the same flows on an after-tax basis.
- What is the effect of taxes on the payback time, break-even time, total cash flow and the net present value?

NOTES

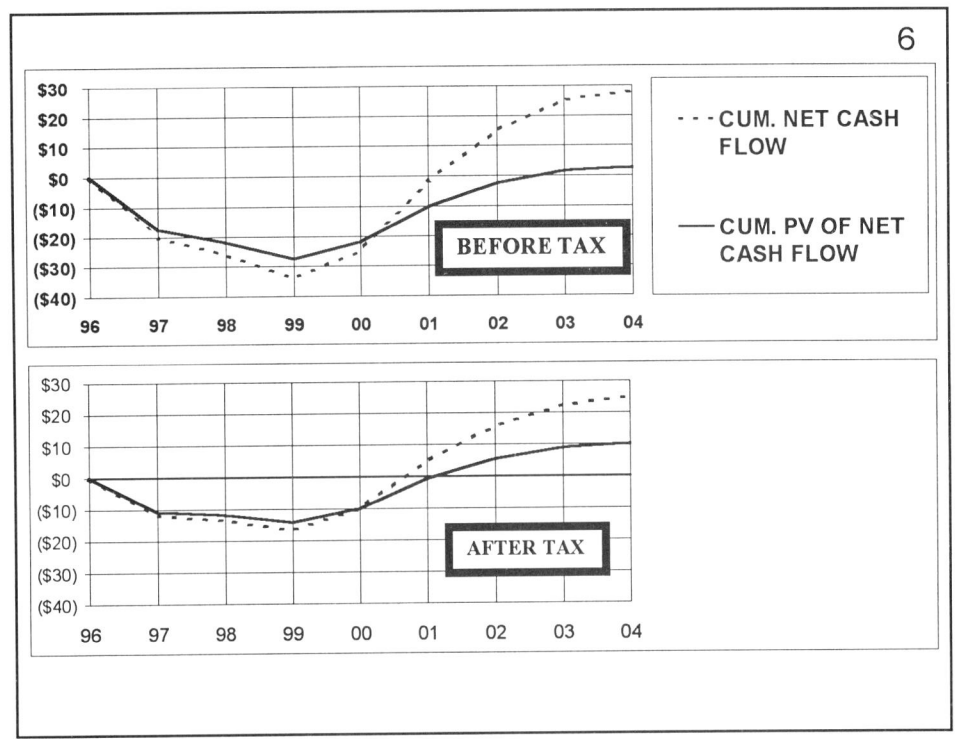

NOTES

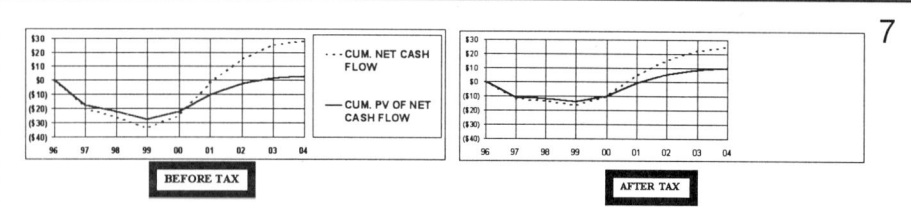

- The payback time decreases from about 4.2 years after the initial investment to 3.7 years. The break-even time decreases from about 6.7 years after the initial product idea was conceived to 5.2 years.
- The cash flow losses are substantially reduced in the early years of the product life cycle due to the tax shield (accelerated depreciation), but, in total, the cash flows are slightly lower.
- The net present value improves when taxes are considered, due to the impact of the tax shield based on accelerated depreciation.

NOTES

Financial Analysis

Complete the financial analysis portion of the project evaluation for the four proposed projects at AIC by giving the payback time, break-even time, and net present value for IC-320 [after-tax basis].

FINANCIAL CRITERIA	IC-318	IC-319	IC-320	IC-321
PAYBACK TIME	3.3	3.5		5.6
BREAK-EVEN TIME	4.1	4.5		8.2
NET PRESENT VALUE	16	-1		13

NOTES

Financial Analysis

- **IC-318 is preferred based on financial criteria. IC-320 ranks third. If AIC can only fund two of the four projects, will IC-320 be rejected? Explain.**
- *IC-320 may still be accepted based on non-financial criteria. Examples of non-financial criteria are given on the next slide.*

FINANCIAL CRITERIA	IC-318	IC-319	IC-320	IC-32
PAYBACK TIME	3.3	3.5	3.7	5.6
BREAKEVEN TIME	4.1	4.5	5.2	8.2
NET PRESENT VALUE	16	-1	10	13

NOTES

Nonfinancial Evaluation Criteria

- **Potential for proprietary position (patent) Patents provide market advantage**
- **Balance between short-term and long-term projects and payoffs**
- **Potential for collaborations and outside funding**
- **Need to establish competency in a market**
- **Potential for spin-off products**
- **Probability of technical success**

NOTES

PowerNotes for Cost Accounting: A Managerial Emphasis, Ninth Edition

24

Measuring Input Yield, Mix, and Productivity

NOTES

Productivity Measurement

Productivity Described

- ***Productivity*** measures the relationship between actual inputs used (both physical inputs and costs) and actual outputs achieved; the lower the inputs for a given set of outputs, or the higher the outputs for a given set of inputs, the higher the level of productivity.

NOTES

What Productivity Measures Do

- Evaluate whether more inputs than necessary have been used to produce a given level of output.
- Evaluate whether the best mix of inputs has been used to produce that output.

Distinguish Productivity Measurement and Variance Analysis

- Productivity measures do not use information from budgets or standards.
- Productivity measures allow for more general substitutions of factors of production (inputs). For example, labor can be replaced by material where more expensive materials facilitate the labor function.

NOTES

Caroline Laundry had the following results for 19_4 and 19_7:

	19_4	19_7
Pounds of laundry processed	1,360,000	1,525,000
Sales revenue	$720,000	$1,394,000
Direct-labor hours worked	45,100	46,650
Direct-labor cost	$316,000	$498,000

NOTES

Caroline used the same facilities in 19_7 as in 19_4. During the past 3 years, however, the company put more effort into training its employees. The manager of Caroline was curious about whether the training had increased labor productivity.

NOTES

The best productivity measure based on the *physical measures* given is:

Pounds of laundry processed ÷ direct-labor hours worked.

19_4	19_7
1,360,000 ÷ 45,100	1,525,000 ÷ 46,650
= 30.2 pounds/hour	= 32.7 pounds/hour

Productivity has increased by 32.7 - 30.2 = 2.5 pounds per hour, an increase of 2.5 ÷ 30.2 = 8.3%.

NOTES

The best productivity measure based on the financial measures given is sales revenue ÷ direct labor cost.

19_4	19_7
$720,000 ÷ $316,000	$1,394,000 ÷ 498,000
= 2.28	= 2.80

By this measure, productivity has increased by 0.52 ÷ 2.28 = 22.8%.

NOTES

Reasons for the large increase in the financial measure:

- **Increase in physical productivity as shown**
- **Increase in revenue per pound at a greater rate than inflation ($720,000 ÷ 1,360,000 = $0.53 in 19_4 compared to $1,394,000 ÷ 1,525,000 = $0.91 in 19_7, an increase of (0.91-0.53) ÷ 0.53 = 72%)**
- **Increase in wage rates per hour less than inflation ($316,000 ÷ 45,100 = $7.01 in 19_4 compared to $498,000 ÷ 46,650 = $10.68 in 19_7, an increase of ($10.68-$7.01) ÷ $7.01 = 52%)**

NOTES

Suppose the following productivity measure were used:

sales revenue ÷ direct-labor hours worked

Suppose the following productivity measure were used:

sales revenue ÷ direct-labor hours worked

Because of inflation, each 19_4 dollar is equivalent to 1.4 19_7 dollars. Compute appropriate productivity numbers for comparing 19_7 productivity with 19_4 productivity.

NOTES

This productivity measure mixes financial and physical measures. Therefore, it is essential to adjust for inflation. Expressing both 19_4 and 19_7 productivity measures in 19_7 dollars:

19_4	19_7
($720,000·1.4) ÷45,100	$1,394,000 ÷46,650
= $22.35 per hour	= $29.88 per hour

This measure shows an increase in productivity of ($29.88-$22.35) ÷$22.35 = 33.7%. It incorporates the increase in physical productivity and the revenue increase at greater than inflation.

NOTES

Control Systems, Decentralization, Transfer Pricing, and Multinational Considerations

NOTES

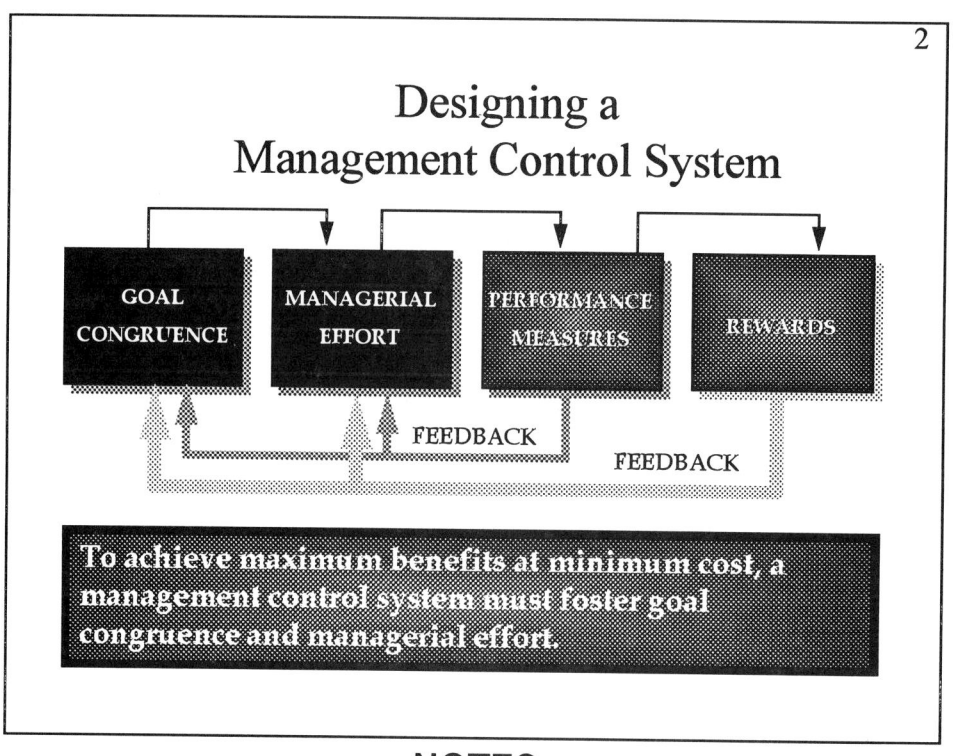

NOTES

MANAGEMENT CONTROL SYSTEMS AND ORGANIZATIONAL GOALS

- A *management control system* is a means of gathering and using information to aid and coordinate the process of making planning and control decisions throughout the organization and to guide employee behavior [Text, page 900].
- Too often, companies depend entirely on financial accounting systems to report data and financial measures to evaluate performance.
- In addition, there may be little integration of goals and success factors, strategies and measurement systems.
- The figure on the next slide shows the relationship between one goal, strategies, and three *financial measures* used in a company's performance measurement system.

NOTES

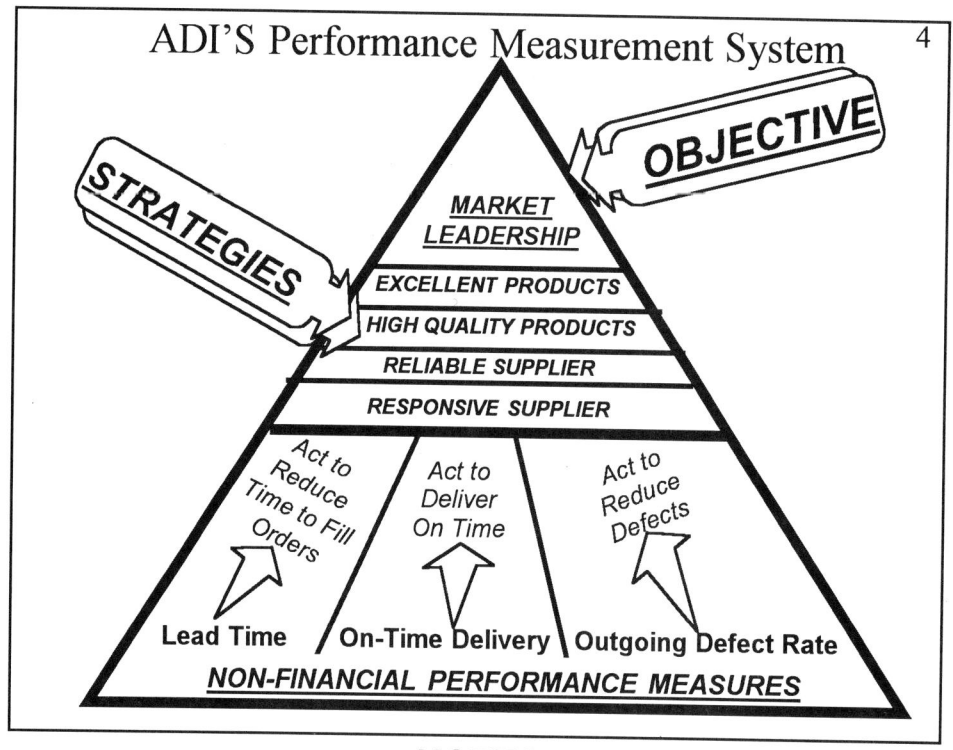

NOTES

Volume Variance

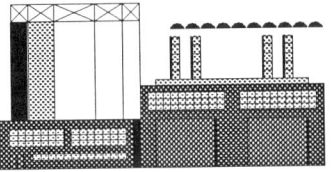

- Volume variance is defined and discussed in Chapter 8.
- It is defined as the departure of actual production volume from planned (budgeted) volume times the fixed overhead rate.
- Unfavorable volume variances are treated as costs on the income statement.
- These variances are largely uncontrollable by managers in the short run. Causes include lower sales, poor production scheduling, breakdowns, and shortages of materials or labor.
- However, by producing more inventory (even if not ordered), unfavorable variances can be reduced or even eliminated.

NOTES

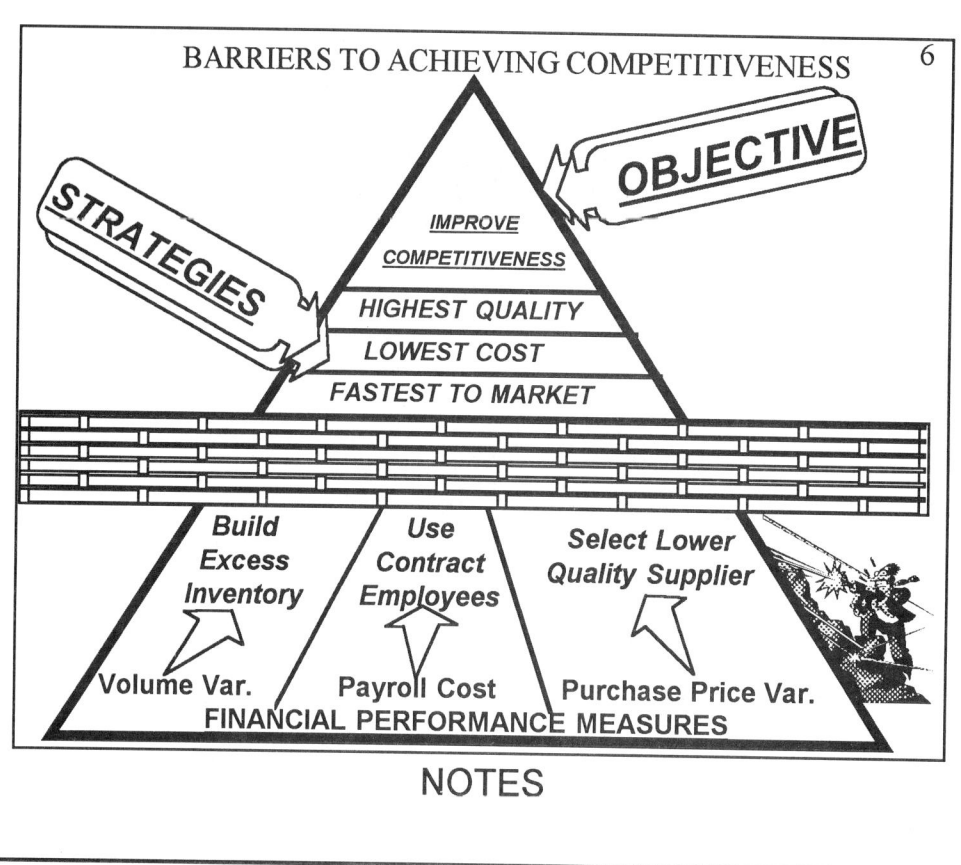

NOTES

Financial Measures as Barriers

FINANCIAL PERFORMANCE MEASURES

- Volume Var. → Build Excess Inventory
- Payroll Cost → Use Contract Employees
- Purchase Price Var. → Select Lower Quality Supplier

- How would the use of these three financial performance measures motivate managers as indicated and how would these actions act as a barrier to executing strategies for improvement in competitiveness?

NOTES

- **Increasing inventories reduces idle capacity (volume variance) and spreads fixed production costs over more units. This reduces unit production costs but many other costs associated with maintaining inventories increase (carrying costs, obsolescence, etc.). Thus, the strategy of being the lowest cost producer is hindered.**
- **To reduce payroll costs, a department could use contract employees or outside vendors. This action can have a debilitating impact on the quality of service as well as response time.**
- **Using lower priced materials (with assumed lower quality) reduces purchase price variance (a financial measure), but quality suffers. Response time can also suffer due to the increased need for rework, downtime, etc.**

NOTES

NOTES

Analog Devices, Inc.

Analog Devices, Inc. [ADI] manufactures precision, high performance, linear integrated circuits. These devices are used to condition, amplify analog signals from sensors that measure physical phenomena (temperature, pressure, velocity), and convert them into digital signals that computers read. ADI sells primarily to original equipment manufacturers [OEMs].

ADI had impressive growth and profitability from its inception (1965) until the mid 1980s. However, due to increasing competition and quality, cost, and service problems, ADI's growth rate had slowed dramatically by the mid 1980s.

In 1987, ADI began to revamp its performance measurement system to bring it in line with new strategic initiatives. One of the most important strategic objectives was to improve *market share* to a leadership position.

NOTES

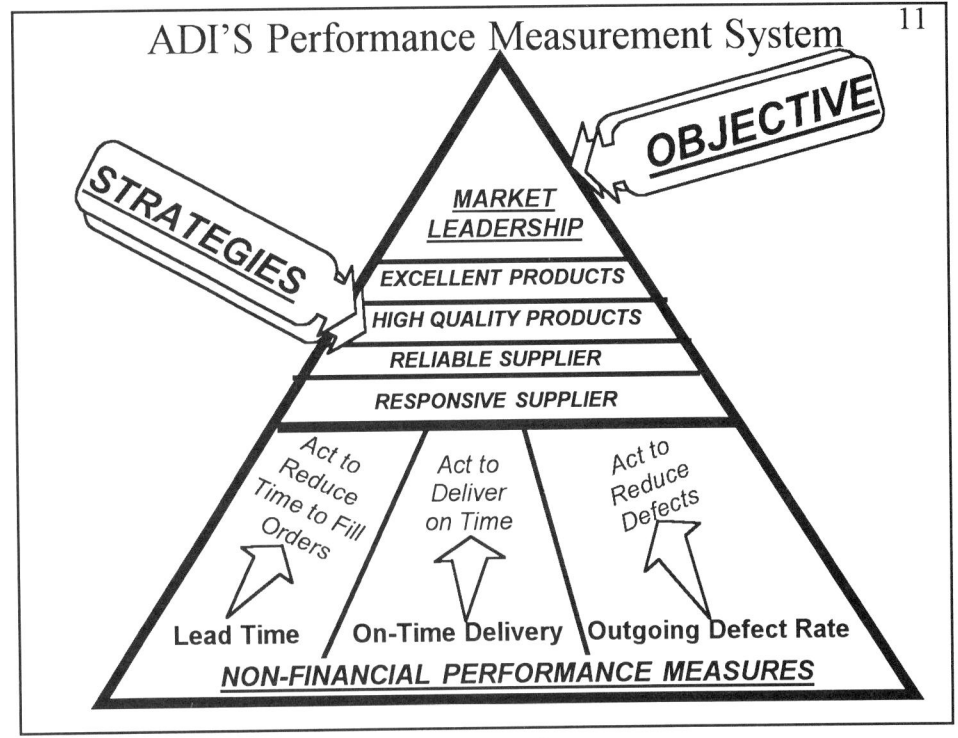

NOTES

Nonfinancial Metrics Pinpoint Customer Satisfaction at Analog Devices, Inc.

- "Our nonfinancial performance measures have all the integrity of the financial metrics. If our delivery metrics are getting better, we're improving customer service. And if we're doing that, it will eventually show up in the financial metrics." -- Art Schneiderman, Vice President of quality and productivity, Analog Devices, Inc. [ADI]

SOURCE: Art Schneiderman, "Metrics for the Order Fulfillment Process," *Journal of Cost Management* (forthcoming).

NOTES

Goal Congruence, Managerial Effort, and Continuous Improvement at ADI

- After performance measures are defined and integrated within the strategic framework, an effective feedback system is designed that facilitates motivation of managers towards continuous improvement.
- A graphical format is used to track performance. Exhibit 1 on the next slide shows a typical graph for percent of lines shipped late.

ch25-1.xls

Exhibit 1 The Half Life of Late Shipments

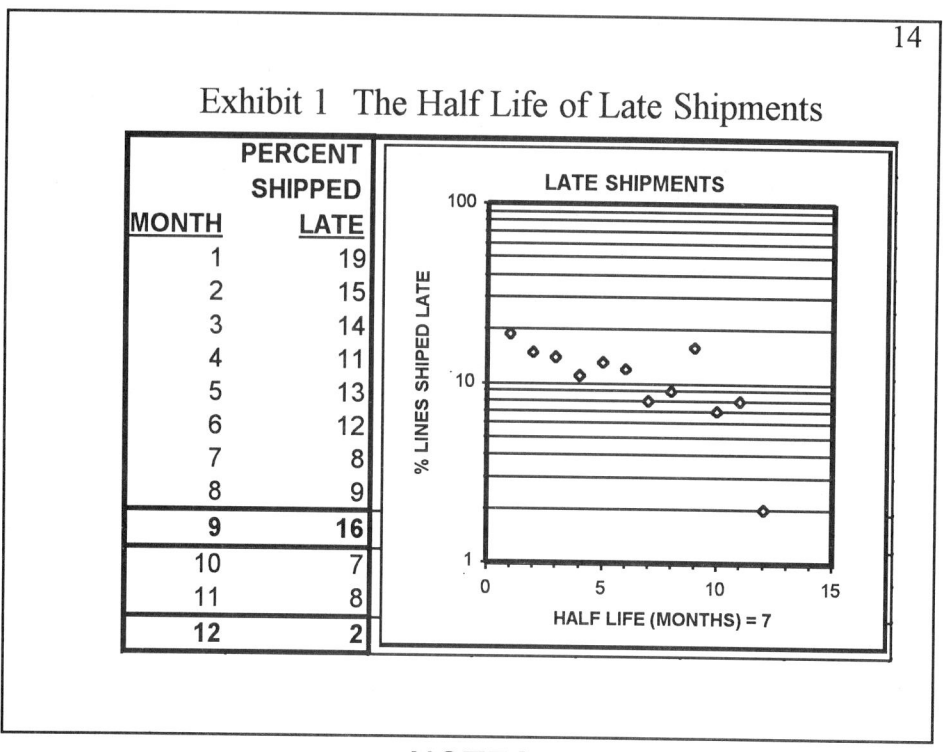

MONTH	PERCENT SHIPPED LATE
1	19
2	15
3	14
4	11
5	13
6	12
7	8
8	9
9	16
10	7
11	8
12	2

NOTES

PowerNotes for Cost Accounting: A Managerial Emphasis, Ninth Edition

The Half Life Concept

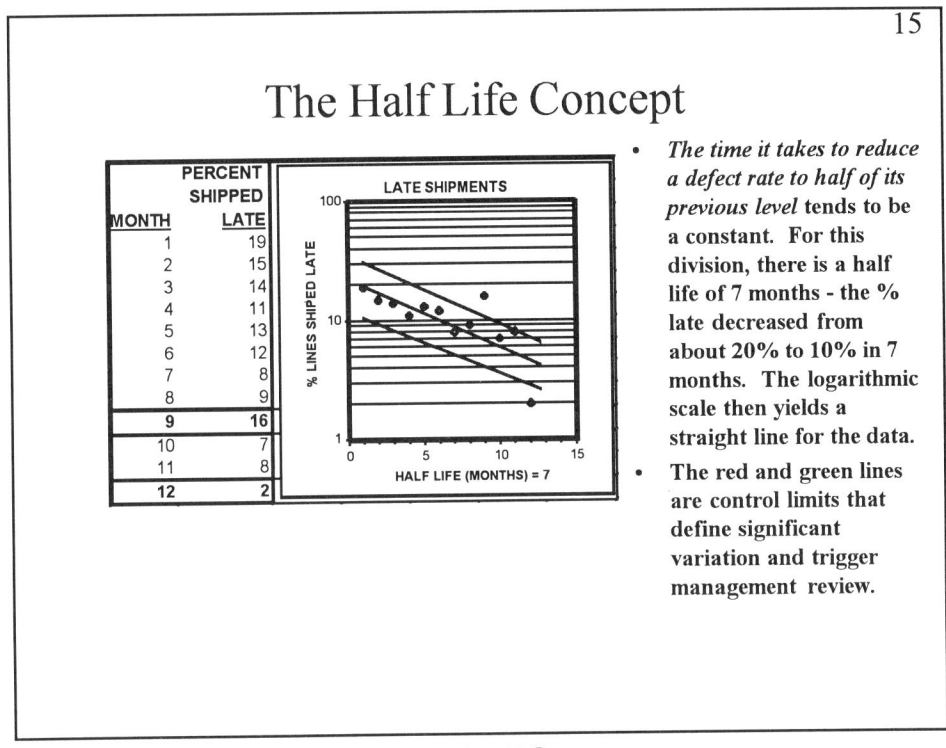

- *The time it takes to reduce a defect rate to half of its previous level* tends to be a constant. For this division, there is a half life of 7 months - the % late decreased from about 20% to 10% in 7 months. The logarithmic scale then yields a straight line for the data.
- The red and green lines are control limits that define significant variation and trigger management review.

NOTES

Advantages of the Graphical Format

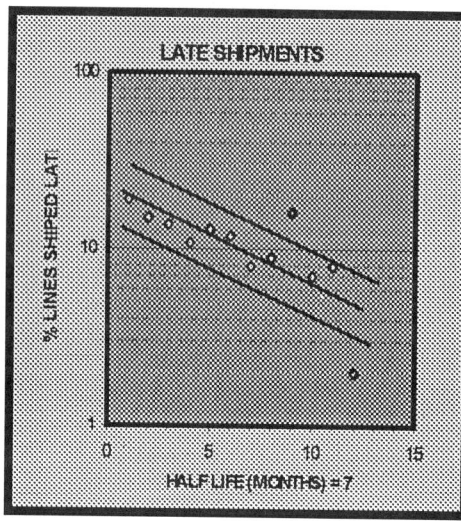

- It shows both the level and trend (half life) of the performance measure
- It distinguishes statistically significant variation from random variation.
- Use of color to focus attention.
- Highlights favorable and unfavorable situations.
- Comparisons across divisions provide for benchmarking.

NOTES

Closing the Feedback Loop at ADI

- **The graphics are the basis for both the quarterly performance review and the annual goal setting process.**
- **Each manager presents the division's quarterly scorecard at a general manager's meeting. Favorable variances from plan resulted in sharing insights and problem solutions. Unfavorable variances resulted in specific action items.**
- **The next two slides give the results of ADI's new management control system.**

The Results at ADI

Measurement	1987	Half Life (months)	1992
External			
On-Time Delivery	85%	9	>99.8%
Outgoing Defect Level	500 ppm	9	<10 ppm
Lead Time	10 weeks	9	<3 weeks
Internal			
Manufacturing Cycle Time	15 weeks	9	4-5 weeks
Process Defect Level	5,000 ppm	6	<10 ppm
Yield	20%	9	>50%
Time to Market	36 months	24	6 months

NOTES

The Results at ADI

- ADI's delivery performance improved from a sub-70% level to over 96% in four years.
- ADI was selected as *Dataquest's* <u>Mid-sized Semiconductor Supplier of the Year</u> two years running.

PowerNotes for Cost Accounting: A Managerial Emphasis, Ninth Edition

Systems Choice:
Performance Measurement, Compensation, and Multinational Considerations

NOTES

PowerNotes for Cost Accounting: A Managerial Emphasis, Ninth Edition

The Importance of the Performance Measurement System

NOTES

PERFORMANCE MEASUREMENT:
The Weight of the In-Box

- Managers tend to focus their efforts in areas where performance is measured and where performance affects rewards.
- "We are basically determined by the weight of what's in our in-boxes, and if everything in the in-box is about cost and efficiency measures, and there's nothing about measuring innovation and quality and service, then the company is going to instinctively focus on what's measured." -- Tom Peters

NOTES

KEY MARKET CHARACTERISTICS IN THE 1990s

- Executives indicate that the global market place of the 1990s is driven by
  - Constant change
  - Intense competition
  - More responsiveness to satisfying customer's demands
- Success factors for these companies are given in Figure 1 on the next slide.

SOURCE: Business International Survey of CEOs and other senior officers -- "Winning in the New Global Market Place: Strategic Redirection for the 1990's," Business International Corp., New York, NY.

NOTES

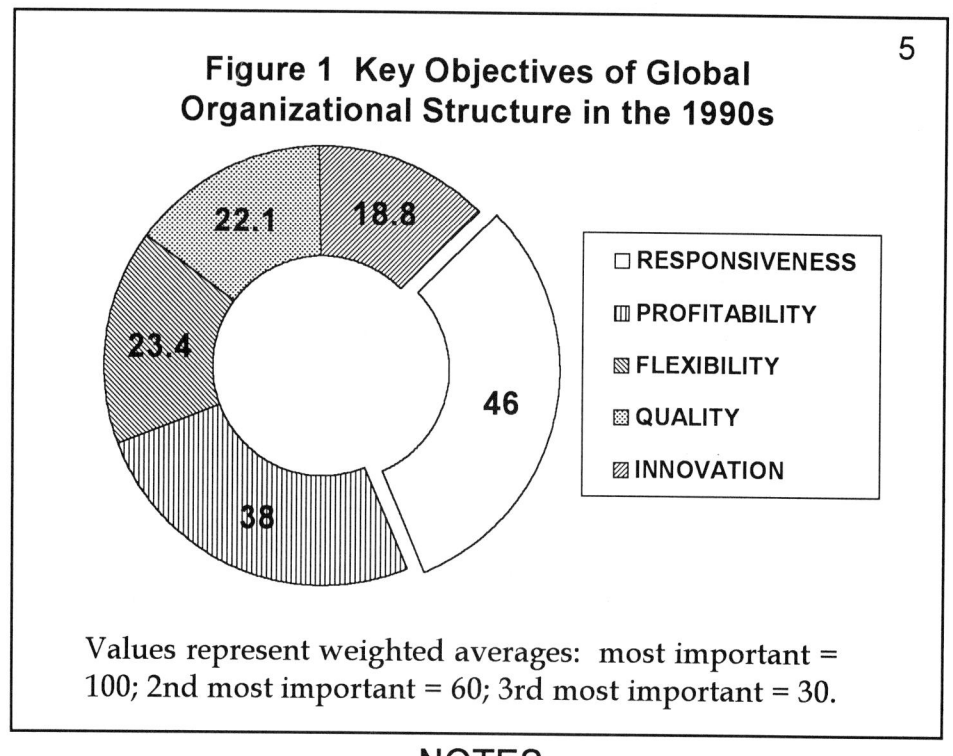

Figure 1 Key Objectives of Global Organizational Structure in the 1990s

- RESPONSIVENESS
- PROFITABILITY
- FLEXIBILITY
- QUALITY
- INNOVATION

Values represent weighted averages: most important = 100; 2nd most important = 60; 3rd most important = 30.

NOTES

Other Survey Results

- Majority of firms have moved toward a more decentralized organizational structure and leadership style.
- Corporate leaders believe that decentralization and employee empowerment improve a company's effectiveness and competitiveness.

THE BALANCED SCORECARD

- A *balanced scorecard* is a performance measurement system that strikes a balance between financial and operating measures, links performance to rewards, and gives explicit recognition to the diversity of stakeholder interests.
- One company that has successfully implemented a balanced scorecard as part of its integrated performance measurement system is Analog Devices, Inc.

NOTES

Nonfinancial Metrics Pinpoint Customer Satisfaction at Analog Devices, Inc.

- Analog Devices Inc., located in Norwood, Massachusetts, is a leading producer of linear integrated circuits for firms such as Hewlett-Packard and IBM.
- "Our nonfinancial performance measures have all the integrity of the financial metrics. If our delivery metrics are getting better, we're improving customer service. And if we're doing that, it will eventually show up in the financial metrics." -- Art Schneiderman, Vice President of quality and productivity, Analog Devices, Inc. [ADI]

SOURCE: Art Schneiderman, "Metrics for the Order Fulfillment Process," Journal of Cost Management (forthcoming).

NOTES

MEASURE TIME AND INNOVATION

- "Certainly any measures of customer service should have a heavy dose - if not a commanding dose - of time. People who are mastering time-based competition are doing things ten or a hundred times faster than their competitors are, and if someone can do something 100 times faster than you, you've got a serious problem on your hands." -- *Tom Peters*
- ADI recognized the importance of delivering products to customers on time and linked time-based measures to key success factors and goals.

NOTES

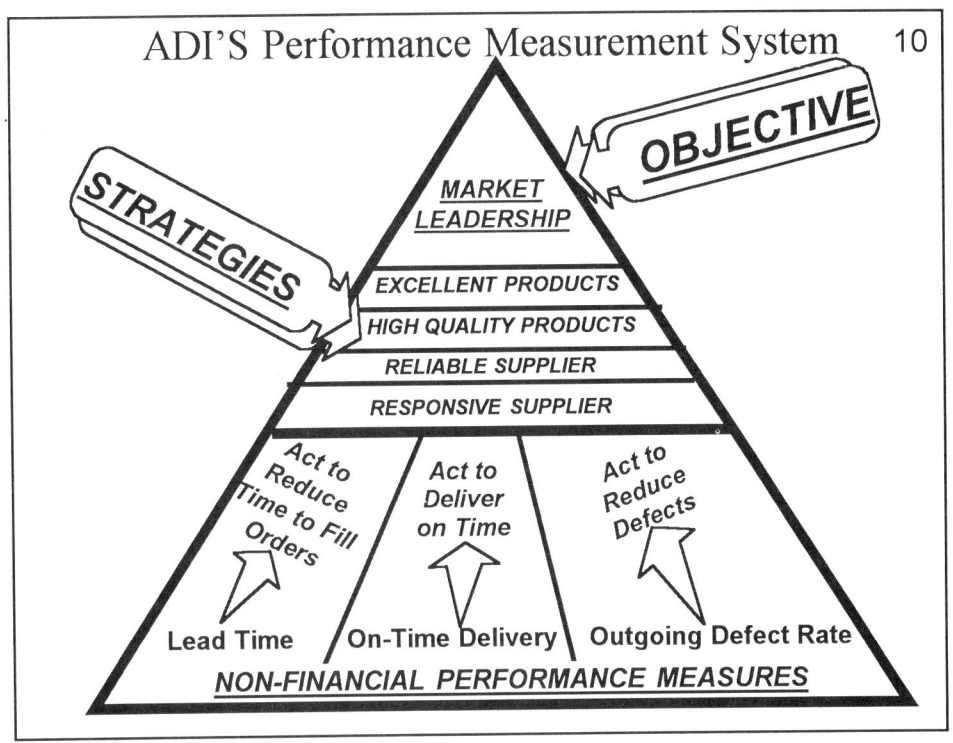

NOTES

DELIVERY MEASURES AT ADI

- ☐ *On-time delivery*-% late, % early, % on time. On time means within a predetermined window around the FCD [factory commit date] that is set at the time of the order and never changed.
- ☐ *Responsibility*-tracking reasons for late delivery.
- ☐ *Lateness/earliness*-0-1 week, 1-2 weeks, etc. Goal is to deliver as close as possible to the FCD.
- ☐ *Lead time*-the difference between the order entry date and the customer request date [CRD]. Measures include % of CRDs matched [CRD=FCD] and excess lead time [FCD - CRD].
- ☐ *Responsiveness*-how long it takes anyone at ADI to answer a customer query or to take action generated by a customer request. Measures include time to schedule an order and failure analysis turnaround time.

NOTES

A PORTION OF ADI'S QUARTERLY SCORECARD

		Actual	Budget	Variance	% Var.
On Time Delivery (To FCD)	%	96	97	-1	-1
CRDs Not Matched	%	52	41	11	27
Excess Leadtime	WKS	2.8	3.0	-0.2	-6.7
Employee Turnover	%	8.4	19	-10.6	-56
IC PRODUCTS					
IC Defective - Outgoing	PPM	1210	908	302	33
IC Defective - In-Process	PPM	1624	1516	108	7
IC Cycle Time	DYS	50	62	-12	-19
IC Yield	%	40	38	2	5
ASSEMBLED PRODUCTS					
AP Defective - Outgoing	PPM	1483	1977	494	-25
Plug In Yield	%	91	90	1	1
AP Cycle Time	DYS	22	29	-7	-24
Scrap/Rework	%	7.7	14	-6.3	-45
FINANCIAL MEASURES					
Sales	$M	120.7	120.2	0.5	0.4
Sales Growth (YTD)	%	6.5	6.0	0.5	8.3
Contribution Margin	%	6.3	8.8	2.5	28
ROA	%	7.8	10.4	-2.6	-25

☐ UNFAVORABLE VARIANCE ☐ FAVORABLE VARIANCE

NOTES

The Results at ADI

- ADI's delivery performance improved from a sub-70% level to over 96% in four years.
- ADI was selected as *Dataquest's* Mid-sized Semiconductor Supplier of the Year two years running.

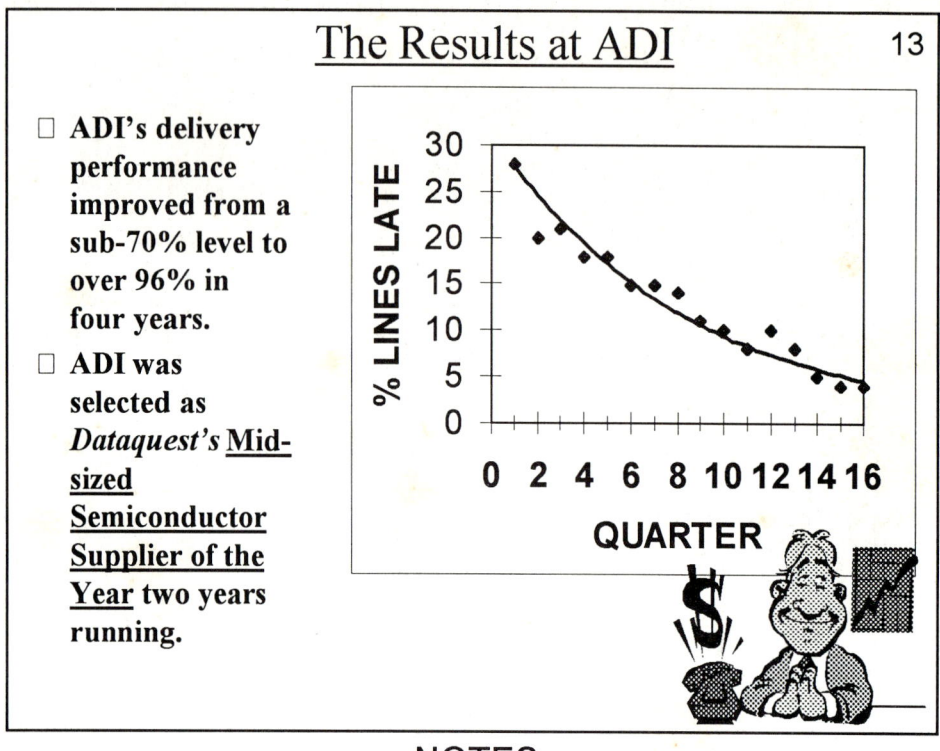

NOTES